WITCHCRAFT AND [ADOLE]SCENCE
IN AMERICAN POPULAR CULTURE

Teen Witches

HORROR STUDIES

Series Editor
Xavier Aldana Reyes, Manchester Metropolitan University

Editorial Board

Preface
Horror Studies is the first book series exclusively dedicated to the study of the genre in its various manifestations – from fiction to cinema and television, magazines to comics, and extending to other forms of narrative texts such as video games and music. Horror Studies aims to raise the profile of Horror and to further its academic institutionalisation by providing a publishing home for cutting-edge research. As an exciting new venture within the established Cultural Studies and Literary Criticism programme, Horror Studies will expand the field in innovative and student-friendly ways.

WITCHCRAFT AND ADOLESCENCE IN AMERICAN POPULAR CULTURE

Teen Witches

MIRANDA CORCORAN

UNIVERSITY OF WALES PRESS

2022

www.uwp.co.uk

British Library Cataloguing-in-Publication Data

A catalogue record for this book is available from the British Library.

ISBN   978-1-78683-892-6
eISBN 978-1-78683-893-3

Typeset by Chris Bell, cbdesign

MIX
Paper from
responsible sources
FSC
www.fsc.org   FSC® C013604

Printed by CPI Antony Rowe, Melksham, United Kingdom

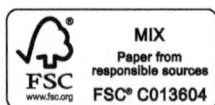

Contents

Acknowledgements   vii

List of Abbreviations   ix

Introduction   1

1. Towards a Teratology of the Teenage Witch   21

2. 'A Pack of "Bobby-Soxers"'
   Marion L. Starkey and the Birth of the Post-War
   Teenage Witch   55

3. 'A guide to life'
   Identity Formation and Perverse Readers in the Long 1960s   91

4. Becoming-Witch
   Makeover Narratives and Glamorous Transformations   127

5. 'How could there not be a choice?'
   Agency and Power in Fourth-Wave Teen Witch Texts   163

   Conclusion
   'By then I might be an entirely different person'   195

Endnotes   205

Select Bibliography   235

Index   243

Acknowledgements

THIS BOOK is the product of three-years' worth of research and writing, but it is also the product of a lifelong interest in witches, horror and the Gothic. I owe an immense debt of gratitude to my mother, Mary Corcoran, who happily indulged her strange daughter with weekend trips to the library and the video store. I am so thankful for her support, guidance and understanding. She has always been there for me, even though the academic world I presently inhabit is a million miles from where we started.

I also want to express my deep, heartfelt thanks to my partner Andrea Di Carlo for his endless love and support. *Ti voglio bene.* I am also lucky to have had the support of wonderful friends. I am immensely grateful to Cara O'Callaghan, Brian Farran, Laura Quirke, Erik Grayson, Edel Semple and Evelyn Hurley for their kindness and ability to distract me from the rigours of research. Equally, I am so fortunate to have had a number of academic collaborators who have also become dear friends: Steve Gronert Ellerhoff, Jeffrey Kahan, Miniature Malekpour and Anne Mahler. I would also like to thank everyone involved with the *New Ray Bradbury Review* and *The Irish Journal of Gothic and Horror Studies* for creating two intellectually enriching, yet always welcoming, communities. I am supremely thankful to Kat Ellinger and everyone at *Diabolique* magazine, not only for publishing my work, but for being an all-round group of wonderful people.

I am incredibly lucky to have worked for the past number of years with kind and compassionate colleagues in the Department of English,

University College Cork. Their support and understanding have been end-less and unfailing. Thank you as well to my students (past and present, undergraduate and postgraduate): you are always so inspiring.

Lastly, I would like to thank everyone who helped and guided me as I worked on this book. I am enormously grateful to the anonymous reviewer whose insightful feedback and constructive criticism shaped the present monograph into its final form. A huge thank you to University of Wales Press (UWP) Head of Commissioning Sarah Lewis for her patience and kindness. I am likewise indebted to everyone involved with the UWP Horror Studies series for giving my first monograph a home. Thank you to Peg Aloi for sending me copies of her previously published work. I would also like to express my boundless appreciation to Steve Gronert Ellerhoff, Jeffrey Kahan and Andrea Di Carlo for reading drafts of this book, whether in whole or in part.

List of Abbreviations

'**AW**'   Ray Bradbury, 'The April Witch', in *From the Dust Returned* (London: Earthlight, Simon & Schuster, 2001), pp. 21–35.

Ca   Stephen King, *Carrie* (London: Hodder & Stoughton, 1974), Kindle edition.

CAS   Roberto Aguirre-Sacasa and Robert Hack, *The Chilling Adventures of Sabrina* (vol. 1) (New York: Archie Comics, 2016).

Cr   Arthur Miller, *The Crucible* (London: Penguin, [1953] 2000), Kindle edition.

CW   Afia Atakora, *Conjure Women* (London: 4th Estate, 2020).

DM   Marion L. Starkey, *The Devil in Massachusetts: A Modern Inquiry into the Salem Witch Trials* (New York: Anchor Books, [1949] 1989).

LOC   Michael Thomas Ford, *Love and Other Curses* (New York: HarperTeen, 2019).

'**SD**'   Ray Bradbury, 'The Sleeper and Her Dreams', in *From the Dust Returned* (London: Earthlight, Simon & Schuster, 2001), pp. 17–19.

STW   *The Complete Sabrina the Teenage Witch: 1962–1972* (New York: Archie Comics, 2017), Kindle edition.

'TT'   Ray Bradbury, 'The Traveler', in *From the Dust Returned* (London: Earthlight, Simon & Schuster, 2001), pp. 159–71.

WBP   Elizabeth George Speare, *The Witch of Blackbird Pond* (New York: Houghton Mifflin Harcourt, [1958] 2011).

WHALC   Shirley Jackson, *We Have Always Lived in the Castle* (London: Penguin Classics, [1962] 2009).

'WO'   Ray Bradbury, 'West of October', in *From the Dust Returned* (London: Earthlight, Simon & Schuster, 2001), pp. 69–86.

Introduction

I N LATE JANUARY 1941, *Life* magazine published a photo-essay
describing a new American phenomenon. Enraptured by the dynamism
of his subjects, yet also somewhat tentative about their cliquish intensity,
the author of the piece approached his objects of study in a quasi-anthropological manner, categorising them carefully and taxonomically as
though he were observing a remote tribe or a strange new species of fauna.
'This is the season of the subdebutante', he warns:

> These are the days when in shrill perfumed coveys they flutter
> through the houses and clubhouses of America's big cities. When
> summer comes they will disperse to the lakes, beaches and moun-
> tains. But now the subdebutante is dynamic, gregarious and at the
> peak of her plumage.[1]

The curious, unwieldly term 'subdebutante' describes 'any socially unini-
tiated but acceptable maiden of 15 to 18 who gallivants around town
with the right young people'.[2] The subdebutante is therefore a sort of pro-
to-teenager, a youth whose voracious consumption, kinetic momentum
and cultish devotion to their social circle marks them off as a distinct social

demographic. While the use of 'the word "teenager" to describe the category of young people from fourteen to eighteen' would not become widespread amongst the American public until around 1944,[3] the subdebutante prefigured many of the concerns that would later accrue around the figure of the teenager: the 'subdeb' was superficial, frivolous and self-centred. Like the teenager who would continue her legacy, the subdebutante was constructed in dehumanising terms. In the pages of *Life*, she is portrayed as an exotic animal, a bird with brilliant feathers at the 'peak of her plumage'. Despite her affinity for the tokens and trinkets of consumerism, the subdebutante is repeatedly aligned with the natural, animal world. In a section describing 'slam books', a diary where teens express their 'frankest' thoughts about their social circle, it is explained that these books are 'circulated privately for *feline* amusement'.[4] Here, *Life* magazine invokes a powerful iconography of female adolescence as shallow, animalistic and precociously sexual.

At the same time, there is something inherently supernatural in *Life*'s description of these girls: they flutter through houses in the winter season, before dispersing to lakes, beaches and mountains in the summertime. The movements of these young women, their swift flight through homes and their eventual mass migration to the natural spaces of seashores and hilltops echoes the frenzy of early modern witches alighting to their sabbaths deep within the woods or high atop the Brocken. The season of the subdebutante could just as easily be the season of the witch! Their hastening collective flock recalls the descriptions of witches' sabbaths offered by the historian Carlo Ginzburg:

> Sometimes, having anointed their bodies, they flew, arriving astride poles or broom sticks; sometimes they arrived on the backs of animals, or transformed into animals themselves. Those who came for the first time had to renounce the Christian faith, desecrate the sacrament and offer homage to the devil, who was present in human or (most often) animal or semi-animal form. There would follow banquets. Dancing, sexual orgies.[5]

There is something in Ginzburg's account of the sabbath – the allusions to dynamic movement, the emphasis on transgression, the references to consumption – that echoes *Life*'s description of teenage girls. The public terror of witches' gatherings and wild speculations on their diabolical deeds anticipates the twentieth-century public hysteria about juvenile delinquency and anti-social behaviour. Moreover, there is a linguistic and iconographic parallel between the sabbath rites and some of the more unnerving aspects of teen-girl behaviour, particularly their cultish devotion to movie stars and singers, their intense friendships, strange rituals and secret languages of indecipherable slang.

Further invoking the image of witches speeding through the night sky, the *Life* essay characterises the girls as boisterous flocks, 'swoop[ing] in and out' of social events:

> They swoop in and out of parties in noisy, cohesive gangs. They love open houses where there are plenty of phonograph records, cigarets [*sic*] and 'cokes'. They never stay home on vacation nights. Their taste in male companionship runs less to steadfast devotion than to a multiplicity of dates and quick turnover. The world at large means nothing to any of them; the microcosm of their gang is everything. They speak in a curious lingo of their own, adore chocolate milkshakes, collect quantities of quaint dolls and soft squishy animals and drive like bats out of hell.[6]

Like the witches' sabbath, the social life of the subdeb begins with a descent from the heavens ('swooping in'), relies upon strange rites of music and dancing and is defined by consumption, though here the banquet is one of 'cigarets' and 'cokes'. Coven-like, these teen girls refuse the wider world, devote themselves to the 'microcosm of their gang' and communicate in their own 'curious lingo'. While it is obvious that the *Life* author had little conscious interest in portraying teenage girls as witches, his lexicon of feathers, swooping bodies and shrillness plays upon a vast cultural store of witches, harpies and she-monsters. There is something about the metamorphic quality of the witch, her ability to play in the space between categories, as well as her historical association with female transgression, that lends itself to the articulation of female adolescence.

It is this iconographic and imaginative connection between girls and witches that constitutes the central preoccupation of this book. The chapters that follow demonstrate how the witch was employed, from the middle part of the twentieth century onwards, as a means of conceptualising female adolescence. When the contemporary teenager emerged amidst the unprecedented tumult of World War II, the phenomenon was greeted with a potent admixture of disdain and intrigue. The teen girl seemed strange, lacking in purpose or definition, and evoked both desire and disgust in her elders. In 1945, *The March of Time* newsreel proclaimed that: 'Of all the phenomena of wartime life in the United States, one of the most fascinating and mysterious, and one of the most completely irrelevant, has been the emergence of the teenage girl as an American institution in her own right.'[7] Although adolescence as a developmental stage had been categorised as early as the nineteenth century, the suddenly ascendant teenager, defined by their 'newly visible spending power',[8] was unprecedented.

Although much ink was spent penning editorials on the problem of male juvenile delinquency, the female adolescent, with her new visibility, caused a distinct set of problems that were often more difficult to speak about. Mary Celeste Kearney claims that:

> teenage girls were represented as challenging the norms of female sexuality and resisting, or at least postponing, their engagement with domesticity, while also blurring the boundaries between the private and public spheres via their increased involvement in school, work and non-familial activities.[9]

Teenage girls posed something of a puzzle: they were imbued with a disruptive potential that strained at the boundaries of what could be publicly expressed in the mid-twentieth century, while at the same time being a nascent demographic, unformed and without a language, history or set of discursive tropes that could easily articulate their nature or social role. My contention here, and indeed throughout this book, is that witchcraft iconography and supernatural imagery provided a means for American culture to conceptualise and understand the figure of the teen girl in the first half-century or so after her emergence. In the popular imagination, witchcraft becomes fused with adolescence, generating a uniquely modern trope: the teenage witch. However, the teen witch is not simply a repository of cultural anxieties about wayward adolescent girls, but rather a vital, fluid and malleable trope that provided, and continues to provide, an imaginative framework for articulating and constituting female adolescent identity.

In the years following World War II, the association between female adolescence and witchcraft was solidified in both literary and historical texts, manifesting in works ranging from Marion L. Starkey's historical study *The Devil in Massachusetts* (1949) to Arthur Miller's play *The Crucible* (1953), as well as appearing in Ray Bradbury's short stories (particularly pieces such as 1952's 'The April Witch') and Elizabeth George

Speare's *The Witch of Blackbird Pond* (1958). A short while later, in October 1962, the most iconic teenage witch, Sabrina Spellman, also made her debut in *Archie's Madhouse #22*. It may seem, then, that the concomitant emergence of the teenage girl and her dark spectre, the teenage witch, is clearly and easily explicable as a reflection of broader societal concerns about female adolescence. And this is what she does, to a degree. It would be futile to claim that the teenage witch does not embody the zeitgeist of an era in which the teen girl flourished as an avatar of America's postwar affluence while simultaneously encapsulating its trepidations about social change. However, in this book, I contest that not only does the teen witch serve, to borrow Catherine Driscoll's phrase, 'as an index of broad cultural changes and continuities',[10] but that she also plays a major role in the discursive constitution of adolescent femininity in the second half of the twentieth century and on into the twenty-first. Born alongside the teenage girl, the adolescent sorceress provides a language through which to name the teen girl and to articulate her behaviour. The teenage witch furnishes American culture with a store of iconography through which to talk about unruly, leaky bodies, as well as a series of historical associations that facilitate the discussion of new forms of femininity, social deviance and girlhood. Rather than passively reflecting a new social phenomenon, the teen witch is a valuable component of the cultural discourse out of which the teenage girl was formed. Appearing in fiction and film, she articulates shifting ideas about the female body, sexuality and group dynamics. At the same time, she also plays a crucial role in how teenage girls shape their own identities and understand themselves. She is an imaginative double, a fictive doppelganger who embodies new modes of being and heralds new identificatory possibilities.

In her book *Mastering Fear: Women, Emotions, and Contemporary Horror*, Rikke Schubart argues that horror fiction frequently serves as an imaginative playground, a 'dark stage' where we can engage with challenging emotions and concepts and in doing so 're-author our self-scripts', imaging new identities and modes of being.[11] Likewise, the adolescent witch not only serves as a means for society to conceptualise and articulate adolescent identity, but she also acts as an avatar through which teenagers themselves can explore their own identities. Perhaps the most famous example of this kind of identificatory exploration through the icon of the teenage witch was the explosion of interest in Wicca and witchcraft iconography in wake of the immensely popular 1996 film *The Craft*. As Christine Jarvis demonstrates, fictional portrayals of teenage witches empower adolescent girls to reconfigure their own identificatory parameters in new, exciting or even challenging ways.[12] Likewise, Darren Elliott-Smith describes how another adolescent witch, Carrie White (*Carrie*, 1974), resonates powerfully with LGBTQ+ spectators, through her status as 'both victim and monster'.[13] Even one of the earliest teen witch texts, Speare's *The Witch of Blackbird Pond*, presents its heroine, sixteen-year-old accused witch Kit, as an avatar of adolescent possibility, encapsulating positive identificatory options for America's young girls. Indeed, as children's author Karen Cushman notes in her introduction to the 2011 edition of the novel, the character of Kit opens up a host of possibilities for young readers who are still forming their identities:

> What Kit learns throughout the book is just what I needed to learn as a young person – the value of being yourself, fighting for what you believe in, taking care of those who need care, seeing beauty in things that might ordinarily seem plain, building friendships and community and the importance of hard work.[14]

The teenage witch is therefore an active figure in twentieth and twenty-first-century American culture. Witchcraft, with its attendant images of subversion, transformation and deviance, provides an ideal language through which to shape popular understanding of the teenage girl, herself a figure associated with delinquency, consumption and rebellion. At the same time, she is an imaginary avatar through which teenagers themselves can play with their own identities and negotiate the boundaries of their selfhoods.

The teenage witch can be considered a cultural 'trope' in the sense of the term deployed by the historian Hayden White. Used in both literature and historical writing, tropes are devices (metonymy, synecdoche, irony and metaphor) that authors employ in order to evoke certain thoughts, ideas and responses in the reader. For White:

> Understanding is a process of rendering the unfamiliar, or the 'un-canny' in Freud's sense of that term, familiar; of removing it from the domain of things felt to be 'exotic' and unclassified into one or another domain of experience encoded adequately enough to be felt to be humanly useful, nonthreatening, or simply known by association. This process of understanding can only be tropological in nature, for what is involved in the rendering of the unfamiliar into the familiar is a troping that is generally figurative.[15]

In *Tropics of Discourse*, White explains that new modes of understanding are ushered into being by literary and conceptual devices that establish unexpected yet potent connections between disparate concepts and generate iconic images based on these connections. The *Life* piece mentioned above engages in this kind of tropological representation, using images of wildlife, exotic birds and vaguely supernatural depictions of swooping bodies to articulate the frenetic movements, hyperactivity and consumerist fervour of the subdebutante. Ilana Nash remarks that the importation of iconography to delineate teenage identity was widespread during the post-war decades: 'A vast discursive field surrounding the teenager emerged in twentieth-century mass culture, which frequently described youth in language that was quasi-anthropological in its discussion of teens' puzzling fads, slang, and "tribal" peer culture.'[16]

Likewise, in her article on post-war media representations of girls on the telephone, Mary Celeste Kearney explores how the image of chatty teens gossiping on the phone helped to solidify a new image of adolescent femininity as straddling the border between liberation and containment. The trope of the teenage daughter furtively whispering to her friends from the hallway or lying on her bed chatting about boys signalled a threat to American social norms around which a plethora of associations with promiscuity, disobedience and consumerist avarice coalesced. Kearney claims that:

> rather than approaching the girl on the phone as a commonly recurring image *that merely reflected* American girls' communicative practices in the mid-twentieth century, it should be analysed as a trope, *a discursive formation that signalled and helped to mediate a significant transition* in how teenage girlhood was being conceptualized during this period.[17]

Operating along similar lines, this book explores the teenage witch not as a mere reflection of US anxieties about adolescent femininity, but as a distinct 'discursive formation' that enabled Americans to conceptualise teenage girls as a unique identificatory category and a new form of female subjectivity, while concomitantly offering adolescent girls themselves a malleable, imaginative space in which to experiment with their own nascent identities.

Thinking with Witches: Conceptualising Female Adolescence
Through Witchcraft

Although many influential ideas about witchcraft derive from antiquity,[18] the image of the witch as a night-flying servant of the Devil emerged only in the early fifteenth century, with the large-scale criminal prosecution of witchcraft existing alongside both the Protestant Reformation and the humanist Renaissance.[19] The composite or cumulative notion of witch-craft that appeared at this time brought together a host of previously dis-tinct ideas drawn from popular folklore, beliefs about heretical sects and theological concepts.[20] The cumulative concept of witchcraft constructed the witch as someone who employed harmful magic (*maleficia*) through the aid of the Devil, with whom they had entered into a pact.[21] As part of this pact, the witch not only agreed to serve the Devil, but to worship him, often collectively in large gatherings called sabbaths. In various continental accounts of the sabbath, witches flew to these meetings on the backs of animals, or on rods, poles and brooms. While the vast majority of histori-ans generally agree that the early modern witch had little basis in reality,[22] witchcraft beliefs formed a meaningful part of the period's cultural and intellectual life.

In his study *Thinking with Demons*, Stuart Clark argues that 'whether witchcraft beliefs did in fact correspond with reality' is ultimately 'a question not worth asking'.[23] Rather, witchcraft and demonological beliefs are impor-tant *as* beliefs, ideas that form part of a broader discursive arena. As Clark explains, demonology engaged with and was sustained by a range of distinct intellectual commitments.[24] Discourses on witches abutted wider debates about history, religious authority and the natural world, often overlapping and intersecting with them. Moreover, ideas about witchcraft regularly con-tributed to ongoing debates about religion, science, politics and history. Clark observes that in many instances, 'the subject of witchcraft seems to have been used as a means for thinking through problems that originated elsewhere and that had little or nothing to do with the legal prosecution of witches'.[25] This is not to dismiss the horror of witchcraft persecutions nor to obscure the suffering of those who were tried, imprisoned and executed as witches. After all, witchcraft beliefs – from antiquity to the early modern period, from the Satanic Panic[26] to the witch hunts that continue in many parts of the world today – have destroyed lives and resulted in countless fatalities. However, alongside and sometimes intertwined with these very real tragedies, witchcraft beliefs serve an important cultural function.

Clark argues that demonology and witchcraft beliefs can be understood as an 'intellectual resource', a framework through which myriad philosophical, cultural and political concerns were investigated.[27] It is for this reason, Charles Zika explains, that the early modern witch could be put to a wide range of conceptual uses:

> representations of witchcraft could support calls for reform of the moral order, stimulate anxieties over female sexuality, support the articulation of male fantasies, forefront the moral lessons of classical literature, reinforce the power of Scriptural precedents, strengthen secular authorities in the disciplining of their states, interpret social crimes as signs of divine displeasure, and help incorporate the New World into the cultural frameworks of the old.[28]

Similarly, in his book, *Demon Lovers*, Walter Stephens claims that early modern witches served an important theological function. Through their reputed physical contact with demons – whether sexual or otherwise – witches provided empirical proof of the veracity of the diabolical and, by extension, of the divine.[29] For Ronald Hutton, one historical function of the witch has been as an embodiment of inversion and deviance, 'an attempt to imagine how human beings can continue to live within communities while secretly rejecting and attacking all of their moral constraints'.[30]

Witchcraft was also bound up with ideas about women. Many early modern witchcraft treatises tacitly assume a link between witches and femininity, while approximately 75 per cent of witches executed in Western Europe and British North America were women.[31] Despite the predominance of female witches, witchcraft was a sex-related rather than a sex-specific crime.[32] The predilection of women towards witchcraft was primarily understood in terms of innate characteristics that made women more lustful, curious and talkative. The seventeenth-century Puritan clergyman Richard Bernard wrote that women were 'tongueripe'; both inquisitive and garrulous, they desired forbidden information but could not keep it to themselves.[33] Pierre Crespet claimed that the power to bewitch derived from vapours emitted by the build-up of melancholic and menstrual blood in the female body.[34] Similarly, early modern thinkers also drew on the Pythagorean theory of opposites in order to associate the male with limitation, light and goodness and the female with unboundedness, darkness and evil.[35] Witchcraft, then, existed within a broader representational schema in which divisions between good and evil, soul and body, light and dark reflected the male/female binary.[36] Witches were simply one expression of female disorder, a category that also included whores, gossips and shrews. Demonological treatises, such as the 1487 *Malleus Maleficarum* that attributed witchcraft to the lustfulness and perceived intellectual weakness of women, were not unique expressions of misogyny. Instead, they formed part of a broader cultural discourse that associated femininity with pollution, instability, carnality and the body, while simultaneously linking men to solidity, consistency, intellect and the mind. Witches therefore provided the early modern imagination with a means through which to articulate ideas about femininity.

Witchcraft has also served as a useful means of discussing female deviance. Serenity Young argues in her study of airborne women that witches provide a potent discursive framework for articulating ideas about womanhood and deviance, observing that:

> beliefs about witches are especially key to a society's concept of womanhood because witches, especially, contradict the characteristics of the ideal woman. The witch is an inversion of the good woman, who embodies the categories of wife, mother, and upholder of morality.[37]

Thus, while witches might enable early modern thinkers to conceptualise femininity broadly conceived in opposition to masculinity, they also furnished a language of inversion that allowed those same individuals to talk specifically about deviant women. Clark describes the early modern 'good' woman as 'pious, patient, silent, acting in conformity to male standards of female sexuality, domesticity, and religiosity, and, above all . . . obedient'.[38] Women defined as 'evil' or deviant in this period were those who acted in opposition to these norms and attempted to snatch control of language, sexuality or authority away from men. Active by night rather than by day, adoring the Devil instead of God, witches upended the natural order and symbolised the inversion of gender hierarchies. During the early modern period, the witch, as a trope, generated new ways of thinking about and articulating femininity, a function that she would continue to fulfil over the next five centuries.

By the middle part of the twentieth century, the witch had accumulated a plethora of distinct meanings in the United States. Early American discussions of witch rials, those published in the late eighteenth and early nineteenth centuries, framed witch beliefs as a product of ignorance and superstition.[39] Novels printed during the first decades of the nineteenth century – including *Salem Witchcraft* (1820), *The Witch of New England* (1824) and *Rachel Dyer* (1828) – attributed witchcraft panics to political and cultural populism.[40] Later works, such as Charles Wentworth Upham's *Salem Witchcraft* (1867), constructed witchcraft hysteria as an allegory for corrupt or repressive authority. In the late nineteenth and early twentieth centuries, feminist authors such as Matilda Joslyn Gage (*Woman, Church and State*, 1893) and Charlotte Perkins Gilman ('When I Was a Witch', 1909) employed the figure of the witch to explore the powerlessness of women in patriarchal society. Likewise, Virginia Woolf in her essay 'A Room of One's Own' (1929) posits that when 'one reads of a witch being ducked, of a woman possessed by devils, of a wise woman selling herbs . . . then I think we are on the track of a lost novelist, a suppressed poet'.[41] As the twentieth century progressed, popular cinema furnished the American imagination with a broad array of witches who served different functions. *The Wizard of Oz* (1939) featured two witches, one a wicked hag and the other an angelic beauty, while Disney's *Snow White and the Seven Dwarfs* presented a witch who was simultaneously an ugly crone and a sensual vamp.[42] The 1942 comedy *I Married a Witch* and the equally light-hearted *Bell, Book and Candle* (1958) presented the courtship between female witches and human males as an analogue for sexual containment. Consequently, by the time the teenage girl emerged in the mid-twentieth century, the witch was already laden with multiple, occasionally contradictory, meanings.

In his work on monstrosity, Jack Halberstam argues that Gothic novels produce fear through a 'vertiginous excess of meaning'.[43] In Gothic fiction of the nineteenth century, 'The monster always becomes a primary focus of interpretation and its monstrosity seems available for any number of meanings'.[44] With reference to *Dracula* (1897), Halberstam argues that to reduce the titular vampire to an avatar of perverse sexuality risks stabilising the identity of perversity, reducing it to a static set of characteristics, when such Gothic monsters 'produce monstrosity as never unitary but always an aggregate of race, class, and gender'.[45] Although Halberstam views the contemporary monster as less indebted to such modes of over-determined meaning, I would argue that the witch remains available 'for any number of number of meanings'. The witch signifies racial Otherness, sexual non-conformity, domestication, consumerism, youthful glamour and the ravages of age. The teenage witch discussed in the following pages is simply one expression of the witch's excess of meaning, and even she is not stable or fixed. Rather, she shifts over time, encompassing new ideas about adolescent identity, sexuality and embodiment. Similarly, the teen witch is merely one way of thinking about adolescence. Even within the realm of horror, adolescence has been signified through the body of the werewolf (*I Was a Teenage Werewolf* [1957], *Teen Wolf* [1985] and *Ginger Snaps* [2000]), the sexual desire of the demon (*Night of the Demons* [1988] and *Jennifer's Body* [2009]) or the madness of the teen murderer (*Scream* [1996]). As with the early modern witch, the contemporary teen witch is simply one framework through which a multitude of different problems and ideas can be thought through. Moreover, like her fifteenth, sixteenth and seventeenth-century predecessors, the teenage witch can be put to a range of conceptual uses, enfolding within herself ideas about adolescent identity, social dynamics, puberty, identity formation and more.

Scope and Content

This monograph will focus heavily on the periodisation of the texts under discussion. Although centred primarily on the post-World War II development of the teenager as a highly visible social phenomenon, it also reaches back to early modern and Victorian antecedents in an attempt to contextualise the association between adolescent girls and the occult. However, the focus of this book remains firmly grounded in late twentieth and early twenty-first-century popular culture. At the same time, the present study also limits itself to representations of teen witches in *American* popular culture. While Barbara Creed notes that in many cultures around the world 'a young girl who had prophetic dreams at the time of her menarche was frequently singled out as a future shaman or witch',[46] this book is firmly rooted in the US context, largely due to the myriad associations between post-war American culture and the birth of the modern teenager. Unfortunately, this means that I will necessarily have to exclude some of the fascinating representations of teen witches produced in other parts of the world, such as the British film *The Blood on Satan's Claw* (Piers Haggard, 1971) or the Czech films *Valerie and Her Week of Wonders* (Jaromil Jireš, 1970) and *The Girl on the Broomstick* (Václav Vorlíček, 1972).

Chapter 1 serves primarily as a theoretical and historical overview of the teenage witch. This chapter maps and clarifies the key theoretical apparatuses utilised throughout this book. I begin by positioning adolescence – the real-world developmental phenomenon – as fundamentally biocultural in nature. Rejecting both constructivist and essentialist positions, bioculturalism is an intellectual paradigm that views cultural and biological processes as inextricably linked. This means that adolescence, for instance, would be understood as a developmental period informed by hormonal fluctuation, pubertal transformation, social norms and environmental factors. However, I argue that while more mundane representations of adolescence can be read through a biocultural lens, the fantastic figure of the adolescent witch requires a more pliable theoretical framework. I maintain that in writing about teenage witchcraft, the biocultural model of adolescence should be supplemented, or even displaced, by alternative conceptions of embodiment that can account for the fluidity and metamorphic power of the adolescent witch.

As such, the first chapter constructs a theoretical model that incorporates conceptions of embodied subjectivity derived from the works of Michel Foucault, Gilles Deleuze and Félix Guattari, as well as new materialist or material feminist thinkers such as Karen Barad, Stacy Alaimo and Susan Hekman. The theories advanced by these scholars can, I believe, serve as a useful supplement to biocultural views of adolescence because they focus on issues of materiality and embodiment, while also attempting to dismantle simplistic forms of mind/body dualism. Drawing on the work of these thinkers, I argue that adolescent witches are regularly portrayed as possessing a vibrant, agentic corporeality that empowers them to demolish dualistic binaries between subject and object, nature and culture, self and Other. Teen witches, rather than being bound to static, monolithic forms of subjectivity, regularly undertake dynamic becomings, or transformations, that bring them into meaningful connections with other (human and non-human) lifeforms. However, where a number of the texts discussed in this book celebrate the metamorphic materiality of the adolescent witch, framing her as a creative force, other texts portray her as a transgressive entity whose ability to destabilise binary categories holds untold potential for destruction.

The chapter closes with an overview of the figure of the teenage witch or girl occultist prior to the mid-twentieth century. It briefly explores supernatural expressions of girlhood such as medieval fasting saints and early modern 'miraculous maidens'. This chapter also expounds on the central role afforded to women in occult movements of the nineteenth century. Here, I place particular emphasis on the part played by the young women who acted as mediums in Spiritualist séances of the nineteenth and early twentieth centuries. This chapter analyses how pre-twentieth-century figurations of mystical girlhood pivoted on notions of corporeal fluidity, transformation and the dissolution of dualisms. It also contextualises the teenage witch within a longstanding tradition whereby female adolescence was associated with and understood through the supernatural.

Chapters 2 and 3 meditate on the function of the adolescent witch. The second chapter initiates this process with a consideration of the teen witch as a trope through which adult authors could conceptualise the novel phenomenon of the adolescent girl. This chapter begins with a discussion of Marion L. Starkey's influential historical study *The Devil in Massachusetts: A Modern Inquiry into the Salem Witch Trials*, which was published in 1949. Starkey's study attributes the Salem witchcraft panic to the hormonal delusions of what she calls a 'pack of bobby-soxers'. As is evident from Starkey's use of contemporary terminology, the purpose of her book is not so much to provide a rigorous historical account of trials themselves, but rather to understand modern female adolescence through the iconography and language of witchcraft. Starkey's book would be instrumental in inaugurating the trope of the teenage witch as we now understand it. Alongside its immensely generative anachronisms, *The Devil in Massachusetts* attributes the accusations of the bewitched girls to a vaguely defined biological upheaval, a conflation of puberty and hysteria that frames adolescent corporeality as fundamentally disruptive.

The chapter then moves on to investigate the relationship between Starkey's study and Arthur Miller's play *The Crucible* (1953), a text that draws extensively on historical material derived from *The Devil in Massachusetts*. Eschewing the familiar discourses about McCarthyism, I focus primarily on Miller's representation of the 'children' at the heart of the witchcraft panic. Here, I discuss why, despite the fact that the accusers spanned a wide range of demographics (including children, middle-aged women and men), Miller depicts them, almost uniformly, as a group of teenage girls. I argue that, like Starkey, Miller attributes the Salem witchcraft panic to the unstable, active materiality of the adolescent body, which is here framed as threatening to the social order. The chapter closes with a discussion of short stories written by the fantasist Ray Bradbury in the late 1940s and early 1950s that, in contrast to Miller and Starkey's work, celebrate the fluid materiality of the adolescent body. These texts, 'The Traveler', 'West of October' and 'The April Witch', centre on a seventeen-year-old witch named Cecy, who holds the power to inhabit other bodies. Employing Deleuzian conceptions of becoming, as well as new materialist ideas about the continuity and agentic capacities of matter, I argue that Cecy's metamorphic abilities enable her to make meaningful, productive connections with the world around her.

Chapter 3 explores another function of the teen witch text: its capacity to serve as an imaginative space in which adolescent readers can explore and develop their own identities. This chapter also represents a chronological step forward, as it focuses on teen witch texts produced during the period that historian Christopher B. Strain terms the 'long 1960s'.[47] According to Strain, the long 1960s refers to the period between 1955 and 1973, an epoch that began with the dissolution of post-war consensus culture and continued through to the early 1970s recession. I begin by exploring instructive young-adult fiction, Speare's *The Witch of Blackbird Pond* and Archie Comic's early *Sabrina the Teenage Witch* series (1962–72), to show how these teen witches serve as identificatory templates through which adolescent readers can learn to model normative femininity. Moving on to more unsettling, self-consciously Gothic works such as Shirley Jackson's *We Have Always Lived in the Castle* (1962) and Stephen King's *Carrie* (written in 1973, but published in 1974), I illustrate how violent, often murderous, teen witches can offer liberatory identificatory options for girl readers who identify with their rage and frustration. These young women, I argue, undertake exciting, dynamic becomings that are initiated by acts of violence. In doing so, they fragment binary constructions of gender and sexuality, while also unsettling dualistic divisions between self and Other, human and animal, animate and inanimate. Drawing on ideas of perverse readership/spectatorship derived from the works of Eve Kosofsky Sedgwick and Janet Staiger, this chapter argues that these sinister teen witches enable young readers to imagine new and potentially subversive selfhoods.

Chapters 4 and 5 shift away from considering the function of the teen witch and move towards an analysis of her abilities, what she can do. Chapter 4 centres on the transformative power of the teen witch, her ability to change shape and appearance, as it manifests through the convention of the magical makeover. Situating this convention in the context of post-feminism, a complex amalgamation of themes and ideas that emerged in the late 1980s and pivoted on the presumed 'pastness' of feminist discourse, I focus on four key texts: *Teen Witch* (1989), *Sabrina the Teenage Witch* (1996–2003), *The Craft* (1996) and *Buffy the Vampire Slayer* (1997–2003). The chapter contends that hegemonic texts, such as the film *Teen Witch*, advocate a restrictive, normative mode of femininity and utilise the makeover trope to fix the teenage witch into a rigid molar subjectivity that depends on ingrained hierarchies and dualistic, binary modes of being. However, I also argue that this kind of static molarity is not the only option available to the fictive teen witch, as a number of the texts discussed in this chapter – the television series *Sabrina* and *Buffy*, the film *The Craft* – imagine such transformation as playful, even liberating acts of becoming that challenge binary constructions of class, gender and sexuality. In these texts, the makeover or transformation is framed as a molecular becoming that enables the teen witch to move away from a conception of identity as fixed, bounded or unified and towards a more fluid, contiguous vision of the self.

In the final chapter, Chapter 5, I analyse the recent surge in popularity of the teenage witch and focus on another of her powers: agency. In the first part of this chapter, I focus on a series of post-millennial teen witch texts: *American Horror Story: Coven* (2013), *The Witch* (2015), Roberto Aguirre-Sacasa's comic-book series *The Chilling Adventures of Sabrina* (2014–present) and its Netflix adaptation (2018–20). Reading these works through the lens of fourth-wave feminism – a movement that emerged in the 2010s and emphasises issues of consent, intersectionality and bodily autonomy – I argue that these works foreground themes of agency and power. Working with theories advanced by Karen Barad and Michel Foucault, I argue that both power agency and power are figured, in these texts, as relational forces. I maintain that in each of these texts, the teen witch engages in complex reconfigurations of phenomenal parameters and navigates broader agential fields in order to construct herself as a specific type of agent. In all of these works, the teen witch must also reframe her relationship with her body, learning to view it not as a passive object, or a negation of consciousness, but rather as part of an identity conceived of as a dynamic, unfolding event. These texts also engage with the convention of the demonic pact in order to frame power, not as a 'thing' to be possessed, but as a complex series of force relations that can be resisted, reinforced or reversed.

The second section of Chapter 5 problematises this optimistic vision of teen witches actively negotiating fields of agency and power. Here, I argue that in contrast to white teen witches, who are free to navigate their identities and engage in exciting, liberating becomings, witches of colour are often pinned to molar subjectivities that bind them to bodies portrayed as mute, passive objects. I argue that many teen witch texts are informed by racist, sexist discourses that reduce Black women to their physical bodies and occlude possibilities for transformation or becoming. Consequently, Black teens are rarely afforded the ability to freely navigate vectors of power and agency. Here, I address the representation of Black witches in works such as *American Horror Story: Coven*, *Chilling Adventures* and Afia Atakora's 2020 novel *Conjure Women* to explore how issues of agency and power are invariably complicated by the legacy of slavery and the endurance of racist ideologies.

Finally, this book draws to a close with a discussion of a recent teen witch text, Michael Thomas Ford's *Love and Other Curses* (2019), which pushed the boundaries of what a teen witch can be. By focusing on a queer male witch, this book troubles the narrow parameters that had defined the teen witch trope over the past seventy years. I use *Love and Other Curses* as a starting point to draw together some of the key themes and ideas that have emerged in my study and suggest some of the ways that the teen witch might evolve in the coming years.

'Thou witch-baby': Limitations and Exclusions

This book focuses on teenage witches and their shifting representation across genres and media from the mid-twentieth century to the present day. However, the category of the female adolescent is not an uncomplicated one. Indeed, as I explain in Chapter 1, both femininity and adolescence are contested states, understood in different ways across cultures and time periods. However, rather than posing a challenge to the scholarship undertaken in the following pages, such instability is an essential part of these analyses. This book foregrounds the complex ways in which both gender and adolescence are mediated and transformed by culture. Today, adolescence is considered to encompass the period between ten and eighteen years of age. However, Catherine Driscoll notes that even in the comparatively short period between the late nineteenth and early twentieth centuries, adolescence expanded to encompass young people up to the age of twenty-one or even twenty-five, before contracting during the following decades to include only those in their teenage years.[48] In many of the texts explored in this book, female adolescence is often connected to menarche and menstruation. While this is simplistic and exclusionary in its failure to account for teenage girls who experience neither of these phenomena, menarche is often used a symbolic shorthand, particularly in fiction, to suggest a transitional moment in the life of a young woman.[49]

Reflecting the historically variable definition of the teenager, the adolescent witches discussed in this book primarily inhabit the transformative years between their early teens and early twenties, with some straining at the borders of this demographic. Because of the propensity of Western European and US popular culture to gender witches as female, these teen witches are *almost* uniformly cis-gendered girls and women.[50] This tendency to exclude male or trans witches is not intended to be prescriptive on my part;[51] rather, it reflects some of the limitations inherent in twentieth and early twenty-first-century representations of the adolescent witch. This book also neglects some of the most popular witchcraft texts produced over the past few decades. Works such as the WB series *Charmed* (1998–2006) and Alice Hoffman's *Practical Magic* (1995) have been excluded from this study because although they incorporate aspects of the 'coming-of-age' plot commonly associated with teenagers, their characters are adults for the majority of the narrative.

This book also ignores the figures of the 'sinister child' and the 'witch child', both of whom are undoubtedly related to the teenage witch. The critic Robin Wood argues that children frequently appear in horror because they embody an Otherness that we, as adults, attempt to repress in ourselves: 'What the previous generation repressed in us, we in turn, repress in our children, seeking to mold them into replicas of ourselves, perpetuators of a discredited tradition.'[52] Childhood, which emerged as a distinct, protected state only at the end of the seventeenth century, was idealised in the works of Romantic writers such as William Blake, Jean-Jacques Rousseau and William Wordsworth.[53] For them, the child was innocent, uncorrupted by the demands of civilisation and intimately connected to the natural world.[54] Horror fiction regularly subverts such notions of pre-cultural innocence, reconfiguring the child's remoteness from civilisation as sinister and threatening. Robert Bloch's 1947 story 'Sweets to the Sweet' and William March's 1954 novel *The Bad Seed* imagine little girls whose pre-cultural states ensure that they are unencumbered by conventional morality. Such texts also employ monstrous children to explore intergenerational conflict and the fragility of the American family. However, because childhood, as both a cultural and biological event, is distinct from adolescence and carries its own set of imaginative associations, evil or supernatural children must necessarily be excluded from this study.

Likewise, the witch child must also be overlooked. Witch children are often born into families of sorcerers, inheriting their powers while lacking the inhibitions of adults. They are often chaotic creatures, causing mayhem with their unrestrained magical abilities. In the television series *Bewitched* (1964–72), the children of Samantha and Darrin Stephens inherit their mother's powers and use them, often unintentionally, to disrupt their parents' ordered suburban existence. Other comedy series, such as *Sabrina the Teenage Witch* (1996–2003), also feature witch children who use their powers to chaotic ends. In more serious texts, such as Alice Hoffman's *Practical Magic*, child witches who have inherited their powers through family bloodlines are used to explore themes of intolerance and prejudice, as these children face discrimination due to their perceived Otherness. Even in less explicitly fantastical works, the witch child has been deployed as a symbol of both childhood innocence and societal intolerance. In Nathaniel Hawthorne's *The Scarlet Letter* (1850), Hester Prynne's illegitimate daughter Pearl possesses an affinity for the natural world and is shunned by a repressive Puritan society that denounces her as an 'imp of evil, emblem and product of sin'.[55] In one passage, a sailor even hails Pearl as 'thou witch-baby'.[56] Witch children serve an important function, reminding us that, 'Across history and literature . . . children have been positioned in relation to witchcraft: as innocent victims, as accusers, as witches, and frequently in the liminal ground between these seemingly opposing statuses'.[57] However, because childhood carries with it a unique set of associations – innocence, inhibition, nostalgia – and because childhood emerged as a concept separately from adolescence, child witches are a discrete subject matter, one already explored skilfully by Kristina West in her 2020 book *Reading the Salem Witch Child*. The witches who inhabit my study exist primarily because adolescence poses a vexing challenge to the rigid distinction between child and adult. Where childhood had, by the middle decades of the twentieth century, accrued a robust imaginative lexicon through which it could be discussed and understood, adolescence was still a novel idea. Images of witchcraft were therefore imported – deployed as metaphor, synecdoche and simile – in order to articulate a concept that was new and without a symbolic language of its own.

1

Towards a Teratology of the Teenage Witch

Between Culture and Biology?: Defining the Teenage Girl

I N ORDER TO explore the evolution of the teenage witch as a cultural trope, it is pertinent to begin by asking the same question that parents, teachers, social workers and policymakers found themselves asking in the middle part of the twentieth century: what exactly is the teenage girl? Is adolescence a physical reality, tangible and measurable, or is it a cultural construction? Over the course of this book, I treat a host of texts that position female adolescence either at the intersection of biology and culture or as a profoundly embodied experience that refuses dualistic models of a biology/culture divide. Indeed, as noted in the Introduction, it is my contention that the corpus of twentieth and twenty-first-century teen witch texts is split between those that imagine the adolescent girl as poised between the natural and the cultural, therefore figuring her as a potentially transgressive entity, and those that understand her in terms of an active, agentic materiality and consequently construe her in terms of creation, connection and growth. This chapter plots a spectrum of theoretical approaches that can be usefully employed to grapple with female adolescence in general and the teen witch in particular. Here, I move from biocultural theories that frame adolescence as *both* a biological phenomenon and a social category through to radical constructions of materiality in which dichotomous notions of the nature/culture, body/mind divide are not only challenged but undone. Drawing on these distinct, albeit inter-related, conceptions of teenage girlhood, I then argue for a teratology – a science of monsters[1] – of the teen witch that pivots on the materiality of the body. Such a framework eschews the psychodrama associated with concepts such as the abject and the uncanny, well-worn cartographies of female monstrosity, to consider corporeality itself as the locus of presumed monstrosity. Finally, this chapter concludes with an overview of the his-torical antecedents, those figurations of mystically inclined femininity, that while predating the teenage witch, nevertheless influenced her devel-opment. In these proto-teenage witches, it is possible to uncover com-plex issues of embodiment and materiality that anticipate those that later accrued around the twentieth-/twenty-first-century adolescent sorceress.

While the theoretical approaches that guide this book centre on bod-ies and the material, it is crucial to note that the teenager is often read as a cultural product. Social constructivist understandings of adolescence are grounded in the belief that the American teenager, as a distinct demo-graphic, was born entirely of discourse, a fantasy of extended youth con-jured into being in the halcyon days of post-war affluence. Certainly, the modern term 'teenager' is a product of the mid-twentieth century, while the conception of female adolescence as a distinct developmental stage originates in the nineteenth century. In her study of girlhood, Catherine Driscoll notes that:

> Adolescence has historically been applied predominantly to con-ceptions (both theoretical and popular) of developing manhood. In the context of increasing nineteenth-century interest in girlhood, discourses framing a female adolescence and new ideas about fem-ininity enable further twentieth-century innovation in theorizing female adolescence.[2]

As a demographic classification, the adolescent appears precisely at the moment in history when systems of scientific knowledge were deployed to both constrain and construct individuals as specific social types, mould-ing them into culturally sanctioned entities that reflected the values and attitudes of their era. According to Michel Foucault, this was a period when the Western world was engaged in the 'transformation of sex into discourse' and dedicated to the eradication of 'the forms of sexuality that were not amenable to the strict economy of reproduction'.[3] As part of this emerging medical gaze, a host of new sexualities, proclivities, 'perversions' and demographics were born: 'from childhood to old age, a norm of sexual development was defined and all the possible deviations were carefully described.'[4] The formulation of adolescence as a distinct developmental phase occurred within this broader Victorian rush to label, categorise and control sexual development. Indeed, the invention of adolescence can be assigned a definitive date: 1904, just as the Victorian era was making way for the twentieth century. The inception of adolescence is generally held to be 1904 because it was in this year that the psychologist G. Stanley Hall – often considered the father of adolescence – published his influential study *Adolescence: Its Psychology and Its Relations to Physiology, Anthropology, Sociology, Sex, Crime, Religion and Education*. Hall's work was key in defining adolescence as a transformative epoch, classifying the teen years as 'the storm and stress period'.[5] For Hall, adolescence occurs between the ages of fourteen and twenty-four, and it is characterised by depressive modes, 'high sensation seeking' and 'susceptibility to media influences'.[6] All of these are, of course, characteristics that would continue to be associated with adolescence, marking it off as a potentially dangerous developmental period.

That adolescence can be seen as an invention of late nineteenth and early twentieth-century psychology seems to suggest that it is a fundamentally constructed, socially contingent category. Furthermore, numerous psychologists such as Perry R. Hinton note that 'the English word "teenager" is a culturally constructed concept with a distinct (culturally based) representation'.[7] Hinton's constructivist understanding of adolescence emerges from a cross-cultural analysis of feminine adolescence, and he notes that adolescent identity is envisioned differently across distinct cultural contexts:

> the categories of the *shouju* [Japan] and *jeune fille en fleur* [France] have very different social representations of emerging womanhood, arising within different cultural contexts, without focus on teen 'deviance', teen 'problems' (requiring adult support) and teens being psychologically 'troubled'.[8]

If adolescence is envisioned as both the product of the nineteenth-century drive towards scientific rationalism and an infinitely malleable social category that transforms as it crosses national boundaries and historical eras, it is logical to imagine that the adolescent is little more than a cultural construct. This mode of apprehension is not only logical but appealing. Constructivism, the anti-essentialist position that denies the primacy of biological factors in the development of the self, is often viewed as liberating, largely because it sees identity as fluid and transitory.[9]

As enticing as a constructivist framework might be, it is ultimately an approach to adolescence that minimises its somatic dimensions and the experience of corporeality. For instance, although it is possible to see the 'teenager' – that is, the modern, post-World War II phenomenon – as a wholly cultural construct, it is important to bear in mind how this construct is connected to puberty and the biological changes that usually begin with the onset of menarche in people with uteruses (and starting with ejaculation, or semenarche, for those with testes).[10] Despite its problematic elision of embodiment, many scholars are reluctant to abandon constructivism, fearing that the only alternative is an essentialist or deterministic framework. Essentialism posits the existence of an inherent, static essence that remains unchanged by history or culture.[11] Because essentialist positions are often imbricated with misogynistic or racist discourses that reduce individuals to a fixed biological principle, most thinkers approach them cautiously. However, while such uneasiness about essentialist perspectives is legitimised by their frequent connection to reactionary ideologies, the biology-culture dichotomy that guides so much of our thinking about identity and being is simplistic. Moreover, I maintain, it is a bifurcation ill-equipped to describe the complexities of adolescence.

Biocultural Theory: A Methodology for Comprehending Female Adolescence

In recent years, many thinkers have begun to reconceptualise adolescence in a manner that takes into account 'both the biological process of puberty *and* psychological, social, and cultural changes'.[12] This 'holistic' methodology is known as bioculturalism, or biocultural theory, and it is a productive method for establishing a dialogue between 'biological and cultural perspectives'.[13] In contrast to constructivist visions of humanity, which conceive of individuals as social products, infinitely malleable and historically contingent, a biocultural approach to human subjectivity imagines the myriad ways in which bodies and brains are influenced by the environment and evolutionary history.[14] However, as Torben Grodal is careful to point out in his study of film and bioculturalism:

The biological approach to culture does not contradict a historicist approach; on the contrary, it offers a radically historical and constructivist view, describing the evolutionary processes and functional concerns that have led to our present human ways of thinking and representing.[15]

Biocultural theory is also distinct from biological essentialism, as it does not seek to negate the influence of social and historical infrastructures on humanity. It posits an understanding of selfhood that is fluid and historically, or culturally, contingent. Bioculturalism is an interdisciplinary paradigm that seeks to bridge the ideational chasm between what C. P. Snow termed the two cultures (science and the humanities) by creating a 'third culture' that unites science with the humanities.[16]

An example of this biological-cultural identificatory nexus is provided by Rikke Schubart who illustrates a biocultural approach to the essentialist claim that women lack the strength or ability to throw an object long distance; or, to put it more succinctly, she deconstructs the notion that a woman will always 'throw like a girl'. Drawing on the work of Iris Young and Erwin Straus, Schubart claims that the cultural imperative for women to be smaller and less visible than men affects the way in which they experience physical embodiment:

Women learn an ambiguous transcendence where we treat our body as an object (a-thing-to-be-looked-at) and a subject. We inhibit intentionality and take up less space than men, we take shorter strides, hold our arms closer to the trunk, and we approach 'physical engagement with things with timidity, uncertainty, and hesitancy'. We restrict our motility, take away self-confidence, tell ourselves to be self-aware – and *then* we throw like girls.[17]

In this way, Schubart articulates an analytical paradigm where body and mind, biology and culture, are not seen as distinct solutions to the problem of identity production. Rather, her conception of selfhood is one that locates identity within a dynamic nexus of influences.

The dynamism of biocultural theory lends itself particularly well to the study of adolescence. Anthropologists who track the often-complex relationship between biology (puberty) and culture (adolescence) during the process of maturation have employed bioculturalism to understand how physiological markers of development are often bound up with culturally constructed values, social roles and rites of passage. Meredith W. Reiches describes puberty as a 'physiological event' that commences with the activation of gonadotropin-releasing hormone (GnRH) pulses from the hypothalamus and leads to transformations in growth, metabolic and reproductive hormones.[18] This period also sees an increase in gonadal steroid hormone levels, as well as a rise in growth hormone (GH) and insulin-like growth factor, which later reduce to a post-pubertal equilibrium, signalling the end of puberty.[19] At the same time, Reiches observes that adolescence is defined not only by physical transformation, but also by social transition. She explains that 'somatic and reproductive maturity and sociocultural adulthood are related and sometimes difficult to disentangle'.[20] Physiological development is regularly marked by social milestones or understood through cultural tropes, while the biological processes of puberty, particularly in terms of timing, are invariably influenced by environmental factors or external stimuli that affect nutrition, diet and energy expenditure.[21]

Biocultural theory is a helpful methodology for explicating adolescence without either reducing it to the immovable bedrock of biology or imaging it solely in terms of highly unstable, continuously shifting cultural representations. Yet, although bioculturalism presents an intriguing view of adolescence as it exists in our mundane world, it may be somewhat limited in its capacity to account for the fantastic figure of the teenage witch. Biocultural theory is a diverse conceptual framework, one that 'can carry a range of meanings and represent a variety of methods, research areas, and levels of analysis'.[22] However, it is also beholden to a somewhat rigid understanding of the biological sciences. As Grodal elucidates, a biocultural embodied approach is distinct from other theoretical figurations of embodiment because it describes the embodied subject 'in its concrete ecology and by means of cognitive science'.[23] For this reason, bioculturalism, strictly adhered to and taken on its own, may be insufficiently flexible when applied to supernatural beings or scenarios. Thus, while biocultural paradigms inform my discussion of those texts (*The Devil in Massachusetts*, *The Crucible*, *The Witch of Blackbird Pond*) that deal with real-world, non-magical adolescent witches, they are less useful and so less frequently applied to texts that present more fantastical permutations of the teen witch archetype (*Sabrina the Teenage Witch*, *The Craft*, *American Horror Story*, etc.).

A framework adequate to describe not only an adolescent but an adolescent *witch* would need to consider her supranormal nature, her capacity for transformation and her ability to traverse existential categories.

Consequently, the theoretical apparatus deployed throughout this book is one that augments, and in places supplants, a biocultural understanding of adolescence, broadly conceived, with more diverse theories of embodiment and materiality. Foucauldian ideas of embodied subjectivity, material feminisms and Deleuzian notions of becoming are useful supplements to bioculturalism as they enable us to comprehend the teen witch's Otherness, her transformative powers and her extensive materiality. Moreover, while bioculturalism explicates a dynamic system for understanding interactions between biological and cultural agents, it rests on a distinction between biology and culture, a sense that they are separate actors, albeit entwined and difficult to distinguish. This poses problems for a number of the teen witch texts discussed later in this book because they imagine biology and culture as co-extensive rather than discrete. Since these works refuse dualistic constructions of the nature/culture, mind/body divide, it is necessary to draw not only on theories that delineate an *inter*action between biology and culture, but also on more radical formulations that posit an *intra*-action – to borrow a neologism from Karen Barad – between the material, the discursive, the human, the animal, the technological and the natural, all of which are figured as contiguous.[24]

'The very "stuff" of subjectivity': Embodiment, Subjectivity and the Deconstruction of Dualist Thought

In her 1994 study *Volatile Bodies: Toward a Corporeal Feminism*, the philosopher Elizabeth Grosz attempts to move beyond binary conceptions of the mind/body split, reworking the ingrained philosophical paradigms that conceive of the mind as both separate from and superior to the physical body.[25] Grosz advocates, instead, a corporeal selfhood where the body is moved from the margins to the centre of analysis so that it is reimagined as 'the very "stuff" of subjectivity'.[26] Moreover, not only is the experience of psychic interiority filtered and transformed by bodily exteriority, but bodies themselves are shaped by cultural discourses, social norms and the demands of particular historical moments. In this way:

> the body, or rather, bodies, cannot be adequately understood as ahistorical, pre-cultural, or natural objects in any simple way; they are not only inscribed, marked, engraved, by social pressures external to them but are the products, the direct effects, of the very social

constitution of nature itself. It is not simply that the body is represented in a variety of ways according to historical, social and cultural exigencies while it remains basically the same; these factors actively produce the body as a body of a determinate type.[27]

Certainly, some of these ideas can be seen as compatible with biocultural theory, dependent as they are on a productive interaction between the cultural and the corporeal. However, where Grosz's theories diverge from dominant strains of bioculturalism is in their far more radical rejection of dualistic thought.

As Grosz explains it, dualism is the view that the mental and the physical, the mind and the body, exist as two mutually exclusive entities.[28] These agents may interact; they may be hostile or harmonious in their intersections, but they remain fundamentally distinct. In her attempt to construct a mode of feminist thought centred on the body, Grosz rejects this model and advances a subjectivity that is 'no longer conceived in binarized or dualist terms, either as the combination of mental or conceptual with material or physical elements or as the harmonious, unified cohesion of mind and body'.[29] Her ideas, therefore, go beyond bioculturalism by imaging the relationship between nature and culture, body and mind, not in terms of intersection, but rather as a continuity. Grosz does not reject notions of interiority, agency or consciousness. Instead, she argues that they can be more productively conceived in terms of corporeality, reimagined not in terms of latency but of surface.[30] By refusing to separate out mind and body, Grosz demonstrates that 'Bodies are not inert; they function interactively and productively. They act and react. They generate what is new, surprising, unpredictable'.[31] Such a view of the body as productive and agentic not only refuses the hierarchical structures of dualism, but it also opens up intriguing new possibilities for reading the metamorphic body of the teen witch. Although many of the earliest teen witch texts (see Chapter 2) frame the adolescent sorceress as sinister or disruptive because of her position between biology and culture, many later works (see Chapters 3, 4 and 5) refuse this binary entirely and figure her as possessed of a generative materiality that has the potential to be surprising, unpredictable and even joyful.

Grosz's model of subjectivity is that of the Möbius strip, 'an inverted three-dimensional figure eight', which allows us to comprehend 'the inflection of mind into body and body into mind, the ways in which, through a kind of twisting or inversion, one side becomes another'.[32] This novel apparatus also informs the structure of *Volatile Bodies*, empowering

Grosz to consider how psychoanalytical, phenomenological and neurological theories of the body (theories that understand embodiment from the 'inside out') can work with theories of corporeal inscription (the 'outside in') while avoiding the reduction of one to the other. This is certainly an intriguing and useful model. However, because this book is concerned primarily with the materiality of the witch's body and its continuity with other bodies, discourses and entities, I will hew more closely to frameworks that move from the 'outside in'. As a book about adolescence and magic, this is principally a work about movement, transformation and fluidity. My interest here lies in what Deleuze and Guattari term 'becoming', which in contrast to the fixed state of 'being', is creative and generative.[33] *Becoming* is a movement that makes something new, maps unfamiliar territories and establishes dynamic continuities. Psychoanalysis, with its static model of the unconscious, is concerned with *being*, with singularity and discontinuity. Psychoanalysis is a model that 'everywhere constricts by insisting on the reduction to unity'.[34] As a critical tradition, psychoanalysis is therefore inadequate to describe the adolescent witch, a figure defined by her metamorphic nature, capacity for flight and her propensity to generate new and exciting connections with the other entities and bodies.

Power, Possession and the Government of Things: The Foucauldian Body

A useful means of augmenting biocultural theory is by turning to one conspicuous part of Grosz's 'outside in' Möbius strip and drawing on Foucault's construction of subjectivity as both embodied and historically constituted.[35] Identifiable as what Grosz terms a theory of social inscription, Foucault's ideas, especially those advanced in his genealogical work, posit a mode of subjectivity that is 'embodied and manifests its self through practices' that 'enable and constrain' while remaining 'situated within material, institutional, and disciplinary matrices'.[36] Foucault's genealogical period encompasses *Discipline and Punish* (1975) and *The History of Sexuality, Vol. 1* (1976), as well as a number of significant essays, articles and lectures. Genealogy is well-suited to an analysis of the teen witch figure because it is 'dynamic, rather than static', incorporating an array of discourses, practices and vectors of power into its account of subjectivity.[37] It allows us to imagine a body that is not inert or passive, but metamorphic, mobile and intimately bound up with subjectivity.

Although remaining alert to the dangers of simplistic conflation or reduction, it is possible to decipher nodes of connection between Foucault's embodied subjectivity and biocultural theory. In his essay 'Nietzsche, Genealogy, History' (1977), Foucault describes the body as 'the inscribed surface of events (traced by language and dissolved by ideas), the locus of a dissociated self (adopting the illusion of a substantial unity), and a volume in perpetual disintegration'.[38] In particular, Foucault affirms that 'descent' – his term for group affiliations related to family, tradition or social class – manifests corporeally.[39] An affiliation of this type is capable of attaching itself to the body: 'It inscribes itself in the nervous system, in temperament, in the digestive apparatus; it appears in faulty respiration, in improper diets, in the debilitated and prostrate bodies of those whose ancestors committed errors.'[40] In this way, if bioculturalism is a paradigm that merges the natural sciences and the humanities, taking into account how bodies are shaped by evolutionary and environmental factors,[41] then Foucault's claim that the body is moulded by 'everything that touches it' – including 'diet, climate, and soil' – can be incorporated, albeit somewhat loosely, into this framework.[42]

Where Foucault's work deviates from biocultural theory – and this is perhaps why it can serve as useful supplement to bioculturalism – is in its ambiguity. As noted previously, proponents of bioculturalism, such as Torben Grodal, laud the paradigm precisely because of its adherence to evolutionary history, cognitive science, endocrinology and biology. Foucault, in contrast, discusses such matters in comparatively vague terms, opening up productive spaces of uncertainty, creation and play. His work has been roundly criticised, often by feminist critics, for its lack of clarity about such matters as the pre-existence of the body (i.e., if the body is socially inscribed, does there exist a pre-discursive body?),[43] the possibility of agency and the sexual or racial specificity of discrete bodies. While such critiques are legitimate and entirely necessary, I would argue that appending Foucault's notion of embodied subjectivity to biocultural theory is a productive project because his lack of clarity undercuts some of the rigidity associated with bioculturalism. When working with mythic, or quasi-mythic, figures such as the adolescent witch, the ambiguity of Foucault's theories makes it possible to discuss the supranormal abilities that distinguish her from the bioculturally constituted adolescent proper. A genealogical perspective moves beyond scientific rigour to incorporate an embodied subject who is capable of flight, transformation and possession.

Beyond their ability accommodate fantastic bodies, such as that of the adolescent witch, Foucault's ideas also facilitate engagement with some of the key themes explored in teen witch texts: power, metamorphosis and the sorceress's relationship with the demonic. Foucault's work is explicitly concerned with power. He is preoccupied with how power – in the form of institutions, practices and discourses – moulds bodies and, consequently, subjectivities, but he is also interested in how those same bodies serve as loci of resistance.[44] When Foucault speaks of power, he does not mean power as it crystallises in authority or as a mode of subjugation emanating from the pinnacle of the social or political hierarchy. Foucault's power is active in relations, it is everywhere at once, and it is productive as well as confining. As he writes in *The History of Sexuality, Vol. 1*, 'power must be understood in the first instance as the multiplicity of force relations imma-nent in the sphere in which they operate and which constitute their own organization'.[45] Power is therefore ubiquitous, complex and multifaceted. It impacts on the embodied subject in a multitude of ways; it 'permeates individual bodies, it sets limits, it simultaneously shapes bodies and indi-viduality'.[46] In the teen witch texts discussed throughout this book, adoles-cent girls are regularly presented as products of such force relations. Their bodies and their selfhoods are shaped by cultural norms, practices, values and institutions. Modes of dress, community surveillance and disciplinary regimes extending from the family to the school inscribe themselves on the bodies of these young women.

At the same time, however, power can be resisted, and its dynamics reversed. Power relations are therefore ensnared within a process 'which, through ceaseless struggles and confrontations, transforms, strengthens, or reverses them'.[47] Employing a number of subversive strategies – rang-ing from playful acts of self-transformation to spectacular displays of demonomania, from casting mischievous spells to committing violent murders – teen witches transform, reverse and resist the power relations that bind them. Similarly, many of these adolescent sorceresses enter into power relations that are productive and capable of creating new modes of being. As Elizabeth Grosz observes, there exist a wide array of 'proce-dures for inscribing bodies' that 'do not function coercively but are sought out'.[48] Such procedures are 'commonly undertaken voluntarily and usually require the active compliance of the subject'.[49] These are what Foucault would call 'technique[s] of self-production'.[50] While such techniques are often associated with exercise regimes and body modification, the teen witch has a much wider array of procedures available to her. Indeed, her magical abilities often enable her to produce, or re-produce, her selfhood in radically different ways: she can makeover her appearance, change her features, switch genders, transform into an animal or become incorporeal. The witch's power of self-production is endless and infinitely variable.

The witch may also reverse, transform or play with power relations via her engagement with the demonic. Although Foucault does not, as a rule, devote much time to the subject of witchcraft, his 26 February 1975 lecture at the Collège de France constitutes one major exception. In this lecture, Foucault discusses the difference between witchcraft cases and demonic possession, elaborating on how these two supernatural occurrences differ in their relationship to power. He explains that while the witch's body is a somatic unity 'in the service of, or penetrated by, the countless armies of Satan', the body of the demoniac (or possessed individual) is 'the seat of an indefinite multiplicity of movements, jolts, sensations, tremors, pains, and pleasures'.[51] Crucially, where the witch engages in a comparatively simple reversal of power relations – '"Give me your soul," Satan said to the witch, "and I will give you some of my power"'[52] – possession is infinitely more complex. For demoniacs, 'different powers and their confrontations manifest themselves within the body'.[53] Theirs is a 'citadel body, the stake in a battle between the demon and the possessed body that resists, between the part of the person possessed that resists and the part of herself that gives way and betrays her'.[54] In the teen witch texts discussed in the following pages, there are examples of both the power reversal that stems from the witch's exchange of her soul for the Devil's gifts and the multiple confrontations and contestations that signify demonic possession. Although these scenarios differ greatly in how they are represented and in the role that they play within the texts, they nevertheless adumbrate the capacity of the adolescent witch to subvert, resist, reverse or play with the force relations that surround them.

Foucault's work is also useful for thinking about teen witches because it refuses binaristic thinking about the relationship between body and mind, corporeality and culture. Thomas Lemke argues that Foucault can be placed in the category of thinkers who ascribe agency and power to the non-human because of how his work 'stresses the materiality of the physical body and focuses on the mundane details of bodily existence and the technologies of power that constitute disciplined and docile bodies'.[55] Moreover, Lemke goes on to demonstrate that Foucault's discussion of a so-called 'government of things', which rather than upholding a distinction between humans and 'things' rests on 'a sort of complex of men and things',[56] signifies an interest in the 'entanglements of men and things, the natural and the artificial, the physical and the moral'.[57] Significantly, Lemke notes that Foucault's use of quotation marks in his references to 'things' suggests a continuity of human and non-human matter whose separation is culturally contingent. Within Foucault's schema, 'the art of government determines what is defined as subject and object, as human and non-human'.[58] Here, Lemke persuasively argues that Foucault's work evinces an understanding that agency is a property not limited to humans, but rather something that emerges as a product of relations between the human and the non-human.[59] Foucault's articulation of the milieu, described as 'a set of natural givens – rivers, marshes, hills – and a set of artificial givens – an agglomeration of individuals, of houses etc', can also be read as a deconstruction of dualistic thought because it articulates the intersection between the natural and the synthetic, the human and the more than human, without separating them into distinct categories of being.[60] Such fluidity provides an appropriately pliable structure through which to analyse the teenage witch, a figure who regularly moves between the human and the non-human and challenges the boundaries between subject and object.

Recuperating the Material: New Materialism and Material Feminisms

To fully comprehend the motility of the adolescent witch, her propensity to flow across bodies, identities and states of being, it is necessary to consider questions of materiality in their dynamic fullness. New materialism and related material feminisms provide a language for discussing the potential of the teen witch through their focus on bodies and their refusal to reinscribe the nature/culture divide. In the introduction to their anthology on material feminisms, Stacy Alaimo and Susan Hekman write that the purpose of such theories is to 'bring the material, specifically the materiality of the human body and the natural world, into the forefront of feminist theory and practice'.[61] Where much recent feminist discourse has been influenced by the linguistic turn, emphasising the role of language in defining dominant constructions of gender, materialist philosophers argue that this preoccupation with language and representation obscures lived experience and corporeality. These modes of thought often associate both the body and natural world with fixity, silence and essentialist positions.

In an attempt to recuperate the body as a subject of philosophical enquiry Alaimo, Hekman and a host of other thinkers argue for the demolition of nature/culture dualism and the related conception of the natural world as a passive resource. Nature, they claim, 'can no longer be imagined as a pliable resource for industrial production or social construction. Nature is agentic – it acts, and those actions have consequences for both the human and nonhuman world'.[62] When thinking about nature, and indeed about the body, it is far more productive to view their materiality as active rather than passive, agentic rather than inert. This concept of material agency generates new modes of apprehension centred on the 'co-extensive materiality of humans and nonhumans'.[63] Drawing on this framework, philosopher Karen Barad argues that it should therefore be possible to replace ideas of 'interaction', which presume 'the prior existence of independent entities/relata', with a conceptual apparatus based on '*intra*-actions' between ontologically inseparable components.[64] Thinking of materiality in terms of *intra*-action, rather than *inter*action, empowers Barad and others to annihilate the distinction between subject and object, imagining instead a world where 'relata do not preexist relations; rather, relata-within-phenomena emerge through specific intra-actions'.[65] Barad is radical in their refusal to understand the material as inert or lacking in agency. They instead describe a world in which active materiality constructs ostensibly distinct phenomena or bounded objects through a series of complex relations.

'Other, more dynamic, ways of being in the world': The Deleuzian Body

In the context of this book and its interest in the teenage witch, the most alluring facet of new materialist thought is its emphasis on continuity, fluidity and movement. Within this schema, the body is contiguous with other objects and phenomena in the world, regularly engaging with them to create new modes of being. The promise of this continuity and its radical capacity is also explored in the work of Gilles Deleuze and Félix Guattari, philosophers who are often enfolded within new materialist discourse. As Rosi Braidotti explains, Deleuze's work, including his collaborations with Guattari, is characterised by 'a form of neo-materialism and a blend of vitalism that is attuned to the technological era'.[66] An immensely rich meditation on change, transformation and difference, Deleuze and

Guattari's work is difficult to parse due to a preponderance of neologisms and its often-unconventional structure. Their 1980 collaboration *A Thousand Plateaus* is, for instance, organised around the model of the rhizome, an underground stem whose roots sprawl in all directions from their connective nodes. The book does not follow a linear, or arborescent, structure and can be read in any order, with readers encouraged to explore its various sections, or 'plateaus', at will. While the experimental nature of their work may be initially off-putting, it nevertheless provides a fertile model for developing ideas about the body in terms of metamorphosis, movement and connection.

Deleuze and Guattari proffer a conception of the body as defined by 'becoming' rather than 'being'. They imagine the body not as a static, bounded entity that undergoes transformative change in order to 'be', but rather as a surface defined by flows, durations, speeds and intensities. Theirs is body that refuses binary divisions between inside and outside, self and Other, mind and body, nature and culture. They do not comprehend the body in terms of what it is, but what it can do. Growth and change are ongoing processes, and they occur largely through machinic connections, which Deleuze and Guattari term 'lines of flight'.[67] Notions of change are decisive here. In their published works, Deleuze and Guattari repeatedly turn to the concept of 'becoming' to describe the tendency towards change. Since they view becoming as a meaningful, ongoing transformative process, Deleuze and Guattari are careful to emphasise that:

> Becoming is certainly not imitating, or identifying with something; neither is it regressing-progressing; neither is it corresponding, establishing corresponding relations; neither is it producing, producing a filiation or producing through filiation. Becoming is a verb with a consistency all its own; it does not reduce to, or lead back to, 'appearing,' 'being,' 'equaling,' or 'producing.'[68]

The body that emerges in their philosophy is defined by the connections that it makes with other bodies, whether human or more than human, animate or inanimate, technological or natural. These connections facilitate becomings.

Moreover, because Deleuze and Guattari are opposed to notions of discontinuity or the atomistic separation of bodies, they maintain that connective possibilities are endless. They do not view nature or the world in terms of rigid categories, nor do they attempt to make sense of it through the application of arborescent systems of hierarchical knowledge. They prefer to consider things – all things – through the model of the rhizome, the previously described root system that can grow in any direction and is defined by heterogeneity and connection. Removed from the field of botany and applied to a much broader ontology, the rhizome 'ceaselessly establishes connections between semiotic chains, organizations of power, and circumstances relative to the arts, sciences, and social struggles'.[69] However, it is important to understand that such connections are not merely superficial imitations. They are meaningful engagements that incite dynamic, unexpected becomings. One example of this kind of fertile connection is put forward by Deleuze and Guattari in the early part of *A Thousand Plateaus*. Here, they discuss a species of orchid that so closely resembles a female wasp that male wasps attempt to mate with it, and in doing so, unintentionally pollinate other orchids.[70] A more simplistic, or arborescent, account of this process might suggest that through the process of natural selection the orchid had evolved to imitate the female wasp and thus ensure the survival of its species. However, the kind of rhizomatic logic espoused by Deleuze and Guattari rejects simplistic notions of representation or mimicry in favour of change brought about via connection. The connections engendered between the wasp and the orchid have, over the course of thousands of years, resulted in parallel transformations in the two entities that can never be conceptualised as discrete, but must instead be understood in terms of the continuous intensities that circulate between them.[71] For the orchid and the wasp, Deleuze and Guattari explain, their corresponding metamorphoses are 'not imitation at all but a capture of code, surplus value of code, an increase in valence, a veritable becoming, a becoming-wasp of the orchid and a becoming-orchid of the wasp'.[72] Becomings are therefore predicated upon movements, lines of flight, between continuous entities that create heterogenous alliances and novel entities.

Deleuze and Guattari's theories are a useful framework for exploring the teen witch because they emphasise multiplicity over unity, becoming over being, as well as continuity over binary divisions. Moreover, as I discuss in subsequent chapters, Deleuze and Guattari are profoundly interested in the girl as an important figuration of becoming. The girl is particularly important because she is a 'line of flight'. She traverses and explodes the binarisms of man/woman and adult/child. As described in *A Thousand Plateaus*:

girls do not belong to an age group, sex, order, or kingdom: they slip in everywhere, between orders, acts, ages, sexes; they produce n molecular sexes on the line of flight in relation to the dualism machines they cross right through. The only way to get outside the dualisms is to be-between, to pass between.[73]

While Deleuze and Guattari frame 'becoming-woman' as an act that, regardless of gender or sex, refuses established subject hierarchies, the 'little girl' is an even more radical being because she is 'constituted in relations of power between statements and visibilities'.[74] The girl is mobile, fluid and connective. She represents a 'moving away from dominant hierarchal understandings of subjectivity'.[75] Crucially, the Deleuzian girl also allows us to reconceptualise female adolescence as something more than a biologically determined transition to womanhood. As Catherine Driscoll explains, within the context of Deleuze and Guattari's philosophy, the girl can be a liberating, playful and profoundly subversive figure. Within their schema, 'Feminine adolescence is not a transition from one state to another but a contingent and in some senses reversible movement'.[76] The girl's body does not lead irrevocably to the maternal body,[77] but remains infused with infinite possibilities for metamorphosis, connection and the explosion of dualisms.

Deleuze and Guattari's theories can be assembled into a productive framework for analysing the teen witch across various cultural texts. Their ideas about the univocity of being and the radical power of becoming undercut ingrained hierarchies and demolish the binary logic that seeks to separate subject from object, mind from body, nature from culture. A significant number of the literary and filmic works explored in this book present the witch's becoming, her metamorphic capabilities, as imbued with what Deleuze scholar Anna Powell terms 'liberatory potential'.[78] These texts present an optimistic vision of how 'Subject/object boundaries meld in molecular fusion to form new entities', and they teach us that 'If we open up to potential transformations, we experience other, more dynamic, ways of being in the world'.[79] At the same time, not all of the teen witch texts explored in these pages present the transformative power of becoming as a positive movement. Indeed, numerous works attempt to uphold the 'binary machines' of masculine and feminine, child and woman, biological and cultural. In these texts, the multiplicity and the tendency towards change evinced by the teen witch become unsettling and disruptive. Indeed, while Deleuze might locate both beauty and terror in the transformative condition, modes of thought that depend on binary structures might instead position becomings as 'the source of horror'.[80]

The Monstrous Girl: A Teratology of the Teenage Witch

The teen witch texts discussed in this book can generally be divided into two categories: those invested in the binary logic that divides nature from culture, material from psychical; and those that imagine all life as a form of active materiality. Consequently, while texts that align themselves with the latter position might present Deleuzian becomings as potent, exciting transformations, those texts that take the former position are more likely to imagine the witch's powers of metamorphosis and connection as a disturbing, unimpeded flow of matter. In these works, the witch is not an emblem of liberatory promise, but a monstrous figuration of disruption and category confusion. In her work on monstrosity, Margrit Shildrick explains that 'any being who traverses the liminal spaces that evade classification takes on the potential to confound normative identity, and monsters paradigmatically fulfil that role'.[81] Likewise, Rosi Braidotti adumbrates popular conceptions of the monster as betwixt and between categories. For, while monsters are often born from malformations of various types, 'They also represent the in between, the mixed, the ambivalent as implied in the ancient Greek root of the word "monsters," *teras*, which means both horrible and wonderful, object of aberration and adoration'.[82] Monstrosity is contingent upon the existence of categories to be confounded or challenged. The teen witch therefore emerges as monstrous only in those works that attempt to uphold dualistic, oppositional categories of being.

When mapping those representations of the teenage witch where she appears as a disruptive, monstrous being it is easy to fall back on psychoanalytic theories that imagine femininity and girlhood in terms of lack, castration and the grotesque maternal body. In this vein, Barbara Creed employs the concept of the 'monstrous feminine' to describe those beings that transgress the boundaries that give meaning to and create order within our civilisation.[83] Creed draws extensively on Julia Kristeva's theorisation of the abject as 'being opposed to I' and incarnate in those entities, materials and actions that destablise the borders of subjectivity: 'It is thus not lack of cleanliness or health that causes abjection but what disturbs identity, system, order. What does not respect borders, positions, rules. The in-between, the ambiguous, the composite'.[84] For Kristeva, the abject encompasses fluids (urine, blood, sperm, excrement),[85] the corpse, moral transgression and religious taboo. Modifying these ideas, Creed argues that not only do women possess a unique relationship to the abject by virtue of their reproductive functions, but that abjection inheres in all acts of border crossing:

the concept of a border is central to the construction of the monstrous in the horror film; that which crosses or threatens to cross the 'border' is abject. Although the specific nature of the border changes from film to film, the function of the monstrous remains the same – to bring about an encounter between the symbolic order and that which threatens its stability.[86]

Both Kristeva's vision of imperilled subjectivity and Creed's threatened border seem to accord with the anxieties expressed in those texts that image the teen witch as challenging binary categories. However, these positions are limited by their reliance on a psychoanalytic framework. Creed is clear that a psychoanalytic analysis of monstrous women is justified by virtue of the horror genre's engagement with psychoanalysis and the reliance of critics on these paradigms.[87] She is also explicit in affirming that women are not monstrous or abject by nature, but are represented as such by the patriarchal ideology that saturates our cultural products.[88] Nevertheless, I do not believe that a psychoanalytical perspective is fully equipped to describe the complex, metamorphic materiality of the adolescent witch.

As rich as theories of the abject may be, they often tend to elide 'the biological aspects of the body and its sensation as such, using bodies instead as emblematic springboards to primal psychic structures'.[89] For this reason, I concur with recent theorists of horror, such as Anna Powell, who argue that this disproportionate focus on the psychic calls for an urgent 'interrogation of the dominance of psychoanalysis in horror theory'.[90] Writing from a Deleuzian perspective, Powell argues that psychoanalysis appears like a 'rigid template' when contrasted with 'machinic cartography' of Deleuze and Guattari's work, which envisions desire, not as grounded in lack, but rather as the productive root of new and exciting connections.[91] Moreover, as Deleuze and Guattari themselves explain, psychoanalysis is dominated by 'binary logic and biunivocal relationships'.[92] The arborescent, hierarchical, structures of psychoanalytical thought imagine the unconscious as 'representative, crystallized into codified complexes, laid out along a genetic axis and distributed within a syntagmatic structure'.[93] Psychoanalysis can therefore be said to reinscribe binarisms that separate mind from body, male from female, subject from object.

Analogously, Jack Morgan criticises the 'over-psychologizing of the horror mode' for its dependency on the myth of a remote, essentially disembodied consciousness.[94] Like Powell, albeit without her reliance on Deleuzian theory, Morgan argues for the importance of embodiment in any theorisation of horror. His book *The Biology of Horror* works to rescue organic matter from the margins of discourse and restore the body to the centre of the Gothic imagination. His claim that 'horror is essentially bio-horror'[95] overlaps with the new materialist project of returning materiality to the forefront of theoretical endeavour. At the same time, though, Morgan's project is not identical with new materialist aims. His work does, after all, depend on a certain anxiety about matter, as he claims that bio-horror necessarily 'involves the tenuous negotiations between rationality and a looming biological plenum that defies rational mapping'.[96] For this reason, Morgan's theories are not applicable to those teen witch texts that celebrate her materiality. However, his description of horror fiction's often embattled relationship with matter can account for teen witch texts that treat the figure as a potentially destabilising threat to binary categories. Indeed, a number of the texts discussed in this book imagine the adolescent girl as poised on the border between the natural and the cultural, or as representing an unsettling intrusion of the biological into the social realm. Theories of bio-horror provide a means through which to understand anxieties about the disruption of boundaries that do not an entail a recourse to psychoanalytical theories such as the abject.

Likewise, Larrie Dudenhoeffer explains that by attending to the biological realities of embodied subjectivity, it is possible to reconceptualise horror's concern with the uncanny, or the 'return of the repressed', in terms that go beyond the rigid strictures of psychoanalysis. While scholars such as Nicholas Royle have, rightly, noted that the 'uncanny' as conceived in the work of Sigmund Freud (1919) 'is and is not psychoanalytical'[97] – holding within it the potential to exist outside the domain of psychoanalysis[98] – the concept is nevertheless welded to the Oedipal psychodrama, the tripartite structure of the unconscious, and the fear of castration. Dudenhoeffer argues that if we engage with horror's iconography of imperilled and mutilated bodies, we can understand the 'return of the repressed' as encompassing not simply 'taboo cathexes, sexual differences, collective nightmares, or "unresolved childhood traumas"', but also 'the flexions, secretions, oxidations, metabolisms, innervations, cell transfers, muscle coactivations, immune responses, and anterograde and retrograde flows that we normally cannot see and do not think about much'.[99] This perspective, which reconceptualises the uncanny in terms of corporeality, is useful for evaluating a number of the teen witch texts discussed in the early part of this book (see Chapter 2) where the adolescent girl is portrayed as radically embodied and possessed of a fluid corporeality that threatens the social order. Her seepages are unsettling not because they undermine the integrity of the ego, but rather because of how they speak to the omnipresence of the hidden biological processes that linger always and everywhere beneath the surface of the skin.

Susan Yi Sencindiver notes that literary horror often differentiates itself from the new materialist framework through which critics might attempt to read it.[100] Although scholars might – as I do in this book – identify texts in which materiality is active and agentic, generating new modes of being through the formation of exciting, machinic connections, many works erect inflexible boundaries between the biological and cultural, the human and the non-human. In doing so, these works often imagine any force that transgresses these binaries as excessive or dangerous. As Sencindiver elaborates, 'literary horror distinguishes itself from new materialist thought by exploring matter in a sensuous, imaginative manner, visualizing matter in the mode of fear, and notably figuring its agency as an ontological scandal'.[101] These works encourage us to treat the agency of matter, whether incarnate in the manoeuvrings of the natural world or expressed through the materiality of our bodies, as abnormal or monstrous. Kelly Hurley is also interested in how certain texts visualise materiality through an iconography of terror. She describes a 'gothicity of matter' that stems from the awareness that

> Matter is not mute and stolid, but rather clamorous and active. In its viscosity, in its oozing mobility, in its unexpected, incessant animation, this 'physical basis of life,' protoplasm, emerges as a testament to the horrific potentialities of a sheerly physical world.[102]

Like Morgan, Hurley imagines that 'our neglected, marginalized organic life'[103] might be a source of fear. Consequently, while I, like many of the authors and filmmakers discussed in this book, imagine the teen witch as a liberatory model possessed of unbounded potential for transformation, movement and connection, a significant number of the works that I discuss frame this motility in essentially Gothic terms. In doing so, they envision the continuity and agency of matter not as an opening up of possibility but as a disturbing violation of the binary logic in which they are so deeply invested.

Our Juvenile Spinsters: Some Historical Antecedents

While the focus of this book lies firmly within those decades when, from the end of World War II up until the early years of the new millennium, the teenage girl entrenched herself as a recognisable part of the American cultural landscape, the connection between female adolescence and the occult is far older. The uncertainty of adolescence, its position between the more cohesive states of childhood and womanhood, has lent the period a unique aura of otherworldliness. Even before the neologism 'teenager' was coined to describe young people in their teen years, there existed a literary and historical image of mystical girlhood that can be understood as a forerunner of the contemporary teenage witch. Although a detailed analysis of pre-twentieth-century constructions of adolescent femininity is beyond the scope of this project, it is important to acknowledge the teen witch's debt to earlier mystical girls. The concluding section of this chapter therefore aims to situate the teenage witch within a broader tradition of supernatural girlhood, emphasising in particular her close links to medieval ascetic saints, the fasting maidens of the early modern period and the youthful mediums of the nineteenth century. By acknowledging these earlier constructions of supernatural girlhood, the teen witch can be enfolded within an evolving series of discursive practices in which femininity was both underlined and undermined by the mysticism associated with female adolescence. At the same time, uncovering a prehistory of the adolescent witch facilitates an exploration of how this figure, even in her earliest incarnations, troubled binary conceptions of a mind/body, nature/culture divide. Accounts of mystical girlhood, from the Middle Ages to the nineteenth century, can also be understood as important precursors to contemporary teen witch texts in their emphasis on embodied experience and their construction of materiality as an active, agentic force.

The ascetic saints of the Middle Ages may be one of the teen witch's most intriguing ancestors. According to Joan Jacobs Brumberg, 'in the years between 1200 and 1500, many women refused their food and prolonged fasting was considered a female miracle'.[104] The fourteenth-century saint Catherine of Siena (1347–80) allegedly ate nothing but bitter herbs and shoved twigs down her throat to induce vomiting. Blessed Columba of Rieti (1467–1501) died of starvation, while Beatrice of Nazareth (1200–68) became physically ill when confronted with the scent of meat.[105] While not all these women were adolescents, or even particularly young, at height of their fame, many were in their teens and early twenties when they began their fasts. The starving saint may seem like an unlikely foremother of the teen witch; however, these pious women were regularly conceptualised in terms of the diabolic. Catherine of Siena was frequently dismissed as a witch and her detractors claimed that she was fed by demons at night, while Columba of Rieti maintained that her compulsive vomiting was a means to purge her body of possessing devils.[106]

Later, the phenomenon of the starving saint evolved into the 'miraculous maid' or 'fasting girl' of the early modern period.[107] Curiosities of their age, these young women ate little or nothing for astonishing lengths of time, yet they remained comparatively healthy. Where they did eat, their diet extended only to those most delicate of foods. Ephemeral and fairy-like, they imbibed flowers, petals, aqua vitae and, in one instance, only the 'smell of a rose'.[108] As the popularisation of printing enabled the stories of miraculous maidens to travel, these young women gained national and international fame as either miraculous phenomena, signs from God or natural curiosities.[109] In 1600, a fourteen-year-old French girl named Jane Balan drew the attention of medical practitioners as a result of her claim to have fasted for almost three years. Almost seventy years later, nineteen-year-old Martha Taylor garnered fame as the 'Derbyshire Damsel', claiming to ingest nothing beyond the occasional drop of syrup, extracted from stewed prunes, water, sugar and raisin juice.[110]

Fasting girls were not merely confined to the early modern period. A number of these wondrous young women make an appearance in later history, with two significant examples appearing in the nineteenth century. The most well-known of these, the 'Welsh Fasting Girl' Sarah Jacob, was caught up in a tragic case where, after gaining fame for her mammoth acts of self-starvation, she died while under observation by doctors attempting to prove the veracity of her feat.[111] During her alleged fast, Jacob was presented by her family as an ethereal, quasi-supernatural being. Curious members of the public, who often travelled long distances by train to see the young woman, described Jacob as sitting in her bed with 'a victorine around her neck, and a wreath about her hair', while the bed itself was strewn with ribbons and flowers.[112] Around the same time, an American schoolgirl named Mollie Fancher found fame as the 'Brooklyn Enigma'. A studious but nervous young woman, Fancher began rejecting food at the age of sixteen, and her continued refusal to eat not only aroused speculations about possible supernatural causes, but it also situated Fancher in the midst of increasingly complex discourses about youth, femininity, modernity and nervous exhaustion.[113] Following serious accidents in the mid-1860s, Fancher's health deteriorated, and she suffered damage to all her senses: touch, taste, smell, sight and hearing. At the same time, Fancher accrued a wide array of supernatural powers, including the ability to read minds and commune with the spirits of the departed.

The motivations, as well as the somatic experiences, of these women exist at an unbridgeable remove, obscured by history and accessible only through accounts that may or may not provide access to their authentic voices. Nevertheless, a number of scholars have made a convincing case for viewing the body of the fasting woman as a site of social domination and resistance. As noted above, the theories of Michel Foucault advance a vision of subjectivity as coterminous with embodiment. The Foucauldian body is one that is not only shaped, trained, engraved and moulded by power relations, as well as by diet, climate, environment and regimes, it is also, as Margaret A. McLaren stresses, a body that 'responds and increases its forces'.[114] This body is active and cannot be understood as a 'passive recipient of social and cultural inscription'.[115] Although cases like that of Sarah Jacob suggest that some of these young women were manipulated and even abused by their families, other fasting girls sought out starvation as mode of embodied agency. Extreme fasting and the somatic process bound up with this act can therefore be read as form of resistance and even situated within the broader category of those technologies of the self whose enactment generates metamorphosis and opens up new, non-normative modes of being.[116] In her study of female food refusal during the early modern period, Nancy A. Gutierrez argues that the body of the starving woman represents more than a physical body. Rather, she maintains, the fasting girl's physicality 'is a political paradigm of this age's crisis of authority, for it brings to light explicit and cultural pressures within family and marital structures'.[177] In this way, the body is located within a complex of relational agency, refusing to be reduced to mute passivity. It is a site where cultural values and norms collide with individual resistance.

Scholars such as Caroline Walker Bynum rightly caution against drawing simplistic parallels between ascetic saints and subsequent diagnostic accounts of anorexia or other eating disorders.[118] This a wise approbation, but later medical and anthropological studies of anorexic behaviours, cautiously applied, can supplement more historically grounded discussions of fasting women. Megan Warin suggests, following Bryan S. Turner, that those suffering with anorexia might not be struggling to escape their embodied condition, but rather trying to overcome dualistic modes of thought that split them into distinct formulations of mind and body.[119]

These women, Warin proposes, might not be attempting the nullification of a body they view as opposed to an authentic, ephemeral self, but instead may be disturbed or even disgusted by a 'medically fragmented' body that has been broken down into distinct processes, organised into discrete systems and reduced to reproductive and sexual functions.[120] In this way, it is possible to view the fasting woman as struggling against the categorisation and hierarchisation of her corporeality, the segregation of its parts into discrete organs and systems. The fasting woman can be seen as moving towards the radical monism described by Deleuze and Guattari, preferring to see her embodiment as mobile and contiguous. She rejects the cultural organisation of her body and effects a movement towards what Deleuze and Guattari term the body without organs, 'an affective, intensive, anarchist body that consists solely of poles, zones, thresholds and gradients'.[121] As Anna Powell explains, the body without organs enables a radical reconfiguration of corporeality. The body is no longer 'a fixed, biological entity', whose organs are organised and hierarchised within a unitary organism; rather it is a mobile entity defined by 'a set of speeds and affects conceived in relation to other entities'.[122] The ascetic saint and the fasting woman can thus be read as a body that has 'blown apart the organism and its organization'[123] and commenced a decisive movement towards a body defined by the flows and intensities that saturate its surface. In this way, the fasting women of previous centuries can be aligned with the later figure of the adolescent witch not simply because she unites (rudimentary) notions of girlhood with the supernatural, but because of how her quasi-supernatural status undermines binaries, challenges conceptions of fixed static corporeality and establishes the body as a locus of power and resistance.

As with miraculous fasting, demonic possession cases recorded during the early modern period often portray modes of corporeality that are dynamic and metamorphic. Moreover, J. A. Sharpe observes that possession cases were often imbricated within a series of proliferating concerns about the tenability of age-based hierarchies, thereby connecting these transformative bodies to contemporary conceptions of youth. Sharpe explains that while a stable conception of adolescence had not yet materialised, early modern observers nevertheless understood youth, the years between fourteen and twenty-eight, to be a particularly difficult period.[124] Contemporary writers fretted that young people were prone to sins such as sensuality, excess, licentiousness and envy, and expressed concern that the youthful propensity towards such behaviours could undermine the preservation of an orderly Christian community.[125] It is perhaps due to the fraught position of youth that young people of this period were viewed as uniquely vulnerable to demonic possession. Moreover, the majority of cases described by Sharpe involved young women and girls, while the historian Erika Gasser notes that roughly 65 per cent of demonic possessions she studied centred around women.[126] The higher proportion of women afflicted by such diabolical incursions is in keeping with both medieval and early modern rhetoric that viewed the female body as closely bound up with the natural world, more apt to licentiousness and more vulnerable to the Devil's temptations than men, who were associated with the intellect and spirit.

The intersection of youth and femininity in a large number of such cases suggests that, to the early modern mind, girls were especially vulnerable to supernatural assault. Sarah Ferber observes that the practical elements of possession and exorcism were generally seen to reinforce its more ideological elements. The greater physical strength of (male) exorcists in comparison to women and children could be seen as contributing to a spiritual drama in which the ostensibly natural authority of adult over child, male over female could be reinforced through the exorcist's subjugation of the unruly possessed body.[127] Yet, while the restoration of order was an essential component of this spiritual performance, the possession itself opened up a subversive space in which existing hierarchies and behavioural norms could be overturned. During the possession, young women and men, unmarried maids and apprentices, were empowered to speak out and act out. They often engaged in forms of self-presentation that would have been deemed inappropriate to their station, contorting their bodies in bizarre or even sexually suggestive ways. In other instances, they spoke directly or confrontationally to adults. Some possessed youths engaged in blasphemy, mocked religious figures or laughed during prayers.

In late sixteenth-century England, the Starkie children, under diabolic influence, not only fell into fits but openly scoffed at the Bible, referring to talk of the holy book as 'bible bable bible bable'.[128] Analogously, Margaret Hurdman was possessed by a spirit who demanded luxurious items of clothing and displayed a vanity inappropriate to a godly youth of the period. As Sharpe notes, the possessed Margaret, in 'the spirit of teenage girls', requested fashionable clothing, including a smock and petticoat of silk, a cap and gown fashioned from black velvet.[129] In 1671, a sixteen-year-old domestic servant from Massachusetts named Elizabeth Knapp became possessed. According to her employer, Rev. Samuel Willard, Knapp began to:

carry herself in a strange and unwonted manner. Sometimes she would give sudden shriek, and if we enquired a reason, would always put it off with some excuse, and then [she] would burst forth into immoderate and extravagant laughter, in such ways, as sometimes she fell onto the ground with it.[130]

Like other young demoniacs, Knapp behaved in a manner suggestive of suppressed adolescent desire. She also displayed inappropriate materialism and avarice, claiming that the Devil appeared to her, 'presenting the treaty of a covenant, and proffering largely to her – *viz*, such things as suited her youthful fancy: money, silks, fine clothes, ease from labor, to show her the whole world'.[131] In this way, possession contained both the power to uphold as well as to challenge gender stereotypes.[132] It likewise provided new opportunities for young people and women to unsettle the hierarchies that ordinarily constrained them.

In as much as demonic possession may have unsettled cultural norms, it also radically reconfigured extant ideas about corporeality. Thus, if women of this period were associated with the body and nature, demoniacs demonstrated that neither the body nor the natural realm is passive or inert. Rather, these demon-inhabited bodies were active, agentic and capable of generating new modes of connection. As noted above, Michel Foucault carefully distinguishes between the body of the witch and that of the demoniac. He argues that where the witch is marginal, banished to woodlands and other peripheral regions, the demoniac resides at the heart of the social order.[133] The witch offers her soul to the Devil, a relatively simple exchange, in return for power. Possessed bodies, however, are infinitely more vexing. They are, Foucault says, caught in a triangular matrix, a struggle between the Devil, the demoniac and the exorcist or confessor attempting to free them.[134] At the same time, the possessed individual is also themselves split, permeated by the Devil's power but also resistant to it. Similarly, the demoniac may yield to or, presumably, withstand the exorcist's power. Foucault thus defines the body of the possessed as a 'resistant receptacle'.[135] It is a body permeated by coercive forces, yet it does not fall passively in line with these forces. It gathers its own forces, struggling and fragmenting in the process.

Within the schema advanced by Foucault, the witch's body is 'a somatic singularity', while the body of the possessed fractures as diverse powers take hold of it.[136] For this reason:

> The body of the possessed is a multiple body that is somehow volatized
> and pulverized into a multiplicity of powers that confront each other,
> a multiplicity of forces and sensations that beset it and pass through it.
> This infinite multiplicity, rather than the great duel between good and
> evil, generally characterizes the phenomenon of possession.[137]

Foucault's vision of possession is one that resists binary thinking and refuses
to cleave inside from outside, self from other, or good from evil. He sees
the body of the demoniac, not as an inviolable monad, sealed off from the
world that it inhabits, but as contiguous with and permeated by that world.
Moreover, this conception of the demoniac's body, while not reducible to
it, nevertheless overlaps with the Deleuzian body, which is imagined as continuous with its environment, as well as with other bodies and entities.
Foucault's assertion that the demoniac's body is characterised by 'infinite
multiplicity' also aligns it, albeit somewhat loosely, with Deleuze and Guattari's theory that what we take to be stable, unified bodies are in fact multiplicities. Crucially, a multiplicity is not a static or discrete entity, but rather
a mobile, shifting series of connections. Multiplicities are never still but
eternally active, entering into and breaking apart combinations with other
multiplicities.[138] Consequently, there are no stable boundaries separating
multiplicities. They meet instead in what Deleuze and Guattari term 'zones
of indiscernibility'.[139] Although not identical with the Deleuzian body,
Foucault's demoniac approaches this form of multiplicity because their
body is not a singular bounded entity, but rather one that draws together
a 'multiplicity' of movements, sensations and experiences.[140] The possessed
body, then, is one that is fully invested in the myriad potentialities of corporeality. It refuses to rest as a fixed or stable unity, operating instead as a
coalescence of motions, phenomena and powers.

The body of the demoniac, infused by motions, jolts and experiences,
is an agentic materiality. It resists the role of passive object and collapses the
binary logic that seeks to separate it from either the mental or the cultural.
At the same time, the resistance offered by the possessed body is often temporary and socially contingent. In much the same way that the demoniac's
disruption of social hierarchies, described above, can exist only as a temporary phenomenon, so too is the radical materiality of the possessed body
repressed or controlled. If possession empowered ordinarily marginal figures,
women and the young, to assume a central position within their community, the successful completion of an exorcism or the banishment of a demon
invariably returned these figures to their original state. The body that had

once seethed in its dynamism, penetrated by new sensations, pleasures and powers, is rendered quiet once again. Like the teen witches of the twentieth and twenty-first centuries, early modern female demoniacs were ambivalent creatures. Under the supposed sway of the supernatural, they were empowered to exercise an abnormal degree of agency, both culturally and corporeally. However, this agency was always limited, temporary and constrained by a complex web of sociocultural or religious discourses.

Describing the shocking acts performed by early modern demoniacs, Ferber argues that while possessed women were empowered to act in ways ordinarily deemed unacceptable, they were understood to behave this way for gender-specific reasons.[141] A female demoniac might be able to speak publicly, even lewdly, or engage in inappropriately sexual acts. However, she was only able to occupy the liberated position of the demoniac because women were viewed as emotionally, physically and intellectually weaker than men, and so they were seen as more likely to fall victim to demonic forces. In a similar manner, Spiritualist mediums of the Victorian era were able to transgress, even collapse, the divide between the private and public spheres, occasionally adopting the masculine personas of male inhabiting spirits. Yet, like their early modern antecedents, they wielded this transgressive power only because women were commonly associated with traits such as physiological weakness and emotional passivity, which made them more receptive to spiritual contact.

As a fundamentally egalitarian faith, Spiritualism, which came into being in the mid-nineteenth century, held that every human being harboured an innate capacity for mediumship. Women, however, seemed to possess a particular affinity for spiritual contact, adapting to new mediumistic techniques more quickly than their male peers. Alex Owen observes that 'the acceptance of women as powerful mediums was built on a nineteenth-century understanding of femininity'.[142] Women could be powerful conduits for the spirit realm, but this power was linked to a vision of femininity as inherently spiritual, vulnerable and, most importantly, passive. Where masculinity was conceived in terms of strength, will power and drive, womanhood was understood as frail and receptive. As Owen explains:

> Spiritualist mediums became the 'repositories', the 'vessels', the bearers of the spiritual message and channels for Divine communication. And what is vital here is that spiritualists assumed that it was innate femininity, in particular, female passivity, which facilitated this renunciation of self and cultivation of mediumistic powers.[143]

In many cases, not only was femininity understood as ideally suited to spiritual contact, but youth was also framed as conducive to genuine mediumistic practice. Spiritualism owes its origins to the apparent supernatural abilities of two adolescent girls, eleven-year-old Kate Fox and her fourteen-year-old sister Maggie. In 1848, the girls began to hear strange sounds in their home in Hydesville, New York. Convinced that their house was haunted, the two girls instituted a system of rapping or knocking through which they could communicate with the spirit inhabiting their home. News of the sisters' spiritual proclivities quickly spread, and the two teenage Fox siblings, along with their older sister Leah, soon found fame as mediums. Although Maggie Fox later confessed that the sisters' performances had been faked, Spiritualism nevertheless continued to grow, and youth remained a desirable quality for mediums. An adolescent or prepubescent medium, it was felt, was unlikely to have composed her own speech or sought to defraud believers.[144] Youth, like femininity, also opened mediums up to genuine spiritual insights. As Ann Braude elucidates, 'Youth associated the medium with the innocence of childhood, just as domestic ideology contrasted women and children with the worldliness of men'.[145] The categories of child and woman were thus conceived as closely interrelated, even overlapping states. Girls and young women emerged as ideal mediums because their position between woman and child ensured that they would be appropriately receptive, pious and innocent. Yet, during the course of the séance, these girls transformed, embodying new figurations of power through their command of unruly, dominant and even masculine spirits.

Much like the demoniac, the body of the medium who opens herself up to the spirits serves as what Foucault refers to as a 'kind of physiological-theological theater'.[146] The medium, despite her cultural representation as a passive vessel, is not an inert receptacle for spiritual occupation. Rather, her body reacts to possession or communion by undertaking an array of surprising movements, connections or actions. She may become rigid or, conversely, increasingly pliable. Her voice may change, or her hands may tremble, her eyes rolling back in her head. She may issue ectoplasmic manifestations from her nose, the top of her head, her breasts, fingertips and, most commonly, from her mouth.[147] Recalling the demoniacs that came before her, hers is a 'body that swallows and spits out and that absorbs and rejects'.[148] She may be penetrated by fields of power, but her flesh also resists such coercion. The medium likewise resembles the possessed woman in her capacity to become Other. The demoniac effects a movement towards becoming-demon, speaking with the voice of an inhabiting devil, while the medium may become spirit or take on otherworldly traits as she communes with spirits. Becomings, as described above and in the work of Deleuze and Guattari, are experiential states in which an entity connects with other entities to produce new forms of heterogeneity and novel formations. As Joshua Delpech-Ramey elucidates, through becoming, the imagined borders that separate sexes and species, dividing groups from individuals, matter from mind blur, becoming ever more imperceptible.[149] The medium who becomes as she connects with the spirits of the deceased does not simply identify with or imitate these spectres. She enters a relation with the spirits, her body is endowed with new 'relations of speed and slowness' that enable her to become the spirit Other.[150] She enters into an assemblage with this Other identity, becoming Other 'neither by resemblance nor by analogy' but through a line of flight that transforms her into something else.[151]

Nevertheless, in as much as the young female medium, like the demoniac and the fasting girl before her, might model radical forms of embodiment defined by agency, transformation and resistance, this embodiment was not normally viewed as liberating or generative within their respective social milieux. Indeed, as described previously, modes of thinking that depend on binary logic – the dualistic division of nature from culture, mind from matter – or conceive of materiality as inert will inevitably view agentic matter, resistant bodies and dynamic becomings as a source of horror. From this point of view, there is something inherently disturbing about bodies defined by multiplicity and change, bodies that refuse unity and stability. The materiality of the medium is, like all such clamorous matter, 'composite and changeful', 'rent from within by their own heterogeneity, and always in the process of becoming-Other'.[152] Consequently, these figures were often approached with anxiety, viewed with trepidation or suspicion. Social norms dictated that they be contained or categorised, returned to the marginal positions from which they might temporarily escape. Indeed, some contemporary researchers even attempted to abrogate the radical potential of the Spiritualist medium by showing that they were merely hysterics. Physician Antoine Barety, for example, conducted numerous experiments aimed at showing that not only did the bodies of hysterics undergo spasmodic consumptions of energy, but that this in turn gave off a 'radiating neural force', a luminescent fluid that seeped out of orifices such as the eyes and mouth.[153]

That the adolescent girl might emerge as a uniquely contradictory entity, figured as both a passive receptacle and as a vital, clamorous materiality, seems appropriate to the shifting demographics and values of the nineteenth century. The medium, as a cultural type associated with youth and femininity, emerged concomitantly with new debates about girlhood, the role of young women in society and the type, if any, of education that they should receive. In *Adolescent Girlhood and Literary Culture at the* Fin de Siècle, Beth Rodgers observes that during the latter half of the nineteenth century, adolescent femininity as a 'stage was being theorized and discussed by a wide range of commentators, including writers appealing to girls themselves'.[154] Terms such as 'teenager' were not in use at this time, but the unique features of youth were nevertheless widely discussed, especially as they pertained to issues such as education, socialisation and relationships. Commentators, writers and social reformers attempted to define what it meant to inhabit the interstitial space between childhood and womanhood. Rodgers describes how, for instance, British periodicals of the late nineteenth century referred to their readership as girls 'on the borderland'.[155] Catherine Driscoll is equally careful to show that in legislation, parliamentary debate, newspapers, fiction and social policy, the nineteenth century witnessed the emergence of 'a new modern girl who forms a crucial precursor for the twentieth-century category of feminine adolescence'.[156] Nineteenth-century girls, like their mid-twentieth-century descendants, were voracious consumers of a material culture created just for them. They read books, magazines and advice manuals, fawned over new fashions, played sports and coalesced into cliques.[157]

Publications for and about girls debated their status and role in society. Both Rodgers and Driscoll reference S. F. A. Caulfield's series 'Some Types of Girlhood; or, Our Juvenile Spinsters', which was published in *The Girl's Own Paper* between 1889–90. Caulfield's series concerns itself primarily with questions of identity, meditating on different types of girl, from muscular, aesthetic and society girls through to 'commonplace' girls and housewives.[158] Such magazines also expounded on processes of self-fashioning, enumerating acceptable modes of presentation and appropriate behaviours for young women. Yet, what the contents of these publications ultimately suggest is that the nineteenth-century girl is not a static, fixed figure, but rather a metamorphic creature, prone to change and uncertainty. The ambiguous identity of the adolescent girl thus makes logical her incorporation into Spiritualism. Much as the medium might shift between performing proper femininity and vocally subverting

existent gender norms, the modern girl of the period was at once obedient and recalcitrant, demure and riotous. The medium might play host to
many identities, both spiritual and mundane. Similarly, the adolescent girl
might embody multiple identities as she navigates the uncertain process
of maturation.

Like the teen witches that would follow them after World War II,
these earlier incarnations of supernatural girlhood function as malleable
cultural tropes, figures through which adolescent femininity, as it has been
understood across historical periods, could be conceptualised and interro-
gated. Significantly, these diverse figures, spanning a vast swathe of time
from the Middle Ages to the late nineteenth century, indicate that the
teenage witch is not a bounded trope. She is not confined to the post-
World War II period, nor is she unique to the United States. Aspects of the
teen witch can be found throughout history, incarnate in diffuse forms of
female mysticism. The adolescent witch is not a stable body. She is prone
to wander and her corporeality is often framed as leaky and sometimes
disturbingly agentic. The teenage witch resists containment. She cannot
be hemmed in chronologically or geographically. She is always caught in
the process of becoming. Recalling the motions of Deleuzian becoming,
the teen witch is not defined by the points between which she moves. She
passes between these points, coming up between them.[159] She is herself
'the in-between, the border or line of flight'.[160] In the subsequent chapters,
I attempt to map, or at least sketch, these becomings, tracing her various
connections, transformations and movements across twentieth and twenty-first-century cultural artefacts. In doing so, I demonstrate that while the
teen witch may have become a more cohesive trope during the post-war
period, she nevertheless remains dynamic, mobile and generative.

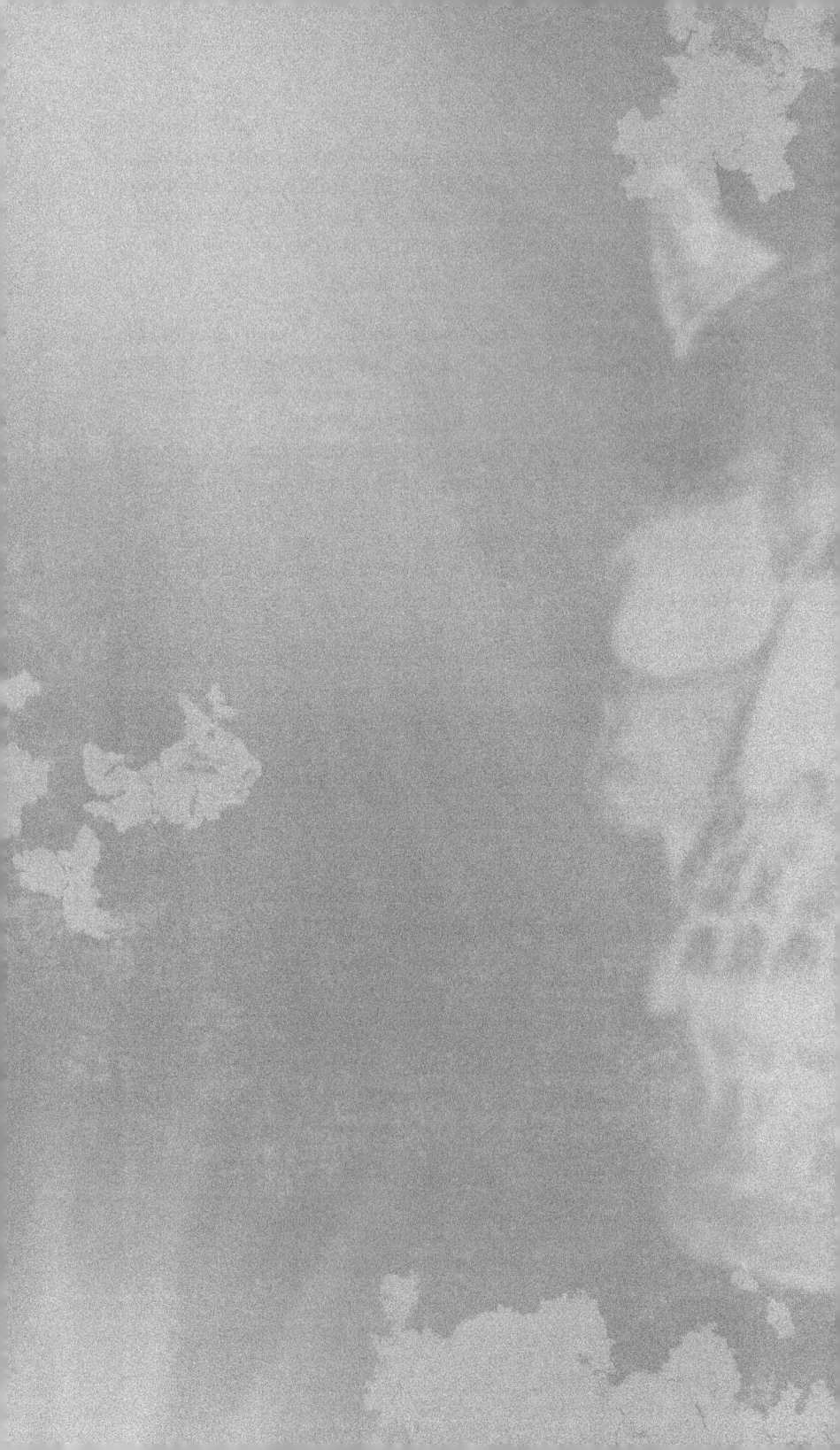

2

'A Pack of "Bobby-Soxers"'

Marion L. Starkey and the Birth of the Post-War Teenage Witch[1]

THIS CHAPTER EXPLORES the origins of the teen witch during the post-World War II period. Although, as discussed previously, diverse figurations of mystical girlhood have existed throughout history, the archetype of the witch who is also a teenage girl, or who mirrors the stereotypical characteristics of a teenage girl, is a comparatively recent phenomenon. Indeed, the teenage witch emerges as a distinct cultural trope at the precise moment in history when the teenage girl proper begins to command the attention of parents, teachers, social workers, policy makers and the media. However, the teen witch is not simply a passive reflection of contemporary anxieties about adolescent femininity (although, she does mirror many of these fears). Instead, the teen witch is a malleable, multivalent trope through which authors in the 1940s and 1950s grappled with the new phenomenon of the teenage girl and attempted to understand her position in American society. By employing the witch as a lens through which to understand the newly visible teenage girl, these authors engaged in a form of tropological representation, which according to Hayden White, functions to transform the 'unfamiliar into the familiar'.[2] 'This process of understanding', White explains, 'proceeds by the exploitation of the principal modalities of figuration, identified in post-Renaissance rhetorical theory as the "master tropes" . . . of metaphor, metonymy, synecdoche, and irony'.[3] In the case of post-war literature, the metaphor of teen girl as witch enabled writers to bring the unfamiliar (the adolescent girl) into the realm of the familiar by couching her in the recognisable language and iconography of witchcraft.

In the pages that follow I analyse three post-war texts that played a part in establishing the teenage witch as a cultural trope: Marion L. Starkey's historical study *The Devil in Massachusetts* (1949), Arthur Miller's play *The Crucible* (1953) and a series of interconnected short stories by Ray Bradbury that focus on a seventeen-year-old witch named Cecy Elliott (1946–52). My analysis commences with a detailed discussion of Starkey's *The Devil in Massachusetts*, a work that was, for much of the post-war period, 'the pre-vailing historical interpretation' of the Salem witch trials.[4] I argue that Star-key's anachronistic treatment of the bewitched girls at the centre of the trials established a new language for discussing teenage girls, that of witchcraft. I then unpack how Starkey frames these young women as positioned between biology and culture, analysing how she draws on contemporary discourses about hormonal fluctuation and the pubertal body to frame the Salem girls as disruptive entities. I then move on to chart Starkey's influence on Miller's *The Crucible*, showing how both authors evince an analogous unease with adolescent embodiment. Miller and Starkey, I maintain, employ images of pubertal upheaval, hysteria and sexual excess to portray the materiality of the adolescent body as destructive and transgressive. Building on the frame-work established in the previous chapter, I contend that Miller and Starkey are deeply invested in a dualistic logic that attempts to separate nature from culture, body from mind, and as such, they view the active materiality of the pubertal body as dangerous because of its power to disrupt these binaries. The final section of this chapter moves away from such anxious construc-tions of adolescent embodiment to explore more positive representations of the body's materiality. In three of his early tales – 'The Traveler' (1946), 'West of October' (written in the late 1940s but unpublished until 1988) and 'The April Witch' (1952) – Bradbury challenges dualistic modes of thought by portraying a young witch whose ability to move between bodies and environmental objects opens up paths to dynamic becomings. These transformations are dependent upon a conception of materiality as active and mobile, but in contrast to Starkey and Miller, Bradbury views agentic materiality optimistically. Here, the metamorphic body is not a source of horror, but rather an invitation to discard fixed, static identities in search of pleasurable new becomings. Although Bradbury, does not fully dismantle binary modes of apprehension, his endlessly transforming adolescent witch productively challenges these rigid structures.

'Unbalanced teen-agers': Marion L. Starkey's Anachronistic Salem

Starkey's *The Devil in Massachusetts* is as much an attempt to comprehend the modern phenomenon of the teenage girl as it is an analysis of the Salem witch trials. The full title of Starkey's study is *The Devil in Massachusetts: A Modern Inquiry into the Salem Witch Trials*, and it is the word 'modern', proudly displayed in the subtitle of the book, that most fully encapsulates Starkey's approach to her subject. While, as Larry Gragg has observed, Starkey's book forms part of a larger scholarly tradition wherein the accusing girls were identified as the epicentre of the witchcraft panic – a tradition that stretches back to Thomas Hutchinson in the eighteenth century and Charles Wentworth Upham in the nineteenth century[5] – *The Devil in Massachusetts* is notable for its anachronistic treatment of the afflicted, whom it figures as fundamentally modern teenagers. On a para-textual level, this conflation of seventeenth-century youth and modern teens is apparent even from the synopsis printed on the interior jacket flap of the first edition. Describing the diverse victims of the Salem witch trials – a plain farmer, a pipe-smoking beggar woman – the blurb informs us that 'Because of the fantasies and hysterical antics of *unbalanced teen-agers* decent men and women were sent to the gallows'.[6] As Marion Gibson observes, the author's language, and indeed that of the publisher, clearly reflects contemporary concerns about post-war American youth and, in particular, the new and somewhat puzzling phenomenon of the teenager.[7] My analysis in this chapter pivots around Starkey's unusual approach to Salem's afflicted girls, her description of them as teenagers, or 'bobby-sox-ers', and her use of contemporary terms and concepts to suggest not so much a continuance of teenage behaviour but a transplantation of mod-ern adolescence to an early modern setting. Moreover, I argue that Star-key's frequent use of the phrase 'bobby-soxers' is evocative of a historical moment in which the teenage girl was new, strange and even threatening to the social order.

In her study of post-war adolescent culture, Ilana Nash explains that the 'general consensus of teen identity manifested very sparsely before the 1930s',[8] while other historians have noted that the word 'teenager' itself did not enter popular usage until around the time of World War II.[9] Likewise, Grace Palladino describes how up until the 1930s most ado-lescents worked – either in factories, on farms or in the home – and, as such, failed to develop a distinct demographic identity.[10] Young people who entered the workforce at this time would not normally have been considered teenagers, or even adolescents, because that descriptor was normally applied only to high school students – those with the kind of financial and familial supports that would enable them to continue their education beyond the primary level.[11] It was not until the scarcity of the Great Depression that the first rumblings of a distinct teenage identity could be heard. With fewer jobs available for adults, teenagers who may have previously worked in industry or agriculture were herded *en masse* into the classroom. This large-scale movement into second-level education proved pivotal, enabling teens to convene as a peer group. The concept of adolescence was no longer reserved for the wealthy, but instead it began to apply to young people from a range of different backgrounds. Palladino notes, that in the rush to the classroom:

> adolescents had become an age group and not just a wealthy social class, a shift that helped to create the idea of a separate teenage generation. When a teenage majority spent the better part of their day in high school, they learned to look to one another and not to adults for information, advice and approval.[12]

By the mid-1930s, secondary education had become the norm rather than the exception, with approximately 65 per cent of the adolescent population enrolled in high school in 1936.[13]

During the 1940s, teenagers further solidified their status as a distinct demographic through the acquisition of increased purchasing power. As the war raged, a thriving economy allowed many teens to re-enter the workforce, and while some dropped out of school in order to engage in full-time employment, many others worked part time, in the evenings after school and on weekends.[14] Nash argues that the ability to remain in school while also earning a regular wage allowed students 'both the financial means and the time to participate in the leisure culture of high school peer groups'.[15] When the conflict ended, America's revitalised post-war economy ensured that many families could afford to shower their children with previously unimaginable luxuries. Yet, even as they were defined by their economic role, post-war teens sought to create new cultural identities, distinct from those of their families and separate from their upbringing. Teenagers moved away from the dominant pre-war notion of adolescents as 'adults in training' towards a more confrontational, rebellious demeanour that signified a desire for peer acceptance and social independence.[16] During this period, teenagers were approached with a great deal of ambivalence. On the one hand, their continued striving for independence, as well as a preoccupation with new music and cultural fads, caused a strain between parents and their adolescent children and contributed to a broad public perception of teenagers as 'potential troublemakers'.[17] On the other, adolescence – imagined as an idyllic period of unrestrained consumption and play – signalled that America had not only won the war, but created a new and better world for its children. However, it is crucial to emphasise at this point that such ambivalence did not extend to young people of colour, nor to working class or migrant youths. It was fully restricted to those whose families and communities benefitted from the post-war economic boom. In her discussion of mid-century adolescent sexuality, Grace Palladino argues that the popular vision of teenage girls as mischievous creatures, vacillating between fresh-faced innocence and threatening, precocious sexuality, was never applied to minority teenagers. Mexican-American girls, or *pachuquitas*, whose fashions consisted of short skirts, sheer blouses and red lipstick, were described by critics as 'little tornados of sexualised stimuli'.[18] Thus, where the sexuality of white teenage girls was often represented in contradictory terms, ethnic-minority teenagers were viewed as unequivocally dangerous.

Composed in the midst of this demographic and cultural turmoil, *The Devil in Massachusetts* addresses itself directly to the cultural concerns of the era. Although Starkey draws numerous parallels between seventeenth-century Puritanism and both the totalitarianism that led to World War II and the paranoia of post-war American culture (*DM*, p. 15), she primarily lays the blame for the panic squarely with a group of female adolescents whom she describes as 'crazed little girls' (*DM*, p. 13). As familiar as a dark fable, the events of the Salem witch trials have been told and re-told numerous times and in different forms over the centuries, and by now, many can recite, almost by heart, the events surrounding the 'bewitchment' of Betty Parris (nine) and Abigail Williams (eleven), children in the home of the village's controversial minister, Samuel Parris. Equally well known is the viral manner in which cases of bewitchment spread throughout the small Puritan community, acquiring a pathogenic quality as more and more of the village's youth fell under a malignant influence. As the ranks of the afflicted grew, numerous young girls were spellbound by the enchantment percolating through Salem. Mercy Lewis (nineteen), Mary Warren (twenty), Abigail Hobbs (fourteen), Elizabeth Hubbard (sixteen) and Ann Putnam, Jr (twelve) all fell under the magic of an apparent diabolical invasion. As teens and pre-teens, these girls existed in an ambiguous space between adulthood and childhood. No longer children but generally too young to marry, they occupied the silent edges of their community and were expected to remain subservient at all times. Claiming harassment by spectral forces propelled the girls into the centre of the community's political and spiritual life. Capable of detecting the presence of witches and evil forces, the girls were viewed by their community as uniquely attuned to the supernatural. Aside from a few members of the circle, such as the rebellious Abigail Hobbs, who were accused of witchery themselves before displaying signs of affliction,[19] the girls were not witches *per se*. Yet, they were able to divine acts of *maleficium* and uncover spectral presences. Starkey refers to them at numerous points in her history of the trials as mediums and seeresses (*DM*, pp. 181 and 211). Thus, while the Salem girls may not have been witches in the strictest sense, they were viewed as intimately connected to the mystical. Even if their abilities were lies or delusions, the mythic status of the Salem panic ensured that in the popular imagination the entanglement between young girls and spiritual forces would remain an enduring cultural trope.

Starkey's unique contribution to the endurance and popularisation of this trope resides in her conflation of the Salem girls and contemporary teenagers, a transhistorical amalgamation that she renders in the new language of teen fads that had grown up in the post-war period. In her most concise attempt to attribute blame for the Salem persecutions, Starkey notes that:

> The tragedy which was once enacted in this pleasant neighbourhood originated in the childish fantasies of some very little girls and was carried to its deadly climax by what one might now call a pack of '*bobby-soxers*' were not the term pictorially incongruous. It was largely the older girls, who inflamed by the terrors of Calvinism as their immature minds understood it, depressed by the lack of any legitimate outlet for their natural high spirits, found relief for their tensions in an emotional orgy which eventually engulfed not only their village but the Massachusetts Bay Colony. (*DM*, p. 14, emphasis added)

The use of the term 'bobby-soxers' is crucial here. It is a descriptor that would have been intimately familiar to contemporary readers, evoking a plethora of associations with youth, irresponsibility and insubordination. Palladino notes in her study of the emerging teenage phenomenon that during the 1940s:

high school students gained national fame as 'bobby soxers', the popular nickname bestowed on swing-crazed fans who were developing a new teenage style. In their saddle shoes, skirts, and sweaters, they became the new symbol of high school life, one that was identified with music, fads, and fun.[20]

The moniker 'bobby-soxer' derives from the style of socks worn by these 'swing-crazed' girls, and as such, it is clear that from the very beginning, teenage girls were reduced to a product, a commodity, a signifier of their 'frivolous' preoccupation with fashion. Moreover, teen girls during the period of their first emergence as a cultural phenomenon were simultaneously fascinating and alienating to adults.[21] Embodying both youthful promise and rebellious dissent, teenage girls were understood as strange, disruptive in their sexuality and fanatical in their devotion to boys and movie stars. Starkey's characterisation of Salem's seventeenth-century bobby-soxers parallels these anxieties. Just as the 'pleasant neighbourhood' of Salem was brought to ruin by the 'natural high spirits' of frustrated Puritan maidens, so too did post-war American adults worry that their pleasant suburban neighbourhoods might be destroyed by the uncontainable energies of unruly adolescent girls. Starkey's portrayal of the Salem afflicted as a threat to the social order echoes, in decidedly modern language, the anxieties about teenage girls that were crackling like electricity in the air of late 1940s America.

Parlaying contemporary fears into her interrogation of the Salem witchcraft panic, Starkey describes, again in quintessentially modern terms, how:

> There was in Salem Village in the winter of 1691–2 quite a store of young girls, unattached teen-agers. The Puritans, sober in all things, quite properly looked on marriage as a serious business and did not favour it for the very young. Thus there were several girls about who had reached the age of sixteen, seventeen, and even twenty still manless and unprovided for, and those girls were instinct with repressed vitality, with all manner of cravings and urges for which village life afforded no outlet. (*DM*, p. 32)

For Starkey, Salem's afflicted were motivated by typical adolescent boredom, by the tedium of chores and the isolation of long winters devoid of company. Moreover, they were 'manless', single girls with no outlet for their burgeoning sexuality, and it was this 'repressed vitality' that would eventually cause them to see witches perched on the beams of the Salem meeting house and feel spectral pins pricking their delicate skin. Here, again, Starkey's portrayal of the Salem girls reflects the standard image of 'bobby-soxers' that proliferated during this period. Ilana Nash notes that one of the most intriguing facets of fictional teen girls, as shown on screen and in the popular magazines of the period, was their tendency to vacillate between 'quasi-angelic creature[s]' and obstreperous 'agent[s] of chaos'.[22] In post-war cinematic depictions of teen girls, their unbounded energy and fanatical devotion to crooners and heartthrobs of all varieties dest-abilises the lives of the adults around them. Popular films such as *Junior Miss* (1945) and *Kiss and Tell* (1945) portray adolescent girls, overcome by crushes and uniquely susceptible to Hollywood-inspired flights of fancy, who lose themselves in day dreams that later prove immensely destructive to both their families and communities.[23] Nash underscores how in numer-ous cinematic texts featuring bobby-soxers, the protagonists are construed as 'silly creatures who cause astronomical, if accidental, damage to their father's stability'.[24] By jeopardising their father's careers, finances and social standing, these girls pose a potent threat to the hierarchy of patriarchal authority. Characterising the young women of Salem as equally susceptible to boredom, mischief and imaginative flights of fantasy, Starkey draws on a store of common social concerns about the American teenager.

Starkey's vision of the Salem afflicted is not, however, a passive reflec-tion of post-war anxieties about adolescent femininity. Her rendition of the Essex County witchcraft panic represents a sustained attempt to com-prehend female adolescence and, perhaps most crucially, to understand the situation of the teenage girl at the intersection between the biological and the cultural. For Starkey, the Salem maidens who inaugurated the witch trials were defined by their peripheral status both culturally, as a store of 'manless' young women on the edge of their community, and corporeally, as marginal beings positioned between childhood and womanhood. Star-key's preoccupation with the unfulfilled cravings and urges of the Salem girls is especially significant in that it is less reflective of Puritan discourses on maidenhood, which were grounded in the idea of preparation for one's wifely duty,[25] than it is of mid-twentieth-century ideas about puberty and the female body. Starkey's formulation of unproductive, directionless female sexuality transforming into destructive energy reflects constructions of femininity inaugurated in the wake of the nineteenth-century 'discov-ery' of sex hormones.[26] Although many scholars have since dismissed the notion that radically different hormonal compositions can fully account for sex differences between men and women,[27] ideas about hormones as the primary source of sexual divergence persist in popular culture, with the image of fluctuating, volatile hormones exerting an irresistible force over both the female mind and body remaining particularly ubiquitous.

Starkey was writing at a time when there was a general awareness of the role of the pituitary glands and other hormonal apparatuses in the modulation of pubertal processes. As Anne Fausto-Sterling explains, the period between 1920 and 1940 could be described as the 'heyday' of hormone research.[28] During these two decades, scientists discovered how to distil active factors from testes and ovaries, learned how to measure the activity of these chemicals, and produced and named pure crystals of steroid hormones.[29] However, *The Devil in Massachusetts* does not reflect the more nuanced elements of this research. Instead, it imagines the relationship between biological (or hormonal) and sociocultural factors as intensely fraught and riven by irreconcilable tensions. Indeed, while her book refers to puberty only in veiled language, a clear position on menarche, menstruation and hormonal change can be deciphered: Starkey's understanding of female adolescence is defined by notions of distress and disorder.

This rhetoric of uncontrollable female biology was a key component of post-World War II conversations about both puberty and menarche. For much of this period, sex education materials aimed at adolescent girls stressed the unruly nature of the pubertal body and outlined steps that could be taken to control its seepages and disturbances. Mid-century discourses on puberty and menstruation regularly emphasised how the disruptive female body must be managed. In her study of twentieth-century puberty pamphlets for girls, Michelle H. Martin discusses the ubiquity of references to containment in these texts, remarking that:

> A consistent theme throughout the puberty pamphlets from Kimberly Clark (makers of Kotex products), Personal Products (makers of Always brand sanitary products and, earlier, Modess), and Tambrands (makers of Tampax) is that although menstruation is 'perfectly natural', women must pay special attention to their body odor, particularly while menstruating.[30]

The discourse surrounding menstruation and embodied femininity was, for much of the twentieth century, preoccupied with a vision of the female body as home to unstable biological forces that perennially threatened to break free. Such materials stress the importance of teenage girls learning to navigate, or mediate, the space between the biological and social realms. The teenage girl is tasked with preserving the border between the cultural and the corporeal, while at the same time embodying the contested site where these disparate realms meet. In 1946, Disney produced a short, animated sex-education film for teenage girls, wistfully titled *The Story of Menstruation*. The film carefully outlines how hormones affect psychology and mood, instructing viewers not to allow such hormonal fluctuations to 'get you down' and reminding them of the importance of looking smart and maintaining a well-groomed appearance.[31] Thus, the teenage girl is asked to fend off the chthonian forces of biology, to present herself as a subject born entirely of culture by suppressing any sign of bodily or hormonal tumult.

Throughout *The Devil in Massachusetts*, Starkey's description of Salem's bewitched girls pivots around such notions of barely contained feminine excess. Although not explicitly referencing menstruation or hormonal fluctuation, her multitude of allusions to the girls' 'high spirits', 'tensions' and 'repressed vitality' are clearly intended to signify pubertal upheaval and frustrated sexual impulses. Describing twelve-year-old Ann Putnam, Jr, Starkey writes that:

> Ann was now on the verge of adolescence, already subject to the preliminary strains of that difficult period, to unexplained pains and heaviness in the limbs, to dizziness and flashes of imagination so vivid that they sometimes resemble hallucinations. (*DM*, p. 38)

Ann's propensity towards fantasy and intense flashes of imagination is explicitly connected to the physical metamorphosis of adolescence, the girl's dizziness and heavy limbs apparently drawing her into soporific flights of fancy. In Starkey's figuration of events, Ann's role as an afflicted girl is intimately connected to her adolescent biology. The listlessness of her body, its mysterious agonies, engender her phantasmagoric hallucinations. Puberty, menarche and hormonal fluctuation are figured as volatile forces, potentially destructive and in need of containment.

Although it is possible to align such images of the leaky, porous female body with psychoanalytic theories of abject,[32] I would argue that these tropes instead reflect a deep-seated anxiety about the materiality of the pubertal body. Starkey's book, while interested in questions of embodiment, appears largely invested in a binary logic that attempts to separate the social from the biological, the rational mind from the riotous body. Her construction of the Salem girls as overcome by biological forces and unstable in their transformative potential echoes Kelly Hurley's vision of the 'undifferentiated body', the body that 'has lost its "proper" configurations and is proceeding towards a state of pure disorganization, or perhaps reorganizing into new configurations, unknown and hence terrible'.[33] In contrast to the abject body, whose permeable boundaries threaten the integrity of the ego, the undifferentiated body is one that generates anxiety by virtue of its 'gross corporeality'.[34] Starkey's representation of the afflicted centres on the physical body as dynamic, agentic and even clamorous in its vitality. Although discussed euphemistically, Starkey figures adolescent corporeality as defined by hormonal secretions, viscous fluids and emotional instability that not only threaten to make themselves visible on the body's surface but destabilise the wider cultural arena. In contrast to those thinkers who celebrate the body's agentic capacities, Starkey appears primarily interested in 'the exorbitant *materiality* of the body and nature',[35] which she views with trepidation. For Starkey, the pubertal body bespeaks the instability of matter, the fact that it 'is intransigent and resists containment within a fixed and unitary form'.[36] The flows and secretions of puberty suggest the impossibility of separating the corporeal from the cultural and illustrate the unease generated by matter's agentic powers.

'Some reddish work done at night': Puberty, Hysteria and Disruptive Materiality in Marion L. Starkey's *The Devil in Massachusetts* and Arthur Miller's *The Crucible*

The Devil in Massachusetts was a tremendously influential book. It was reprinted by Time Books in the 1960s, and so identified as a significant modern work, and it remains in print even today, more than seven decades after its initial publication. Much of its cultural impact stems from the anachronistic tendencies that have led many modern historians to criticise its presentism,[37] but those same anachronisms also enabled Starkey to devise a new language – that of witchcraft – through which to discuss female adolescence. Starkey's ideas also seeped into the popular imagination via their incorporation into literary texts. William Carlos Williams' play *Tituba's Children* (1950) quotes directly from Starkey's book and uses her work to establish a series of parallels between mid-century anti-communist crusades and the Salem witch trials. More influential, however, was Arthur Miller's play *The Crucible*, published only three years later and equally invested in establishing connections between early modern witch hunts and the then-contemporary Red Scare. Crucially, Miller draws extensively on Starkey's portrayal of the Salem bewitched as modern-day bobby-soxers. Indeed, Miller's text not only applies Starkey's anachronistic approach to his characterisation of the Salem girls, he also echoes her unease regarding adolescent embodiment. Miller portrays the afflicted as contemporary teenagers and explains their behaviour in terms of hormonal fluctuation, sexual frustration and unruly corporeality. Moreover, as outlined below, Miller utilises Starkey's diagnosis of the girls as hysterics in his depiction of their behaviour and motivations, while both authors articulate the disruptive power of the adolescent body by positioning the afflicted between the categories of witch and bewitched.

In his essay 'The Crucible in History', Miller ruminates on the origin of his famous play. Describing the moment in which the connection between post-war American anti-communism and seventeenth-century witchcraft hysteria crystallised in his mind, Miller writes that the germ of the idea took root when, on a 'lucky afternoon', he came across a copy of *The Devil in Massachusetts*.[38] Although intended as an allegory of the McCarthy-era's persecution of suspected communists, *The Crucible* nevertheless locates the source of Salem's witchcraft panic in the chaos of hormonal adolescence. A recurring linguistic motif that runs throughout Miller's play is the regularity with which the words 'girls' or 'children' are used to describe the afflicted. While it has been observed that the circle of the spectrally harassed was indeed defined by this appellation, despite a seemingly incongruous variation in the ages of those involved, the afflicted girls in *The Crucible* are portrayed as just that: a gang of teenage girls inflamed by intense adolescent crushes, peer pressure and petty jealousy. The historian Margo Burns notes that despite Miller's characterisation of the young women at the centre of the Salem trials as a homogenous group of teenage girls, the core group at the nexus of the panic was, in reality, far more diverse:

> The alleged 'afflicted' comprised not just a group of a dozen teenage girls – there were men and adult women who also claimed 'affliction', including John Indian, Ann Putnam, Sr., [mother of the listless Ann, Jr.] and Sarah Bibber – and there were more in Andover, where the total number of people accused was greater than any other town, including Salem Village.[39]

Miller's play erases these older accusers, reducing the core group to a gaggle of teenage girls, who in the pettiness of their motivations and the intensity of their relationships mirror popular 1950s representations of high school girls. Here, the leader of the afflicted girls is Abigail Williams, her age raised for the purposes of drama from eleven to seventeen. No longer a mischievous pre-teen, Miller's Abigail fits perfectly with Starkey's description of Salem's primary troublemakers as 'bobby-soxers', older teenage girls whose minds were nevertheless immature. Likewise, Miller echoes Starkey's characterisation of Ann Putnam, Jr as prone to the lethargy and physical discomfort of the teenage years when his fictional Ann, Sr complains that her daughter, renamed Ruth here, has become a remote, etiolated creature: 'A secret child she has become this year, and shrivels like a sucking mouth were pullin' on her life too' (*Cr*, p. 12). In *The Crucible*, as in *The Devil in Massachusetts*, adolescent girls are regularly overcome by unruly physical and emotional symptoms. Located at the nexus of childhood and womanhood, culture and biology, the interstitiality of the Salem girls is constructed in the writings of Miller and Starkey as an irresistible invitation to chaos; it was, apparently, the very in-betweenness of these young women that opened the door to imagined or feigned bewitchment.

Beyond their mutual emphasis on the pubertal corporeality of the afflicted, Miller and Starkey share a common interest in the role of hysteria in stimulating their fantasies and accusations. In her diagnosis of the girls, Starkey observes that the force of their delusions – spectres balanced on courthouse beams, malevolent birds, the dark presence of a sinister 'black man' – combined with spectacular displays of physical affliction – fits, fainting, the sensation of spectral pin pricks – suggests that the girls were suffering from that most indefinite and all-encompassing feminine disorder: hysteria. Starkey claims that despite the strangeness of the girls' behaviour, 'the general pattern of their conduct is clear enough; in *modern terms* they all of them, in one degree or another, had hysteria' (*DM*, p. 45, emphasis added). For Starkey, this diagnosis of hysteria is in keeping with 'the findings of modern psychology, particularly the Freudian school' (*DM*, p. 17). Although the connections she forges between witchcraft, hysteria and psychology owe much to late nineteenth and early twentieth-century discourse,[40] her work self-consciously capitalises on America's post-war fascination with all things psychoanalytical and the zeitgeist of an era when cinema, theatre and the popular press were dominated by positive portrayals of Freudianism.[41]

Based on the argument presented in *The Devil in Massachusetts*, Starkey's understanding of hysteria is vague. However, as many historians have noted, hysteria has always been a nebulous, even unstable, diagnosis. In Ancient Greece, the physician Hippocrates attributed hysteria to the propensity of the womb (*hystera*) to wander throughout the body causing various blockages and disturbances. Associating hysteria with virgins, widows and spinsters, doctors often linked the illness to a 'drying out' of the womb.[42] Later, the physician Galen identified the aetiological roots of hysteria in the accumulation of blood and humours, a theory that persisted well into the eighteenth century. In the nineteenth century, neurologist Jean-Martin Charcot linked hysteria to psychic trauma, a position later adopted by Pierre Janet (albeit with the acknowledgement of a preceding organic aetiology) and, for a time, Sigmund Freud.[43] Consequently, as Rachel P. Maines elucidates, hysteria, while remaining a fundamentally feminine pathology, has, over time, been associated with:

> a set of symptoms that varied greatly between individuals (and their physicians), including but not limited to fainting (syncope), edema or hyperemia (congestion caused by fluid retention, either localized or general), nervousness, insomnia, sensations of heaviness in the abdomen, muscle spasms, shortness of breath, loss of appetite for food or for sex with the approved male partner, and sometimes a tendency to cause trouble for others, particularly members of the patient's immediate family.[44]

This construction of hysteria as a loosely defined disease affecting both the patient's physical body (edema, hyperaemia, breathing difficulties), mind (insomnia, nervousness) and social relations (causing trouble for family members) highlights the categorical instability of the illness. Much like adolescence, hysteria occupies an interstitial position between the mental and the physical, traversing the border between the cultural and the biological while drawing attention to active vitality of the body.

Starkey's employment of the hysteria diagnosis alludes vaguely to Freudian ideas, and her representation of sexually frustrated young women succumbing to delusion chimes with Freud's belief that 'where hysteria is found there can no longer be any question of "innocence of mind" in the sense in which parents and educators use the phrase'.[45] For the most part, though, she tends to conflate hysterical outbursts with pubertal symptoms so that any aetiological distinction between the two is obscured. Patterns of behaviour – ranging from sexual mania to lethargy, from hallucinations to convulsions – appear equally attributable to either diagnosis. Starkey's propensity to collapse somatic distinctions between hysteria and puberty is, however, explicable in terms of the cultural shifts and medical advancements of the post-World War II period. Despite the fashionable status of Freudian psychoanalysis during the mid-twentieth century, hysteria was already becoming an outmoded diagnosis by the late 1940s. The scientific legitimacy of hysteria was seen to have officially 'ended' in 1952, when the illness was excluded from both the first edition of the *Diagnostic and Statistical Manual of Mental Disorders* (1952) and *The Standard Classified Nomenclature of Disease*.[46] Yet, just as the primacy of hysteria was waning, a new all-encompassing diagnosis emerged to account for perceived emotional, physiological or psychological irregularities in women. As Jane M. Ussher observes:

> the focus on the premenstrual phase of the cycle as a time of vulnerability, and on premenstrual changes as symptoms of psychiatric illness, can be traced to 1931, when the diagnostic category 'premenstrual tension' (PMT) was first described. Robert Frank, the gynaecologist commonly credited with establishing the existence of PMT, attributed the combination of physical and psychological symptoms he observed occurring in the days immediately prior to menstruation to accumulations of 'the female sex hormone', oestrogen.[47]

While PMT was rechristened 'premenstrual syndrome' (PMS) in 1953, the construction of the female body as vulnerable, both psychically and physically, to accumulations of hormones and invisible biological manoeuvrings remained essential to contemporary understandings of sex differences. Starkey's vision of hysterical teenage girls unleashing chaos in a formerly stable community appears at a decisive moment when the diagnostic category of hysteria was giving way to a new, modern emphasis on premenstrual disorders stemming from hormonal discord. Yet, by associating hysteria with young women in the midst of pubertal upheaval, Starkey elides this diagnostic transformation, and the distinction between hysteria and premenstrual tension collapses into a singular, iconic image of chaotic feminine corporeality.

In as much as she is destructive, the hysteric can also represent a desire for freedom, and the disorder's subversive connotations may explain Starkey's investment in the diagnosis. In the nineteenth century, hysterics, as well as witches, were associated with suffragists.[48] Physicians frequently linked hysteria to historical accounts of witchcraft, often retroactively diagnosing accused witches as hysterics, as well as to the 'phenomenon of contemporary women's pursuit of new opportunities for work and education'.[49] A century later, the work of Michel Foucault suggested clear parallels between the body of the hysteric, which he described in *Psychiatric Power* (1974) as 'the front of resistance' in the face of nineteenth-century psychiatry,[50] and the contested body of the demoniac, whom he defines in *Abnormal* as a 'resistant receptacle'.[51] Similarly, in *The Newly Born Woman* (1975), Hélène Cixous and Catherine Clément figure hysteria as a manifestation of repressed female energy. To them, the figure of the hysteric is inextricably intertwined with that of the witch. Hysteria is a liberating force that can be compared to the practice of witchcraft precisely because it represents a return of what society represses, namely female corporeality and creative energy. In *The Newly Born Woman* witches and hysterics are portrayed as 'stylized channels into which excess demonically flows – excess desire, excess rage, *excess* creative energy – only to be annihilated by the society that drove her in such directions'.[52] Although the sorceress is able reach back to a paganism repressed by Christianity and revel in the ecstasy of nature, while the hysteric extends herself back to forgotten scenes of childhood, both are liberated only temporarily from the constraints of society and patriarchy: the witch is invariably hanged or burned, and the family of the hysteric closes in around her, reabsorbing her into their dynamic.[53] Despite the brevity of their liberation, these women are nevertheless enabled to 'escape the misfortune of their economic and familial exploitation' by choosing 'to suffer spectacularly before an audience of men'.[54]

Starkey's figuration of the Salem afflicted as hysterics therefore bridges not only the rhetorical and aetiological categories of hysteria and puberty, but also a third category: that of bewitchment. By portraying her bewitched girls as hysterics, Starkey folds these categories in on each other, so that the Salem afflicted are seen to be consumed by both their biology and their proximity to imagined supernatural forces. This rhetorical conflation solidifies the connection between the profoundly and visibly biological metamorphoses of puberty, a state of excessive corporeality akin to that of hysteria, and the transformative power of the occult. Thus, there is a suggestion that whether escaping into the theatrics of supernatural possession or the public spectacle of hysterical performance, the girls are enacting a form of adolescent rebellion, a rejection of social strictures and patriarchal rule.

Taking its cue from Starkey, *The Crucible* also portrays the Salem girls as hysterics. The afflicted girls enact a spectacular retreat into visionary states and elaborate physical performances that temporarily release them from the constraints of a rigid social order. Miller's descriptions of New England Puritanism, although noting the propensity for communal celebration and occasional levity, is grounded in the popular notion of the Puritans as strict, sombre and austere. His introductory historical note defines the New England settlers as serious-minded and averse to fantasy, describing how 'They had no novelists – and would not have permitted anyone to read a novel if one were handy' (*Cr*, p. 4). Adherence to theological and communal norms was enforced not merely by religious dogma, but by the hostility of the landscape and the panoptic nature of a society where the 'predilection for minding other people's business was time-honoured' (*Cr*, p. 5). Although Miller does not allude directly to the patriarchal structure of seventeenth-century New England, he does show that the Salem girls occupy a marginal position within their community. Many of them are serving girls in the homes of neighbours, and this reflects the historical practice whereby New Englanders regularly sent their daughters to work for other families if there was not enough work for them at home.[55] Despite the pragmatism of this, these young women, sent to strange houses just as they were entering adolescence, were left in a decidedly uncertain position. Neither family members nor servants in the conventional sense, they occupied an ambiguous role in their new homes. In *The Crucible* their performance of bewitchment enables these girls to command attention where once they were expected to remain silent; it allows them to act out, to vocalise frustrations and upend the existing social order. When the accusations begin, Elizabeth Proctor expresses a newfound fear of her serving girl, Mary Warren. After her husband, John, queries how she could possibly find such an inconsequential little 'mouse' intimidating, Elizabeth responds that 'It is a mouse no more' (*Cr*, p. 36). The young women of Salem are imagined as a nightmarish rendition of the archetypal post-war rebellious youth, contemptuous of authority and fundamentally uncontrollable. Yet, while the afflicted girls are portrayed as spiteful, bored and resentful, it is through their retreat into hysterical and corporeal excess that they truly defy the behavioural and gender norms that circumscribe their reality.

Hysteria and hysterical behaviour are mentioned numerous times throughout the play. Notably, references to the pathology are confined to the stage directions so that they appear to be a contemporary diagnosis informing the actors' movements and expressions without ever intruding upon the dialogue of the play's seventeenth-century characters. Although bewitched girls like Mary Warren are often described as 'hysterical' with fright (*Cr*, p. 75), male characters and authority figures, such as Judge Danforth, are also occasionally described as 'hysterical' (*Cr*, p. 73). Yet, while both men and woman are described as hysterical, the play's teenage girls are the only characters to manifest actual hysterical symptoms. Betty Parris, the first of the girls to experience bewitchment, is portrayed as suffering from a sort of hysterical paralysis, an immobility that has been recorded in cases of hysteria stretching from the early modern period through to Freudian psychoanalysis.[56] In the stage directions for Act One of the play we are told that 'BETTY PARRIS, aged ten, is lying on the bed, inert' (*Cr*, p. 4). In her soporific state, Betty retreats inwards, away from society and into the body. Upon waking, her behaviour is erratic and unstable: she embodies the liberating excess described by Cixous and Clément. Betty 'darts off the bed' and 'flattens herself against the wall', crying out for her deceased mother (*Cr*, p. 14). Asserting that she will 'fly to Mama', Betty 'raises her arm as though to fly, and streaks for the window, gets one leg out' (*Cr*, p. 14). Betty's paralysis giving way to an excessive physicality in which the girl runs, jumps and even attempts to fly suggests that, like Clément's witch/hysteric, Betty is channelling repressed forces of creativity, corporeality, frustration and desire. She suffers spectacularly before the controlling gaze of male authority figures: her father, the minister, and Reverend Hale, the man of learning. Yet her antics and contortions, while confirming both their Puritanical beliefs in the veracity of the diabolical and the unique susceptibility of women to such forces, also undermine the authority of these men through an explosion of uncontainable feminine excess. Through their hysteric outbursts, Miller's afflicted are permitted to resist, albeit briefly, the power structures that bind, constrain and shape them.

Reading corporeality from a Foucauldian perspective in which the materiality of the body is not denied but rather situated within a disciplinary framework,[57] it is possible to understand Miller's bewitched girls as imbricated within power structures that shape their subjectivity through control of the body. Miller explains, early in the play, that the young people of Salem are expected to 'walk straight, eyes slightly lowered, arms at the sides, and mouths shut until bidden to speak' (*Cr*, p. 4). Their bodies are inscribed by social norms, and this exterior discipline produces an interior that is quiet, submissive and docile. However, the afflicted girls are empowered to reconfigure those same bodies as sites of resistance through their performance of hysteria and/or bewitchment. In a January 1974 lecture at the Collège de France, later collected in the book *Psychiatric Power*, Foucault frames the hysteric as a 'blazon of genuine illnesses'.[58] The hysteric resists the diagnostic power of the medical establishment because 'she pursues a game such that when one wants to fix her illness in reality, one can never manage to do so, since, when her symptom should refer to an organic substratum, she shows that there is no substratum'.[59] Although Foucault's position could be accused, in the words of Elaine Showalter, of 'romanticizing and endorsing madness as a desirable form of rebellion',[60] it also facilitates a conception of corporeality as active rather than passive.

In an analogous manner, Foucault frames possession as a mode of corporeal resistance. While the Salem girls were 'bewitched' rather than possessed, these categories of diabolic affliction often overlap in early modern accounts. Erika Gasser explains that during this period 'there was considerable slippage between possession and bewitchment', as the symptoms of possession were regularly understood as produced through witchcraft.[61] Consequently, the behaviour of the Salem girls often recalled that of victims of possession. Their cataleptic stasis, spectacular fits and disconcerting performances of affliction are all characteristic of demonic possession. Significantly, both the possessed body and the bewitched body are defined by convulsive movement. Foucault describes the convulsion as 'the plastic and visible form of the struggle taking place in the body of the possessed'.[62] More importantly, however, the convulsive flesh is one that rebels against the powers of either medical examination or religious confession. Within the context of early modern religiosity, this body is one 'that counters the rule of obedient direction with intense shocks of involuntary revolt or little betrayals of secret connivance'.[63] In doing so, it resists the corporeal investments of Christianity, refusing supplication or confessional surrender. In *The Crucible*, the bewitched girls resist both medical and religious power through their confounding behaviour. Indeed, one of the first lines of dialogue in the play establishes that the local physician 'cannot discover no medicine for it in his books' (*Cr*, p. 8), while even the ministrations of Reverend Hale fail to rouse the insensible Betty by the end of the first act.

Although the early part of *The Crucible* frames hysteria/bewitchment in terms of individual resistance to mechanisms of power – Betty's inert form lying prone in the face of both the doctor and minister's entreaties – the latter half of the play moves beyond this individualism to explore post-war concerns about the tribalism of teenage girls and their intense peer relationships. The girls' hysteria often manifests in ways that recall the quasi-anthropological studies of teen girls that appeared in the media in the middle part of the twentieth century. Just as these portrayals often foregrounded the symbiotic nature of friendships between adolescent girls, as well the rigidity and homogeneity of their social groupings, so too does Miller present the Salem bewitched as embroiled in a form of group thought that enables each girl's hysteric excess to transcend her own corporeality and infect those around her. When Mary Warren, the Proctor's servant, attempts to extricate herself from the accusing circle, Abigail Williams and the other girls respond as if bewitched, imitating Mary's words and actions in unison:

> MARY WARREN [*pleading*]: Abby, you mustn't!
> ABIGAIL AND ALL THE GIRLS [*all transfixed*]: Abby, you mustn't!
> MARY WARREN [*to all the girls*]: I'm here, I'm here!
> GIRLS: I'm here, I'm here!
> . . .
> MARY WARREN [*screaming at the top of her lungs, and raising her fists*]: Stop it!!
> GIRLS [*raising their fists*]: Stop it!!
> [MARY WARREN, *utterly confounded, and becoming overwhelmed by ABIGAIL's – and the girls' – utter conviction, starts to whimper, hands half raised, powerless, and all the girls start whimpering exactly as she does.*] (*Cr*, pp. 73–4)

This sequence, in which the girls appear infected by Mary's terror, harkens back to Starkey's description of the bewitchment as a 'malady' and a 'contagion' spreading through the village of Salem (*DM*, pp. 41 and 40).

At the same time, however, the girls' behaviour – their unthinking adherence to the cruel demands of their leader, Abigail, and the viciousness with which they ostracise those who fail to conform to group norms – suggests that Miller has imbibed, at least to a degree, the popular contempt directed towards teenage girls during this period.[64] His portrayal of the afflicted echoes mid-century images of adolescent femininity as spiteful, impulsive, conformist and mean-spirited. Yet, following Starkey, Miller merges this understanding of the teenage girl with the iconography of seventeenth-century witchcraft beliefs. His adolescents, like Starkey's, are decidedly anachronistic and, while drawing on archival and secondary

historical sources, Miller's afflicted girls nevertheless behave like the contemporary teenagers who were, in the 1950s, commanding so much attention from teachers, social workers and journalists. The intense physicality
of their subversion – their hysterical symptoms, contortions, mimicry and
shrieking – combined with the rigidity of their group dynamics suggests
that for Miller, as for many of his contemporaries, adolescent femininity
was a phenomenon that bridged the social and the biological realms. Their
bodies, refusing stolid passivity, reject the notion that materiality exists
simply as a passive resource distinct from the cultural realm. Rather, the
vital materiality of these bodies, their capacity to disrupt the social order,
suggests a continuity of the cultural and the biological that troubles dualistic modes of apprehension.

In both Starkey's and Miller's representations of the Salem trials,
members of the accusing circle embody not only the characteristics of
the hysteric, but also those of the sorceress, a figure viewed in both nineteenth-century psychology and twentieth-century feminist discourse as the
ancestor of the hysteric. In *The Devil in Massachusetts*, Starkey relies on
anecdotal evidence about the girls' involvement in fortune telling and divination (*DM*, p. 272); however, Miller takes this presumed occultism even
further as he imagines the young women of Salem slipping out of their
homes under cover of darkness to dance and cast spells deep in the New
England woods. Extrapolating from Starkey's version of events, Miller's
older, more worldly, Abigail is explicitly associated with the occult, having
been observed by her uncle, Reverend Parris, 'dancing like a heathen in
the forest' (*Cr*, p. 8). While Miller does not present the supernatural as an
objective reality in his play, Abigail does engage in practices that would
certainly have been denounced as witchcraft by her community, and her
uncle accuses her of having 'trafficked with spirits in the forest' (*Cr*, p. 9).
Her cousin Betty reminds her later that she went to the forest and 'drank
a charm to kill John Proctor's wife' (*Cr*, p. 15). In this way, through the
character of Abigail, Miller combines the figure of the sorceress and that
of the afflicted, creating an identificatory slippage between the witch and
the bewitched, a contiguity of identity that refuses to polarise these states
of being.

In *The Devil in Massachusetts*, the Salem girls are repeatedly described
in terms of mediumship. Their capacity to identify suspected witches and
their ability to determine the presence of invisible spectres affords them a
quasi-supernatural status. While this aspect of the trials has been described
by other historians – Stacy Schiff even goes so far as to describe Salem as

the 'Lourdes of New England'[65] – Starkey's emphasis on the girls' status as bobby-soxers creates a sense that their imagined powers of divination are somehow related to their girlhood; that the in-between status of these creatures poised between girlhood and womanhood somehow affords them unique insights into the spiritual realm. This blurring of categorical distinctions between the afflicted and their tormenters has roots in historical instances of witchcraft and witchcraft-possession cases. Diane Purkiss describes an 'uncanny homology between the witch's body and the bodies of the bewitched', noting how 'bewitched women and animals give blood instead of milk, and the witch's teat dispensed blood'.[66] Likewise, both Miller and Starkey portray the afflicted girls as closely tied to the figure of the witch and not merely as victims. Writing of the collapse of the Salem trials and the new spirit of incredulity roving through the village, Starkey foregrounds a shift in public discourse that began to frame the Salem girls as deluded by the devil (*DM*, p. 214). As more influential individuals were accused by the girls, many began to consider that the false nature of their claims was the result of diabolical interference: the girls were being led astray by Satan. As the afflicted were now associated with the demonic, they were relegated to that uncertain space between witch and bewitched. Significantly, the manner in which the Salem girls were afforded the somewhat anachronistic status of mediums by writers such as Starkey also suggests a conflation of affliction and magic.

This evisceration of conceptual categories reoccurs throughout *The Crucible* because, as mentioned above, Abigail and her vicious clique are described as participants in, as well as (self-professed) victims of, malefic magic. In one of his comments on the historicity of the play, Miller challenges the assertion that there were no witches at Salem. Stating that he disagrees with this assessment, the playwright argues that the young women of the village did engage in occult rituals, even if these did not produce any real magical effects. Miller claims that the testimony of Reverend Parris's slave Tituba is proof of this, as is the 'behaviour of the children who were known to have indulged in sorceries with her' (*Cr*, p. 25). To Miller, the Salem girls are witches by virtue of their involvement in rituals taught to them by Tituba. Attempting to contextualise the propensity of the Puritan maidens to acts of diabolism, Miller maintains that, 'There are accounts of similar *klatsches* in Europe, where the daughters of the towns would assemble at night and, sometimes with fetishes, sometimes with a selected young man, give themselves to love, with some bastardly results' (*Cr*, p. 25). Miller claims that the Church condemned these orgies and meetings as witchcraft and, as such, he suggests a connection between witchcraft and the sexuality of young women. For him, the witches' sabbath was little more than an expression of overzealous female sexuality. Witchcraft is the seeping sexual excess of the 'daughters of the town' whose energies must be controlled and contained for the good of the social order.

This vision of witchcraft as an eruption of feminine excess reverberates throughout *The Crucible* and crystallises in the figure of Abigail Williams. When Abigail drinks a charm intended to harm John Proctor's wife, she becomes, for want of a better term, a witch in her own right. Upon waking from her paralysis, Betty reminds Abigail of her ultimate transgression: the ingestion of *blood* as part of a ritual to kill Goody Proctor. In this way, Abigail is associated not only with witchcraft, but with blood. Attempting to silence the frightened Betty, Abigail warns the child that if she speaks of their woodland rituals:

> I will bring a pointy reckoning that will shudder you. And you know I can do it; I saw Indians smash my dear parents' heads on the pillow next to mine, and I have seen some reddish work done at night, and I can make you wish you had never seen the sun go down! (*Cr*, p. 15)

Although its proximity to Abigail's description of her parents' murder by 'Indians' suggests that her knowledge of violence stems from her experiences as a refugee from the Second Indian War (1688–97) that was then raging on the Maine Frontier, the term 'reddish work' evokes imagery of blood magic such as that used on Goody Proctor. Abigail is associated with blood and consequently with feminine excess that threatens to spill over and infect the social order. This recalls post-war figurations of female adolescence as defined by the omnipresent threat of seepage – odours and fluids that must be contained – and the impetus on teen girls to learn how to properly control their bodies. Thus, Abigail's connection to blood and 'reddish work' gestures towards a subversive femininity in which the corporeal is not repressed for the sake of the social order. Such embedded references to effluvia also recall early modern conceptions of the witch as essentially Protean, capable of unfixing the 'limits of her own body by shifting her shape'.[67] In contrast to the contemporary emphasis on the need for corporeal control and the importance of the teen girl imbibing strategies to enact this control, Abigail's association with all things sanguine suggests an erosion of bodily boundaries and a disregard for the separation of the social and the biological.

There is clearly a symbiotic relationship between Starkey's history of the Salem witch trials and Miller's dramatic rendering of the events. Miller draws explicitly on Starkey's work and is undeniably indebted to her anachronistic portrayal of the Salem afflicted. Concomitantly, he also shares her interest in and uneasiness about the materiality of the adolescent body. Hormonal fluctuations, the flows and seepages of menstruation, excessive sexual desire, as well as the unruly body of the hysteric all emerge in these texts as sources of anxiety. In *The Crucible* and *The Devil in Massachusetts* the body's active flows attest to the agential or 'non-innocent nature of all matter'.[68] They suggest that neither the body nor the material, figured more broadly, can be understood as passive, inert or subsumable within the mental/cultural. The natural and the corporeal are agentic forces that interact with and transform each other, shaping and being shaped by social reality as they do so. However, while it is possible to read the agentic capabilities of the material as a liberating rejection of dualistic binaries, both Miller and Starkey display an unease with the threatened breakdown of mind/body or biology/culture distinctions. Wedded to positivist or humanist modes of thought, they view matter as something to be used, transcended, suppressed. The seepages of the adolescent body – mirrored in the transgressive, resistant power of the witch, the hysteric and the demoniac – collapse the borders associated with dualism, opening up the social realm to incursion by the very biological forces it seeks to suppress. The radical materiality of the teen witch's (or afflicted's) body is disquieting precisely because, as Kelly Hurley notes, this materiality, or 'Thing-ness' draws attention to 'the inescapable fact of embodied-ness, and to the ineluctibility [*sic*] of matter that resists and exceeds form'.[69] In these texts, the agentic powers of the adolescent body, the connections it makes with other bodies and its perceived seepage into the stable, ordered social arena is a source of terror that recalls contemporary concerns about the disruptive power of youth and teenage sexuality.

'She was all the senses of all the creatures of the world': Productive Becomings and Joyful Materiality in Ray Bradbury's Cecy Stories

In Starkey's *The Devil in Massachusetts* and Miller's *The Crucible* corporeal flows are tempered by binary structures that frame the seepage of the biological into social reality as a monstrous transgression. However, in other texts, those less beholden to dualistic constructions of a mind/body or biology/culture divide, such movements are imagined as productive, liberating and exciting. This final section explores a series of short stories written by Ray Bradbury between the mid-1940s and the early 1950s that offer a vision of materiality as joyful and productive. Like their contemporaries, *The Devil in Massachusetts* and *The Crucible*, these texts focus on an adolescent witch and imagine her as possessed of an unruly, leaky vitality. However, where Starkey and Miller frame the flows and seepages of adolescent femininity as dangerous, Bradbury reconfigures these movements as magical powers that enable his teenage heroine to enter into novel relationships with both human and non-human organisms, as well as a variety of animate and inanimate entities. These relationships also facilitate exciting transformations that can be mapped onto Deleuzian notions of becoming to reimagine the adolescent witch as a positive entity, one whose fluidity is generative precisely because it resists a fixed or static identity in favour of endless metamorphosis. Where Starkey and Miller portray the materiality of the body as disruptive, Bradbury depicts the materiality of bodies and environmental objects as productive, even pleasurable. Consequently, as I argue below, while Bradbury never succeeds in completely dismantling binaristic logic, he does challenge these modes of thought. His stories show that not only can boundaries be crossed, but that this kind of border-crossing can be positive, enlightening and generative.

This section focuses primarily on three stories: 'The Traveler', 'West of October' and 'The April Witch'. The first two of these were composed in the mid-1940s, with 'The Traveler' being published in the March 1946 edition of the magazine *Weird Tales*. The second, 'West of October', was originally written for Bradbury's debut short story collection *Dark Carnival* (1947). However, it was cut from that publication and did not appear in print until it was included in *The Toynbee Convector* in 1988. The final major story discussed here, 'The April Witch', was originally published in *The Saturday Evening Post* in 1952 and later collected in *Golden Apples of the Sun* (1953). These three tales are part of an ongoing narrative, beginning in 1945 and concluding in 2001,[70] that centres on a family of Midwestern ghouls known as the Elliotts. The stories featuring the Elliott Family treat a wide variety of themes, from familial relationships to prejudice and displacement. For the purposes of this chapter, I will focus solely on those stories that employ witchcraft as a lens through which to explore the mid-century adolescent experience.

Bradbury, like Starkey and Miller, utilises the figure of the adolescent witch to grapple with and attempt to understand the teenager as a novel

American phenomenon. Although both 'The Traveler' and 'West of October' were composed prior to the publication of *The Devil in Massachusetts*, it is possible that 'The April Witch' may have been influenced by Starkey's book, which Bradbury read in the autumn of 1949.[71] However, Bradbury's stories differ markedly from Starkey's, and indeed Miller's, vision of unsettling adolescent corporeality. This may be explicable, at least in part, by the conventions and limitations of genre. *The Devil in Massachusetts* is a historical study, while *The Crucible* sits comfortably within the category of historical fiction. While both works treat history in a relatively loose manner, they are nevertheless grounded in mundane reality, albeit in a time and place where witches, demons and familiars were viewed as verifiable facets of existence. Conversely, the Bradbury texts explored in this chapter are not only fiction, but fiction deeply influenced by the author's childhood love of Edgar Allan Poe and dark fantasy of all varieties. They are essentially Gothic works, dark and autumnal entries in the oeuvre of an author known primarily for his gleaming chrome rockets and exotic Martian landscapes.[72]

The Gothic preoccupation with transgression and ambiguity thus lends itself to a more open engagement with issues of embodiment and materiality. Indeed, Hurley observes that 'In its obsession with abominations, the Gothic may be said to manifest a certain gleefulness at the prospect of a world in which no fixity remains, only an endless series of monstrous becomings'.[73] Likewise, Anna Powell, in her Deleuzian account of horror cinema, suggests that a move away from dichotomous ontologies engenders a more radical apprehension of being, wherein 'intimacy between anomalous life-forms need not constrain the viewer to horrified repulsion, but initiates more congruent becomings'.[74] Consequently, Bradbury's Elliott Family stories utilise the ambiguous space of the gothic to imagine productive, joyful becomings and to challenge binary logic.

The primary vehicle through which Bradbury tests the boundaries of dualistic thought is the character of Cecy Elliott, a seventeen-year-old girl and beloved teenage daughter of an 'odd family that flies nights like black kites' ('AW', p. 22). Cecy's parents are vampires who 'work nights' and pilfer blood from their family-operated funeral home ('TT', p. 160), while the family matriarch is a surprisingly vital Ancient Egyptian mummy. Cecy herself is described as a 'last-of-summer-witch' ('AW', p. 27), and her magic consists of her ability to 'travel' in astral form. Reflecting bored, dissatisfied teen girls the world over, she lies on her bed and dreams herself elsewhere, projecting her essence beyond her the limits of her body and into the immense, undulating world outside. Cecy, however, diverges from mundane adolescent girlhood in that her supernatural status allows her to inhabit and *become* any being in existence, whether animate or inanimate. In 'The April Witch',[75] the reader is informed that Cecy can 'live in anything at all – a pebble, a crocus, or a praying mantis' (p. 22), while an earlier tale – 'The Traveler' – emphasises that her power is 'more than telepathy, up one flue and down another' (pp. 161–2). Rather, Cecy's abilities facilitate 'entry to lazing cats, old lemony maids, hopscotch girls, lovers on morning beds, then unborn babes' pink, dream-small brains' ('TT', p. 162). She does not simply read the minds of other beings; she enters and becomes them.

Cecy's abilities, at least initially, appear to function as a metaphor for adolescent embodiment and the teenage propensity for fantasy: she resides primarily in the sanctum of her bedroom, dreaming away the days and nights, and only emerging at mealtimes to gossip with her family. Her father even complains, in one early story, that she does nothing beyond 'Sleeping all night, eating breakfast, and then sleeping again all day' ('TT', p. 159). Yet, at the same time, as we learn in another short text, entitled 'The Sleeper and Her Dreams', Cecy's family views her as a 'goddess of wisdom' ('SD', p. 18). Her travels imbue her with a preternatural knowledge that belies her youth and housebound status. Indeed, the young witch's name 'Cecy', if pronounced 'see-see' recalls the mythological witch Circe, who in the *Odyssey* 'commands esoteric knowledge about both the Land of the Living and the Land of the Dead'.[76] Cecy's mind is equally expansive and receptive to knowledge. While her physical body is confined to the high attic room of her family's rambling Midwestern home, Cecy's witchcraft empowers her to become other people and visit remote regions of the world. She can become animals, plants and even inanimate objects. She can use her magic to experience thrills ordinarily inaccessible to adolescent girls in rural, mid-twentieth-century America. In this way, her power of astral travel serves as fantastic literalisation of the adolescent propensity towards fantasy.

Elizabeth Grosz has described how the discomforts of puberty often compel teenagers to seek relief in the world of fantasy. Because the 'adolescent body is commonly experienced as awkward, alienating, an undesired biological imposition', teenagers are tormented by the 'discord between the body image and the lived body'.[77] She goes on to note that 'the philosophical desire to transcend corporeality and its urges may be dated from this period'.[78] Yet, while this analysis may suggest a flight into asceticism, it is more often the case that teenagers escape the pains and bodily eruptions of adolescence by giving themselves over to fantasies in which the self is whole, unified and in control of its functions. Tellingly, in 'The April Witch' Cecy uses her power of travel to enter the body of an older, more sophisticated girl named Ann because, as she laments:

> *I've never known what it's like to be in a woman, dancing; Father and Mother would not permit. Dogs, cats, locusts, leaves, everything else in the world at one time or another I've known, but never a woman in the spring, never on a night like this.* ('AW', pp. 25–6, emphasis in original)

Once ensconced in Ann's body, Cecy takes pleasure in the older girl's more mature sexuality. While bathing Ann's body, Cecy seems to relish the opportunity to explore her physicality: 'the soap creaming on her white seal shoulders, small nests of soap beneath her hands and the flesh of her warm breasts moving in her hands' ('AW', p. 26). Later, Cecy uses Ann's body to attend a dance and share her first kiss with a young man named Tom. Although Cecy's occupation of Ann's body gives rise to troubling questions of consent, it can also be read as a marvellous evocation of the power of fantasy and its centrality to the adolescent experience. For Cecy, fantasy is a liberating force that enables her to explore her identity and sexuality, free from both corporeal and familial constraints.[79]

It is appealing to interpret Cecy's astral travel as an analogue for teenage fantasy, and this is certainly a productive approach to unravelling Bradbury's symbolism. Concomitantly, though, it is also possible to understand Cecy's flights and transformations as modes of becoming that enable her to make generative connections with other entities, both animate and inanimate. These becomings trouble the kind of binary modes of thought that in Starkey's and Miller's texts frame transformation and fluidity as disruptive. Although Bradbury ultimately falls back on dualistic notions of an internal essence, a soul-like entity that can separate itself from the physical body, his Cecy stories nevertheless posit a continuity of being that allows the teen witch to flow across diverse locations, bodies and experiences. Her movements rather than suggesting a grotesque seepage of matter, are more indicative of a vibrant contiguity of existence where change is desirable, productive and surprising.

As she leaves her own body and connects with other entities, settling softly within them, Cecy mirrors the process of becoming described by Deleuze and Guattari. Becoming, as noted in the previous chapter, occurs when singularities extend themselves and meld with other entities, absorbing and incorporating environmental objects. In this sense, entities are not fixed, static or bounded, but can open out onto other objects, identities and sensations. Becomings are not simply about understanding or imitating another entity; they are decisive movements towards that entity. Bradbury's adolescent witch effects numerous movements of this type. Her powers are not mere telepathy, and she does not simply apprehend the thoughts or emotions of others. She undertakes a line of flight that brings her into transformative proximity with other humans, animals and objects. When she inhabits a dog, she does not play the role of a dog, but enters into relations of speeds and slowness characteristic of that particular canine. Bradbury writes that Cecy's 'mind would pop into dogs to sit, all bristles, and taste ripe bones, sniff tangy-urined trees to hear as dogs hear, run as dogs run, all smiles' ('TT', p. 161). Indeed, Cecy becomes-dog in a manner similar to how Deleuze and Guattari describe Penthesilea's becoming-dog in Heinrich von Kleist's 1808 play of the same name. Penthesilea does not become dog by transforming into a pet or a particular species. She does not imitate the behaviour of dogs, but instead she channels a canine affect.[80] Penthesilea, although still recognisably human, becomes frenzied, foaming at the mouth and leading a pack of dogs. Cecy, likewise, does not simply resemble or imitate a dog, she creates an alliance with the animal and circulates the same affect as the dog: moving, running, tasting and hearing as it does.

Cecy's affinity for Deleuzian becomings can also be seen in her proclivity for inhabiting amoebas and other unicellular creatures. In 'The Traveler', Bradbury notes that 'On sweltering summer noons, Cecy would thrive in amoebae, vacillating, deep in the philosophical dark waters of a kitchen well' (p. 168), while in the later 'April Witch', Cecy moves from a leaf to moss, to 'a fluttering, invisible amoeba' (p. 23). Deleuze and Guattari, like the earlier monist philosopher Henri Bergson, employ the amoeba to construct becoming as movement. Amoebas move through extensions of the cell membrane called pseudopodia. These projectiles reach out and incorporate surrounding matter, which then conjoin with the animalcule to become a part of the amoeba.[81] Similarly, becoming entails a movement away from one's current singularity towards a zone of proximity with another entity, a motion that facilitates an incorporation of that entity's particles:

> Starting from the forms one has, the subject one is, the organs one has, or the functions one fulfills, becoming is to extract particles between which one establishes the relations of movement and rest, speed and slowness that are *closest* to what one is becoming, and through which one becomes.[82]

In this way, as Anna Powell elucidates, 'Becoming is not concerned with identification or formal relations, but with the dynamic movement of life between and through congruent singularities'.[83] Cecy's capacity to become-amoeba, as well as the pleasure she takes in this metamorphosis, suggests that her transformative powers run deeper than mere imitation. The young witch moves in an unimpeded flow that allows her to enter into a generative proximity with other entities, incorporating aspects of their being in order to establish new relations of motility.

Although Cecy regularly takes up residence within the bodies of other humans, she most often finds herself inhabiting the forms of animals. She enters cats, dogs, birds, frogs and insects, embarking on a line of flight that brings her into a meaningful connection with these creatures. In doing so, Cecy engages in what Deleuze and Guattari term 'becoming-animal'. As with the above example of the dog, becoming-animal is not about imitating or resembling animals. It is, as Peter Heymans demonstrates:

> a reciprocal process of desubjectification and designification that explodes the human-animal dualism and configures an extremely volatile and protean concept of identity out of its debris, an identity fluctuating along the constantly changing dynamic of becoming, not firmly based on the ontological stability of being.[84]

In becoming-animal, the individual creates a new identity, a molecular (changing, fluctuating) self, removed from molar (static, monolithic) conceptions of the human. Moreover, all metamorphoses, all tendencies towards change must pass through a becoming-animal. Correspondingly, when an individual becomes-animal, they do not simply transform into a new species, exchanging one molar stability (human) for another of a different genus (animal). *Becoming*-animal is never a *being*-animal, for there is never a final identity at which one arrives.

Deleuze and Guattari utilise motifs borrowed from folklore to explain the experience of becoming as a fluid process that never solidifies into a fixed identity. 'Man,' they tell us, 'does not become wolf, or vampire, as if he changed molar species; the vampire and the werewolf are becomings of man.'[85] Cecy, in her constant shifting between forms, refuses the rigidity of being in favour of the liberating potential inherent in becoming. If, as Deleuze and Guattari claim, the becoming-animal of Franz Kafka's insect-man Gregor Samsa allows him to 'stake out the path of escape',[86] then so too do Cecy's transformations enable her to exist in a perpetual, dynamic state of endless becoming. Indeed, the freedom afforded to her by her ongoing metamorphoses is addressed explicitly in the first paragraph of 'The April Witch' where, in a single, ecstatic line of flight Cecy becomes an array of diverse creatures:

> She soared in doves as soft as white ermine, stopped in trees and lived in leaves, showering away in fiery hues when the breeze blew. She perched in a lime-green frog, cool as mint by a shining pool. She trotted in a brambly dog and barked to hear echoes from the sides of distant barns. She lived in dandelion ghosts or sweet clear liquids rising from the musky earth. ('AW', p. 21)

Cecy *is* motion and flight, entering into relations of speed and slowness, movement and stillness that enable her to circulate the same affect as the creatures she enters: the softness of the dove, the coolness of the frog, the rough brambles of a dog. She displays an affinity for these species, but she never finally becomes a dove, a frog, or a dog. Rather, she is always becoming-animal.

The previously quoted paragraph also alludes to Cecy's ability to engage in even more novel becomings through the connections that she forges with inanimate environmental objects. In her travels, Cecy projects herself into dandelions, mist, water, pebbles and leaves. Thus, as she moves about the world, Cecy refuses to distinguish not only between human and non-human life, but between animate and inanimate objects. For her, all of these possess a vital, agentic materiality that she can inhabit and manipulate. Just as dogs are defined by their barking and frogs by their cool mint skin, so too are dandelions characterised by an ephemeral spectrality and mists by their translucent sweetness. This refusal to separate apparently inert environmental objects from their sentient counterparts is characteristic of Bradbury's treatment of the natural world in his Elliott Family stories. As Fernando Gabriel Pagnoni Berns elaborates, the Elliott tales evince 'a posthuman ecological conscience: undead humans, cats, spiders, and mice are part of the Family', while Cecy's capacity to exist in an array of non-human lifeforms reveals 'a posthuman attitude that decenters the anthropocene'.[87] The meaningful engagements that Cecy forges with objects in the world suggest a conception of materiality that imagines all matter as rich, complex and active.

In this way, it is possible to align Bradbury's characterisation of Cecy with new materialist accounts of the natural world. Her capacity to settle within inanimate objects, to become part of them, to feel and taste them, recalls the agential realist account of matter hypothesised by Karen Barad. For Barad: 'matter does not refer to a fixed substance; rather, *matter is substance in its intra-active becoming – not a thing but a doing, a congealing of agency. Matter is a stabilizing and destabilizing process of iterative intra-activity.*'[88] Agency is not merely a feature of the human will, but a meaningful aspect of all matter. Significantly, Barad stresses that bodies: 'are not objects with inherent boundaries and properties; they are material-discursive phenomena. "Human" bodies are not inherently different from "nonhuman" ones.'[89] The 'boundaries' that appear to delineate individual bodies coalesce through the ongoing intra-actions of material agencies. Cecy's singular witchcraft, the connections that she forges with environmental objects, indicates a continuity of matter. She engages in meaningful interactions, or intra-actions, with human and non-human animals as well as with unicellular and ostensibly inanimate matter. However, the intense feelings that Cecy experiences while ensconced in these forms – the dampness of an amoeba in a well, the lightness of the dandelion, the joyful dance of falling leaves – suggest that matter can never be passive or inert. Even the most basic lifeform possesses agentic capabilities in which Cecy finds pleasure, while the ease with which she slips between these forms suggests an absence of fixed boundaries separating material phenomena.

Cecy is a deeply complex character. She regularly vacillates between kindness and cruelty, and her powers likewise defy easy categorisation. When the young witch travels, Bradbury writes as though it is she, Cecy, in all her dynamic materiality, who takes flight and settles into the forms of other entities. The opening lines of 'The April Witch' stress Cecy's airborne acrobatics: 'Into the air, over valleys, under the stars, above a river, a pond, a road, flew Cecy' (p. 22). Yet, Bradbury also emphasises that as Cecy soars through the night sky and settles in crickets and dew drops, her physical body lies sleeping in her high attic room. Her abilities seem to rely on the separation of her internal essence from her corporeal self. Despite the liberating continuity of matter that enables Cecy to experience the agentic capabilities of unicellular organisms as fully and intensely as she does those of more complex beings, Bradbury's stories nevertheless revert to a mode of dualism that envisions the self, or the soul, as distinct from the vessel that it inhabits. This vision of an ephemeral essential self naturally problematises any attempt to read the Cecy stories as works that fully resist, or dismantle, dualistic binaries. However, while Bradbury does not demolish binaristic logic, Cecy's travels and the connections that she makes with other entities productively trouble ingrained divisions between self and Other, inside and outside, nature and culture.

Indeed, Cecy is repeatedly figured in the Elliott stories as a multiplicity, an ambiguous entity irreducible to a single characteristic or meaning. In 'West of October', Bradbury describes her in terms of multitude, proposing that she encompasses many experiences, modes of being and sensations at once. He writes that she 'was as seedpod full as a pomegranate. She was all the senses of all the creatures of the world. She was all the motion-picture houses and stage-play theaters and all the art galleries of all time' (p. 70). Each body she occupies, each sensation she experiences transforms her and becomes a part of her. In this way, Cecy recalls the Deleuzian notion of the multiplicity, that which 'has neither subject nor object, only determinations, magnitudes, and dimensions that cannot increase in number without the multiplicity changing in nature'.[90] Moreover, like the Deleuzian multiplicity, Cecy is not a 'discrete, static unity', but something constantly entering into and breaking off combinations with other multiplicities'.[91] Although, Bradbury's reliance on a soul-like essence does reaffirm certain elements of dualistic thought, Cecy is simultaneously capable of challenging these kinds of binaries. The self that she projects out into the world is not remote, unchanging or transcendent. When she inhabits other entities, she experiences the fullness of their materiality and relishes the sensations associated with matter. If Cecy's selfhood is fundamentally intangible, it is not separate from earthly matter, but is instead contiguous with more mundane forms of materiality. Bradbury may articulate a distinction between the body and the soul (essence), but his stories nevertheless allow them to interact in a manner that troubles rigid dualistic separations. Moreover, in contrast to works like *The Devil in Massachusetts* and *The Crucible*, the Cecy stories frame the vitality of matter – whether human, animal or object – as exciting. Here, clamorous, seething materiality does not represent a threat to social order, but instead offers new opportunities for connection, transformation and becoming. In Cecy, Bradbury reconfigures the metamorphic nature of adolescence as a generative line of flight that frees the individual from fixed, bounded or monolithic identificatory positions.

Conclusion

During the years immediately following World War II, the teenage witch engaged in important conceptual and tropological work. The adolescent sorceress was conjured into being just as greater access to second-level education and an abundance of disposable income enabled many middle-class youths to delay adulthood and establish a normative peer culture. Originating in Marion L. Starkey's *The Devil in Massachusetts*, mid-century teen witches functioned as tropes through which the unfamiliar figure of the teenage girl could be rendered familiar and comprehensible. In both historical studies and literary fiction, the adolescent witch is largely defined by an active, agentic materiality. She is often a figure whose bodily seepages and corporeal resistances pose a threat to the social order. In works guided by dualistic modes of thought her pubertal body, intimately linked to sexual, hormonal and hysterical excess, threatens the cultural realm through its myriad fluctuations, leaks and overspills. Conversely, though, in texts where such binary logic is challenged, if not fully dismantled, her fluidity can lend itself to fantastic becomings that explode the divide between human and animal, subject and object, animate and inanimate.

Yet, in as much as the teen witch acts as a medium through which adult authors might begin to conceptualise adolescent femininity, she also serves as an imaginative avatar for teenage girls themselves. Indeed, these youthful sorceresses regularly provide teenage readers with an imaginative space in which they can experiment with and negotiate their own identificatory parameters. Likewise, for many readers, the often-transgressive power wielded by the teenage witch serves as a pleasurable site of fantasised boundary crossing. The next chapter explores the generative power of the adolescent witch, her capacity to not just represent, but ignite, imaginative becomings on the part of teen girls themselves. This chapter analyses both explicitly pedagogical teen witch texts and some more subversive manifestations of the trope. In doing so, I argue that whether intended to educate or titillate, many teen witch texts act as imaginative playgrounds for their teenage readership, allowing them to craft their identities through fiction.

3

'A guide to life'

Identity Formation and Perverse Readers in the Long 1960s

I N THE PREVIOUS chapter I analysed the tropological function of the teen witch, how she has been utilised by adult authors, writing primarily for an adult audience, as a means of conceptualising feminine adolescence. These writers employed images and ideas associated with witchcraft to render familiar, or at least comprehensible, the new phenomenon of the teenage girl. In this chapter, I want to move beyond texts that represent an adult attempt to comprehend adolescent femininity in order to analyse a number of works that open up space for teenage girls to explore their own identities and imagine new possibilities. The texts explored here are all products of a period that the historian Christopher B. Strain designates the long 1960s (1955–73) and include works written for both adults and teenagers.

Following an overview of the cultural shifts that transformed the perception of the teenager as well as the popular representation of witchcraft, this chapter commences with a discussion of the pedagogical role of literature and its capacity to inform individual identificatory development. I then move on to explore literary texts that present 'positive role models' through whom adolescent readers can explore their identities. I argue that the first of these works, Elizabeth George Speare's young-adult novel *The Witch of Blackbird Pond* (1958), instructs readers on how to navigate expectations surrounding embodiment, behaviour and social responsibility.

The second text – or, more accurately, series of texts – explored here is the early body of *Sabrina the Teenage Witch* comics (1962–72). These comics, which are uniformly light-hearted in tone, espouse the importance of beauty, popularity and consumerism in an attempt to instil ostensibly rigid notions of normative femininity. However, as I demonstrate below, young readers would not have imbibed these texts passively, but would have used them as templates through which to negotiate questions of self-presentation, social power and cultural expectations. Next, I investigate two novels that offer more subversive points of adolescent identification: Shirley Jackson's *We Have Always Lived in the Castle* (1962) and Stephen King's *Carrie* (published in 1974 but written in 1973). These works, although not written specifically for a teenage audience, nevertheless present intriguing models of adolescent girlhood. Drawing on theories of perverse readership/spectatorship, I position the protagonists of these novels as alternative identificatory templates through which teen readers might discover the cathartic, liberatory power of violence as well as new avenues for dynamic, generative becomings.

Anno Satanas: Changing Conceptions of Adolescence and Witchcraft in the Long 1960s

This chapter represents a forward chronological movement, away from the early years of the adolescent phenomenon and towards a more cohesive flourishing of the teenager both as a demographic and as a cultural signifier. In the following pages, I focus on a period that Strain terms the long 1960s, an epoch that began with the emergence of the civil rights movement and the first challenges to mid-century consensus culture in 1955 and ended in 1973, with the collapse of the post-war economic boom.[1] During these years, there was a marked shift in how teenagers were imagined and represented in popular culture. As noted in the previous chapter, following the 'invention' of the teenager during the immediate post-war period, teens were initially viewed as strange and novel. However, there was an ambivalence – at least for white, middle-class teenagers – in their popular portrayal and how they were understood by adults. Thus, while magazines published light-hearted features throughout the 1940s and 1950s that decoded teen fashion and slang for the benefit of bemused adults, by the 1960s these 'happy-go-lucky stories' were often outweighed by more alarming explorations of teen sexuality, drug use and rebellion.[2] An increasingly irreverent popular culture, combined with tensions unleashed by the Vietnam War and fermenting domestic unrest, meant that the dominant image of American teenagers had changed since the phenomenon first emerged. As Grace Palladino notes, 'The innocent energy that had defined teenagers since the word was coined in the 1940s had given way to hostility'.[3] Adults who had once been amused by the bizarre rituals of teen girls – their Byzantine dating practices and addiction to the telephone – suddenly found themselves discomfited by a counterculture centred on drugs, sexual experimentation and radical politics.[4]

Just as the teenager morphed into an increasingly threatening figure, so too did the witch assume a more sinister aspect. In his study of the long 1960s, Strain notes how the collapse of consensus culture after the mid-1950s resulted in a profusion of new religious movements.[5] For many young people 'alternative' spiritual paths, ranging from Hinduism and Buddhism to Native American mysticism, offered a degree of freedom unknown in conventional Judeo-Christian faiths. Paganism and witchcraft emerged at this time as exciting alternatives to mainstream religious practices. Modern neopagan witchcraft, which was developed in England by Gerald Gardner, arrived in the United States amidst the tumult of the 1960s. Popularised by Wiccan pioneers, such as Raymond and Rosemary Buckland, who brough English witchcraft to Long Island, New York, in 1962, the faith found a receptive audience in North America. As Jeffrey B. Russell and Brooks Alexander note in their history of witchcraft, Wicca's 'oppositional identity' was readily embraced by members of the US counterculture, although the individualism and eclecticism of that movement ensured that its adherents would eschew Gardner's traditionalism and hierarchical framework.[6]

Witchcraft and neopagan spirituality were not the only indicators of a social and spiritual transformation occurring during the 1960s and 1970s. The entire period was defined by a vibrant occulture. A portmanteau of 'occult' and 'culture', occulture involves what philosopher Patricia Mac-Cormack terms 'a reimagining and embracing of a decidedly fabulated form of spirituality'.[7] She describes occulture as a 'bricolage of *fin-de-siècle* magick', esoterica, Luciferianism and popular culture.[8] One of the most enduring and imaginatively fertile examples of this kind of occulture is Satanism, a religious movement that was, for all intents and purposes, invented in the late 1960s and early 1970s.[9] Asbjorn Dyrendal, James R. Lewis and Jesper Aa. Petersen categorise Satanism as a 'self religion', a spiritual system whose lodestar is 'Not a God distinct from and outside human life, but a this-worldly focus that sacralizes the individual self'.[10] Modern Satanism owes its origins to Anton Szandor LaVey, an eccentric showman who claimed to have performed in orchestras and nightclubs, acted as a lion tamer, and served as both a police photographer and a psychic investigator. In 1966, on May Eve, one of the traditional witches sabbaths, LaVey publicly announced the formation of a satanic church, declaring that 1966 was Year One, *Anno Satanas* – 'the first year of the Age of Satan'.[11]

Although the occult was a subject of widespread fascination during this period, it was particularly alluring to young women. In an article published in the early 1970s, sociologist Marcello Truzzi described popular occultism as a youth phenomenon, with close links to university campuses.[12] More striking still, many contemporary commentators noted that college-aged women and young suburban housewives were the most ardent occultists. In 1969, Andrew Greeley, a Catholic priest, published an article for *Time* magazine entitled 'There's a New Time Religion on Campus'. Here, Greeley describes typical occult adherents as 'miniskirted suburban matrons' who 'cast the I Ching or shuffle tarot cards before setting dates for dinner parties'.[13] Truzzi, likewise, stresses that the individual (as opposed to coven-affiliated) practitioner of witchcraft is usually 'a young high-school or college-age girl who, for a variety of reasons, self-designates herself as a witch to her peers'.[14] While Truzzi concludes his study by arguing that 1960s occultism is merely a 'pop religion',[15] the connection he and other contemporary observers identified between girls and the occult is one that captured the cultural imagination of the period. The proliferation of new religious movements and an expanding real-world interest in witchcraft, Satanism and the occult markedly influenced literary and filmic representations of teen witches. No longer confined to an imagined colonial past or cast adrift in a timeless fantasy space, teen witches of the 1960s and 1970s were regularly imagined as facets of the contemporary sociocultural arena. Indeed, the texts explored in this chapter depart significantly from those discussed previously in that only one of them takes place during the early modern period; the others all situate their adolescent witches firmly within the context of twentieth-century America.[16]

Positive Role Models: Teen Witches and Identity Formation
in Young-Adult Fiction

This shift in periodisation coincides with a general transformation in the
function of the teen witch trope. As outlined above, teen witch texts of
the long 1960s undergo a general metamorphosis in that they no longer
serve as a means through which adults can familiarise the strange new
phenomenon of the teenage girl, but instead open up an imaginative space
where adolescents themselves can play with and construct their own identities. While the second half of this chapter focuses on texts that enable
subversive experimentation with identity, the first part explores works that
attempt to inculcate more socially desirable values and behaviours. Theorists of children's and young-adult literature have long identified fictional
texts as spaces where readers learn and develop social capabilities by engaging with imaginative scenarios. As Chloé Germaine Buckley notes, the
standard mode of theorising children's fiction is grounded in the belief that
'through identification with (or against) the protagonist, the child reader
learns the valuable lessons the book has to teach'.[17] Likewise, Elizabeth
Bullen observes that, historically, children's fiction has been understood
not just as a form of entertainment but as a means of shaping values and
educating its readers about cultural norms.[18] When young-adult literature
emerged as a distinct genre in the 1950s,[19] books aimed at teenagers naturally sought to reflect the concerns of their readership while at the same
time hoping to inculcate values that would transform these teenagers into
good citizens and, in some cases, good consumers.

In a series of interviews conducted with teen girls in the 2000s, Jessica
Kokesh and Miglena Sternadori investigated how adolescent identity formation is influenced by young-adult fiction. The authors discovered that
teenage readers tend to employ young-adult novels as 'a guide to life'.[20]
When reading these books, Kokesh and Sternadori argue, teenage girls
often engage in a process of identification whereby they receive and understand the texts from the inside. Contrasted with spectatorship – a more
distanced form of reception – identification enables readers to interpret
the text from inside, 'as if the events were happening to them'.[21] This kind
of identification is 'one of the main mechanisms through which people
develop their social attitudes and construct their identities'.[22] Kokesh and
Sternadori stress that such acts of identification also contribute to the
reader's gender identity construction, as young-adult fiction often models socially acceptable modes of gendered behaviour.[23] In the young-adult

literature of the late 1950s and 1960s, teen witches embody culturally desirable values such as independence, self-reliance, compassion and generosity, as well as more alluring traits such as popularity and beauty. These teen witches serve a pedagogical function, teaching young girls how to be proper American teenagers via an imaginative engagement with diverse situations and experiences.

According to Ramona Caponegro, Elizabeth George Speare's *The Witch of Blackbird Pond* was written in response to increased concern about antisocial behaviour amongst America's youth. During the post-war period, FBI director J. Edgar Hoover went so far as to describe juvenile delinquency as a threat to American freedom on a par with communism.[24] Yet, where public and media discourses framed juvenile delinquents as a growing social problem, Speare's novel critiques the popular panic about juvenile delinquency through its portrayal of compassionate, socially responsible youth. Like Arthur Miller's *The Crucible*, written just five years earlier, *The Witch of Blackbird Pond* displaces mid-twentieth-century anxieties onto the imaginatively rich arena of colonial New England. However, where Miller's play denounced the anti-communist hysteria of the early 1950s, Speare's book critiques contemporary anxieties about America's wayward youth.

The novel follows a sixteen-year-old girl named Kit Tyler who, in the spring of 1687, leaves Barbados, where she had been raised by her grandfather, to live with austere Puritan relatives in Connecticut. Kit is spoiled and wilful, arriving in the devout colony with trunks full of silk dresses and delicate kid gloves. She arouses envy and fascination in her teenage cousins Judith and Mercy, and she raises the ire of both her deeply religious uncle Matthew and the wider community. Before even setting foot in the town, Kit is suspected of witchcraft because she demonstrates her ability to swim and the townspeople believe that 'a true witch will always float' (*WBP*, p. 13). Kit is not literally a teenage witch. She does not practise witchcraft or possess magical powers. Instead, the identity of an adolescent witch is projected onto her by the townspeople. She is labelled a witch because of the complex ways in which she both conforms and fails to conform to mid-twentieth-century ideas about teenage girls. Kit initially draws suspicion because she swims and wears strange clothing, but also because she is vain, spoiled and ill-suited to housework. Yet, while she is first accused because of qualities that align her with the figure of the post-war juvenile delinquent, Kit is only arrested after she transcends these more selfish inclinations and uses her determined spirit to help others. At the novel's climax, Kit is tried for witchcraft because she teaches a neglected local girl to read and befriends a lonely old Quaker woman who has been ostracised and branded a heretic. The label of 'witch' is thus revealed to be an extraordinarily ductile one, having been applied both to Kit's arrogant vanity and her compassion for the village's poor and marginalised.

Over the course of the narrative, Kit evolves from a self-centred and spoiled girlchild into a socially conscious young woman. The values that she comes to embody by the novel's end reflect those held by liberal Americans during the post-war years: independence, self-reliance, empathy. Kit's witchcraft trial teaches the townsfolk to mimic her compassion for the disenfranchised, and it also teaches them to embrace mid-twentieth-century notions of equality: the court case ends with one of the community leaders pronouncing, 'Well, this is a new country over here, and who says it may not be just as needful for a woman to read as a man?' (*WBP*, p. 221). Kit teaches her community to reject superstition and embrace progressive ideals such as education and gender equality. The wisdom that Kit imparts upon her community may be anachronistic, but the use of witchcraft as a vehicle through which to espouse modern values is not unprecedented. In 1862 the French historian Jules Michelet published *La Sorcière* (usually translated as *Satanism and Witchcraft*). In this study of the early modern witch trials, Michelet argues that witchcraft was a form of populist rebellion against both the aristocracy and the Catholic Church that anticipated the widescale upheavals of the French Revolution: 'The "Marseillaise" of that time, sung by night rather than day, was perhaps a Sabbatic chant.'[25] In the same century, the American feminist Matilda Joslyn Gage published her book *Woman, Church and State* (1893) in which she argued that the European witch trials represented yet another example of patriarchal oppression and that women accused of witchcraft were the precursors to contemporary suffragists. Speare draws on this tendency to rewrite historical witches as pioneers and progressives by using the identity of the witch as a liberatory space in which her heroine Kit can develop her identity as a responsible and socially conscious young woman.

Drawing parallels with biocultural theories of adolescence, Speare constructs Kit's experience of teenage girlhood as both physical and social in nature. The transitional period of Kit's teenage years is one during which she must learn to control her physical body and shape her behaviours in accordance with community norms, while also remaining true to herself. As noted above, when Kit arrives in Connecticut she is immediately suspected of witchcraft after she dives into the river to rescue a little girl's lost doll, earning her a reputation as a sorceress because 'no respectable woman could keep afloat in the water like that' (*WBP*, p. 13). The initial witchcraft accusations arise out of Kit's failure to restrain and monitor her body in keeping with the cultural norms of womanhood. Kit, having spent her life in Barbados with her highly permissive grandfather, was an enthusiastic swimmer in childhood, but as a young woman her athleticism is deemed inappropriate. This is in keeping with how pubertal girls are often encouraged to regulate their own bodies. In her study of embodied femininity, Jane M. Ussher observes that 'Menarche brings a young woman into her body, its sexual and reproductive function no longer able to be denied or ignored'.[26] Moreover, young women, upon entering puberty, are expected to engage in practices of 'self-policing' that bring their bodies in line with 'idealised scripts of femininity'.[27] Many of these scripts are based on the assumption that the female body, especially when menstruating, is sick, vulnerable or leaky. Self-help pamphlets produced during the 1940s and 1950s specifically warn young women to avoid strenuous activities like horse riding, vigorous dancing and, of course, swimming in case they experienced a prolapsed uterus.[28] Ussher notes that such prohibitions reinforce a vision of the 'fecund body as [a] site of debilitation'[29] and encourage girls to view their bodies as vulnerable or ill.

Although *The Witch of Blackbird* does not explicitly reference menstruation, its emphasis on the cultural prohibitions that prevent Kit from swimming suggests that at least part of the book's coming-of-age narrative is concerned with Kit's changing body and the expectation that she contort it to adhere to social norms. Since contemporary self-help booklets and conventional wisdom recommended abstaining from swimming during menstruation,[30] Kit's discovery that the mores of her new home forbid such activities to women functions as a metaphorical conceit, alluding to the ways in which women's relationships to their bodies might change during puberty. In one especially poignant scene, Kit is forced to stay aboard the ship on which she sailed from Barbados on a hot spring day. Conversely, the teenage boys who work on the ship are free to swim in the river, 'thrashing about like porpoises' (*WBP*, p. 22). If Kit's movement from her childhood home in the Caribbean to the oppressive environs of New England represents a painful journey towards maturity, a significant part of that journey involves learning how to live in a body that is considered vulnerable and has suddenly accrued a panoply of new regulations to govern its movements. In her work on embodiment, Niva Piran argues that a key feature of early adolescence is a reduction in the range of ways that a girl can inhabit her body.[31] Piran labels this restriction of bodily possibility 'corseting', using the term to denote how girls entering puberty are confronted with 'growing physical restrictions and constraining molds of femininity'.[32] Further, such limitations, as they are internalised, have the power to inhibit motility and impact on the girl's relationship to her body.

The powerful sense of dislocation that attends Kit's arrival in Connecticut can be read as symptomatic of the constraints placed upon her body and the attendant shift in her self-perception. Yet, while Kit initially struggles with the self-policing required to keep both her body and behaviour in line with her community's rigid norms, she does not passively imbibe these dictates. Much of Kit's story, her growth towards womanhood, involves discovering how to become a compassionate, socially responsible individual. She learns to rein in her impulsivity and moves beyond her early selfishness through her engagement with marginalised members of the community. She comes to reject her initial materialism, no longer valuing fine clothes and wealth above all else, but she does not simply replace her formerly selfish attitude with the pious obedience of the ideal Puritan woman. Kit actively reauthors the social scripts made available to her. She reflects on her ideas about the world around her and develops 'alternative frameworks for attributing meaning to experiences, which emphasise agency, self-sufficiency and competency'.[33] Thus, by the end of the novel, she is no longer spoiled or short-tempered, but has instead reconfigured these attributes into the more positive characteristics of determination and independence.

In the final pages of *The Witch of Blackbird Pond*, Kit is humble, loving and more appropriately feminine in her behaviour and outlook. Crucially, for the readership of the time, she has also learned to develop appropriate heterosexual relationships with young men and to care for others. Despite these transformations, Kit does not lose her sense of self. Instead, she carves out a path that runs halfway between social expectations and her own ambitions. As the novel closes, Kit is about to marry the rebellious sea captain Nat, a young man who shares her sense of social responsibility. He vows to take her sailing on his ship, appropriately named *The Witch*, bringing her south to the West Indies in the winter while providing a cottage so that she can assume the role of housewife in the summer. With this, Kit's future promises to be one of balance: she will be both wife and sailor, conventional woman and defiant adventurer. Kit therefore serves as an identificatory template through which young female readers can learn to moderate their own behaviours while retaining a connection to their authentic selves. She shows the reader that while mature femininity brings new responsibilities, social norms and even restrictions, it is possible to negotiate these expectations in a meaningful and productive manner.

Comparable to the way in which reader identification with teen witch Kit Tyler imparts the value of compassion and courage, the popular Archie comics featuring Sabrina the Teenage Witch also serve to teach young readers about the proper performance of adolescent femininity. However, while Kit acts as a prototype for liberal mid-century values related to individuality and compassion, Sabrina Spellman models a version of young adulthood centred on popularity, beauty and diligent consumerism. Created by George Gladir and Dan DeCarlo and debuting in *Archie's Madhouse #22*, in October 1962, Sabrina is a teenage witch who lives with her aunts, Hilda and Zelda, and her wisecracking familiar, Salem. Unlike her aunts who sport long, warty noses and pointed hats, Sabrina is not a conventional Halloween hag. She is an outwardly normal teen girl who, in her first appearance, is drawn wearing fashionable clothing and surrounded by the accoutrements of affluent post-war teen culture: a television set, records, a record player. Cheerily addressing the reader, Sabrina introduces herself by playing with popular ideas about witchcraft: 'Hi! My name is Sabrina! I hope I haven't disappointed you! I mean . . . I hope you didn't expect to find me living on some dreary mountain top . . . wearing some grubby old rags, and making some nasty old brew.' (*STW*, p. 11.) Sabrina explains that she is a modern witch who believes that 'life should be a ball' (*STW*, p. 12). Sabrina's concerns are with the superficial signifiers of American adolescence and her magic is usually directed towards materialistic aims. Her spells conjure new outfits, enchant attractive boys, whip up magical dates and entertain her friends.

Sabrina's simplistic goals are closely aligned with the ethos of the Archie Comics publications from which she emerged. Archie Comics was established as MLJ Comics in the late 1930s, and the characters that the company is most famous for – the eponymous Archie Andrews, Betty and Veronica, Jughead – were created in 1941 to capitalise on the popularity of teen movies such as *Love Finds Andy Hardy* (1938) and *Life Begins for Andy Hardy* (1941). Archie Comics were popular not only because they mirrored the tropes of early teen cinema, but also because of what Luisa Colón describes as 'Archie's peculiar dichotomy – an obedient adherence to cultural norms coupled with the ability to successfully evolve'.[34] Essentially, Archie and his friends, while changing with the times and reflecting popular teen trends, never push beyond the parameters of conventional

American values. While their fashionable attire and modern slang endear them to teen readers, the Archie characters have historically promoted conformity, consumerism, traditional gender roles and, until recently, heteronormative relationships. According to Sharon Scholl, in an outline provided by Archie Enterprises, Archie Andrews is described as 'an assertive, optimistic, conventional person who is unquestioningly loyal to American institutions'.[35] Archie, then, promotes conventional American values clad in the guise of modern teen culture.

Sabrina Spellman, who has appeared in both solo comics and alongside Archie and his friends, also exemplifies an ethos of fashionable adolescent conformity. From her first appearance, Sabrina positions herself as a rebellious character. Echoing a taboo found in films such as 1958's *Bell, Book and Candle* and Ray Bradbury's 'The April Witch', Sabrina stresses that witches are forbidden to love: 'Still another trait we have is that we can make others fall in love . . . But we're not permitted to fall in love ourselves . . . That would make the head witches very angry.' (*STW*, p. 13) In a comic published in 1963 Sabrina is arraigned for kissing a boy and chastised by her fellow witches. Sabrina presents herself as a rebel amongst witches: she is pretty, popular and enjoys appropriately chaste mid-century dating practices. Ironically, the manner in which Sabrina rebels against the strictures of the witch community is by embodying the cultural norms of the early 1960s. Indeed, high school sex education programmes during the middle decades of the twentieth century presented adolescence as a crucial period during which young people must adjust to sex, gender and heterosexuality.[36] Susan K. Freeman points out that mid-century pedagogies 'exalted normative femininity, masculinity, and heterosexuality as tools for resolving the concerns and problems of adolescents'.[37] Consequently, the Sabrina comics generally promoted narrow ideals of beauty, popularity and consumption as signifiers of normative femininity. Most of Sabrina's adventures involve her using magic to procure consumer goods, summoning up a closet full of fashionable clothing or instantly conjuring parties to enjoy with her friends.

Sabrina enacts consumerism as fantasy, a chimera of instant fulfilment that delivers on the promises of advertising and consumer culture. Mark Jancovich observes that mass culture is predicated on the promise of immediate gratification: 'It awakens fantasies and desires and offers to satisfy them, but in fact the satisfaction of these desires only creates deeper misery.'[38] Jancovich explains that advertising operates by stimulating dissatisfaction in the consumer base 'in order to offer one the possibility of satisfaction and self-transformation through the purchase of consumer products'.[39] While the reality of this strategy is the creation of a self-perpetuating cycle in which new dissatisfaction must necessarily be created in order to sell new products, the Sabrina comics portray a vision of consumerism based on instantaneous and perpetual fulfilment. Any new desires that Sabrina might have can be immediately sated: 'One advantage in being a teen witch is that you don't have to keep a big wardrobe! All you have to do is find a picture of an outfit you like . . . and say abracadabra shindigabaloo!' (*STW*, p. 67.) For Sabrina, there is no waiting, no financial constraints. She can immediately procure the latest fashions, and her trendy outfits, alongside her all-American beauty, make her popular amongst her peers. Sabrina's ability to engage in instantaneous consumption is also what precipitates her many adventures: she plays with Archie's band, attracts attention on the beach and has multiple suitors fight over her, all because of her power to immediately summon into being the latest consumer goods and popular diversions. Sabrina not only embodies the notion of the adolescent as a marketing demographic, defined by shopping habits and homogenous trends, but she also makes consumption appear enticing to readers. Discussing Disney's use of merchandising in the 1930s, Bullen observes that 'The conflation of the pleasures of entertainment with the pleasures of consumption is a key mechanism in the enculturation of the young into consumer society'.[40] In the case of Sabrina, a character whose adventures are regularly incited through her magical attainment of consumer goods, the pleasure of entertainment is intimately intertwined with that of consumption.

The centrality of consumerism within the Sabrina comics also reflects new ideas about the role of girls during the Cold War and a broader reconfiguration of adolescent consumerism as essentially patriotic. Jennifer Helgren observes that the years between 1945 and 1970 witnessed the emergence of an economy, as well as a culture and politics, built on a perceived connection between consumption and democracy.[41] Because the availability of consumer goods in America contrasted sharply with the supposed deprivations of Soviet communism, buying became a 'citizen's duty', and shopping – with its overtly feminine connotations – was viewed as a key activity through which young women could express their patriotism.[42] In the early 1960s, Sabrina was not the only fictional character promoting rampant consumerism to a teenage audience. Around the same time, a series of 'clean teen' movies, exemplified by wholesome films like *Gidget* (1959) and *Beach Party* (1963), represented adolescents as normalised consumers.[43] Thus, while cultural attitudes towards teenagers had become more complex over the course of the long 1960s, mainstream Hollywood images of young people portrayed them 'as fun loving, clean living and most of all, good consumers'.[44] In these more sanitised depictions of youth, some of the teenage girl's more problematic features – her excessiveness, her expansive desire – were reimagined as useful, even patriotic, characteristics, as shopping and spending became weapons in America's anti-communist arsenal.

Yet, while Sabrina Spellman may have served as an identificatory template, created to inculcate values associated with normative femininity and diligent consumerism, she also functioned as a more complex imaginative avatar onto which young readers could map their desires and negotiate their burgeoning identities. Indeed, her body and fashionable self-presentation can be read as a contested site in which social norms are simultaneously inscribed, manipulated and mediated. In her discussion of adolescent embodiment, Piran describes how teenage girls respond to and negotiate appearance-related norms. Rather than passively adhering to expectations of how they should look, dress and behave, teen girls often weigh these expectations carefully and consider how they might enhance or limit their social power. One teenage girl interviewed by Piran made it clear that she was acutely aware that conforming to appearance expectations could increase her social power (i.e., popularity) while diminishing her sense of authenticity (individual power).[45] Teen girls, in modelling their appearances and identities, do not passively adhere to the norms or templates that they are presented with. Rather, identifying with characters such as Sabrina allows them to imaginatively explore and consider the power exchanges involved in acts of normative self-presentation.

Considering these negotiations from a Foucauldian perspective, it is possible to imagine that identification with Sabrina and related (or expected) practices of self-transformation might reframe the body as a site of resistance or, at the very least, contestation. As discussed previously, Michel Foucault's notion of power disregards more conventional notions of top-down oppression and instead figures power as something that functions through more complex systems of surveillance, supervision, discipline and the construction of norms. Power relations deploy distinct technologies (ranging from nutrition to education to population control) to produce docile bodies and compliant subjectivities. Yet, power can be resisted in a variety of ways. Indeed, for Foucault, resistance is in inherent within power. In a posthumously published essay, Foucault distinguished what he calls 'techniques of the self' from techniques of production or domination.[46] Techniques of the self, he explains, are those that:

> permit individuals to effect by their own means or with the help of others a certain number of operations on their own bodies and souls, thoughts, conduct, and way of being, so as to transform themselves in order to attain a certain state of happiness, purity, wisdom, perfection or immortality.[47]

While the consumer-driven femininity promoted in the Sabrina comics may initially appear to represent a gendered form of disciplinary technology, it can also be read as offering the opportunity to reinscribe the body in new and meaningful ways, even enabling the construction of powerful social identities. Sabrina does not simply capitulate to ostensibly 'voluntary' disciplinary procedures – the wearing of make-up, high heels, fashionable clothing – that produce the normative feminine body, she actively configures her own body in a way that invests it with useful social power. Identification with socially acceptable role models can therefore be considered part of a complex process of self-production whereby cultural norms are incorporated, negotiated, resisted and utilised.

Kit Tyler and Sabrina Spellman are characters created to appeal to adolescent girls. Despite their many differences, both model ideal figurations of femininity that readers are encouraged to mimic. While Kit embodies more nuanced conceptions of adolescent femininity, growing over the course of the novel from a spoiled, immature girl into a considerate, courageous young woman, Sabrina's characterisation remains relatively static throughout the early Archie comics.[48] Sabrina models a vision of female adolescence predicated on beauty, popularity and consumerism. Nevertheless, both are overtly pedagogical. They present constructions of femininity in line with contemporary values that young readers might identify with and imitate. At the same time, it cannot be assumed that readers engaged with them in a manner that was either passive or uniform. As Buckley explains, the 'reading child', the presumed audience of children's or young-adult fiction, is a 'construction (of the critic, the book, the writer)', and it is ultimately impossible to predict how 'active or critical' the reader's identification will be.[49] Moreover, young readers did not always identify with the kinds of positive role models incorporated into works written primarily for their age group. As such, the long 1960s also offered more subversive identificatory models for adolescent readers. Removed from the pedagogical obligations of young-adult literature, horror fiction written primarily for an adult audience frequently opened up imaginative spaces in which adolescent identity could be constructed or at least played with in a more seditious manner.

Perverse Pleasures: Subversive Identification in *We Have Always Lived in the Castle* and *Carrie*

Lacking the affirming messages and overtly pedagogical objectives of either *Sabrina the Teenage Witch* or *The Witch of Blackbird Pond*, Shirley Jackson's *We Have Always Lived in the Castle* (1962) and Stephen King's debut novel *Carrie* (1974) portray teen witches who complicate both the label 'teen witch' and normative constructions of adolescent femininity. More significantly, these texts present adolescent bodies and identities as fluid and metamorphic in a way that goes beyond the intersection of biology and culture discussed previously. Both novels move towards a conception of the body as a series of flows, energies, processes and events in order to challenge the binary oppositions that are projected onto the body by mind/body, nature/culture, subject/object and interior/exterior dualisms.[50] Foregrounding protagonists who actively dismantle the boundaries between human and animal, animate and inanimate, interior and exterior, these texts approach a model of the body defined by its capacity for connection and transformation.

While neither Jackson nor King writes specifically for an adolescent audience, the unconventional teenage witches they create are perversely appealing to teenagers, presenting unsettling yet liberating visions of young womanhood. The alternative model of adolescent femininity offered by both works is intimately bound up with questions of reception, how they are experienced by both adult and adolescent audiences. Indeed, *Carrie* and *We Have Always Lived in the Castle* lend themselves to the unique pleasure of perverse readership and invite creative forms of reception. In his study of horror and queer reception, Andrew Scahill argues that cinematic representations of monstrous children are particularly appealing to queer viewers because they empower those viewers to fight back against the cultural insistence on normalisation and 'imagine themselves as *de facto* children run amok'.[51] Analogously, I argue that morally ambiguous, or downright monstrous, representations of witchy young women provide adolescent readers with an equally broad canvas on which to imagine alternative – often taboo – identificatory possibilities for themselves. By opening up such subversive imaginative spaces, these works highlight the complexity of reader identification. Rather than operating passively or according to expected patterns, identification can be disorganised, multivalent and even contradictory. The book is, in Deleuzian terms, a multiplicity into which the reader is drawn and within in whose proximity they may embark on new lines of flight and dynamic modes of transformation.[52]

Eve Kosofsky Sedgwick's theorisation of 'perverse readers' can help to illuminate this notion of the text as a multiplicity. Sedgwick describes a form of reception in which readers and audiences eschew expected responses or modes of identification, deriving unexpected meanings from texts and projecting themselves onto characters other than conventional protagonists. She observes that her own experience of perverse readership derived from a practice of reading 'against the grain' in order to find meaning in literary texts originally created without marginal identities in mind:

> the need I brought to books and poems was hardly to be circumscribed, and I felt I knew I would have to struggle to wrest from them sustaining news of the world, ideas, myself, and (in various senses) my kind. The reading practice founded on such basic demands and intuitions had necessarily to run against the grain of the most patent available formulae for young people's reading and life – against the grain, often, of the most accessible voices even in the texts themselves. At any rate, becoming a perverse reader was never a matter of my condescension to texts, rather of the surplus charge of my trust in them to remain powerful, refractory, and exemplary.[53]

To be a perverse reader one must uncover the multitude of potential, often suppressed, meanings embedded in a text, listening for the marginal voices consigned to the perimeters of a work. Janet Staiger further expounds on perverse reception in her work on film and spectatorship. Staiger notes that in addition to searching out submerged meaning, 'Viewers also project their personal, sometimes marginalized, identities into the sense data'.[54] Perverse spectators 'rehierarchize from expectations',[55] deviating from normative modes of engagement, such as identifying with the hero and reviling the villain. In *We Have Always Lived in the Castle* and *Carrie*, the reader is confronted with monstrous girlchildren who have the capacity to serve as perverse templates through which they might construct and imagine alternative selfhoods. These works function as dark playgrounds in which murder, intrafamilial violence and the destabilisation of gender binaries create new, often subversive, identificatory possibilities.

Shirley Jackson is a writer frequently associated with witchcraft and the occult. Jackson was famously intrigued by these topics and in college was an avid reader of works such as Émile-Jules Grillot de Givry's 1929 book *Witchcraft, Magic and Alchemy*, an illustrated collection of demonology and witchcraft lore.[56] She was also fascinated by Joseph Glanvill's 1681 treatise *Saducismus Triumphatus*, a scholarly argument for the existence of witches, and borrowed passages from the book for her short story collection *The Lottery* (1949). In 1953, Jackson was asked to contribute a book on the Salem witch trials to the Random House Landmark young-adult history and biography series. Like her contemporary, Arthur Miller, Jackson focuses primarily on the young women at the centre of the trials. Unlike, Miller, she presents the girls in a sympathetic manner, emphasising how exciting the spectacle of the hearings, accusations and public performances of affliction must have been, both for the accusing circle themselves and for other young people in the village.[57] Alongside violence and paranoia, witchcraft brings excitement, fantasy and imagination to Salem. For the village's Puritan maids, there is a promise of liberation bound up with the violence of the trials.

A similar sense of chaotic liberation tinged with violence also pervades Jackson's 1962 novel *We Have Always Lived in the Castle*. According to Bernice M. Murphy, the novel's narrator Mary Katherine (Merricat) Blackwood, can be understood as a partial fictionalisation of the nineteenth-century alleged murderer Lizzie Borden,[58] who despite being in her thirties when she was accused of killing her parents, is frequently portrayed in popular culture as a child or teenager, a perennial monstrous girlchild. In the opening passage of *Castle*, Merricat introduces herself to the reader in a manner that is at once childlike and sinister:

> My name is Mary Katherine Blackwood. I am eighteen years old, and I live with my sister Constance. I have often thought that with any luck at all I could have been born a werewolf, because the two middle fingers on both my hands are the same length, but I have had to be content with what I had. I dislike washing myself, and dogs, and noise. I like my sister Constance, and Richard Plantagenet, and *Amanita phalloides*, the death-cup mushroom. Everyone else in my family is dead. (*WHALC*, p. 1)

Merricat is a strange addition to the pantheon of mid-twentieth-century teenage witches. Aged eighteen, she is on the cusp of adulthood, at least from a legal perspective. Her behaviour, however, is that of a child: she climbs trees, plays make-believe games and craves sweet treats from her caregiver Constance. Unlike the other adolescent witches explored in this book, Merricat is neither associated with historical witch trials nor in possession of verifiable supernatural powers. As Joyce Carol Oates writes in the afterword to the 2009 Penguin Classics edition of *Castle*, Merricat's witchery is 'self-invented'.[59] Merricat utilises sympathetic magic – burying dolls and coins or nailing books to trees – in order to arrest the forward movement of time and remain an eternal child. Her magic is unique and idiosyncratic, inhabiting a strange borderland between witchcraft and obsessive-compulsive behaviour. If she has a good day on one of her shopping trips to the nearby village, she makes 'an offering of jewellery out of gratitude' (*WHALC*, p. 5). She positions totemic objects in strategic positions around the property that she shares with Constance, checking them regularly to ensure their continued adherence to her own private rituals.

Echoing the early modern belief that one of the defining features of the witch is a propensity to commit *maleficium* (malevolent magical acts), Merricat also curses the villagers that she encounters on her twice-weekly shopping trips: 'I thought about burning black painful rot that ate away from inside, hurting dreadfully. I wished it on the village' (*WHALC*, p. 6). Later, following an unpleasant meeting with a man named Jim Donnell, she imagines that 'Perhaps someday soon Jim Donnell would die; perhaps there was already a rot growing inside him that was going to kill him' (*WHALC*, p. 12). Merricat's most accomplished act of malefic magic occurs, however, before the narrative proper even commences. While the villagers believe that her older sister Constance poisoned the rest of the Blackwood family six years ago – leaving herself, Merricat and their now-infirm uncle Julian as the only survivors – the poisoner was, in actuality, Merricat. Obstinate and contemptuous of her parents' rules, the young Merricat, who was then only twelve years old, murdered her family by poisoning the sugar bowl. That the girl poisoned her family serves to bring her into further concordance with the historical figure of the witch. In the classical world, from whose legal systems many early modern European witchcraft laws developed, witches and poisoners enjoyed a close proximity. Indeed, they were often interchangeable. The historian Livy (59 BCE–17 CE) described how approximately 5,000 Romans were executed for *veneficium*, a crime whose literal meaning, 'poisoning', was then evolving into something closer to *maleficium*, the use of harmful magic.[60] Significantly, the dictionary defines *veneficus* as 'connected with sorcery/ charms, sorcerous, magic; poisoning'.[61] Much like Merricat, witches have, throughout history, been associated with the interchangeable acts of poisoning and the working of wicked spells.

Merricat's witchcraft, I argue, provides her with a line of flight that enables her to escape static gender and class identities. Her sympathetic magic and affinity with nature empower her to enter into a series of generative becomings through which she unsettles binary divisions, rejects the rigidity of adult womanhood and commits herself to an eternal becoming-girl. Mapping the feminist applications of Deleuzian theory, Elizabeth Grosz observes that molar unities – divisions between classes, races and sexes – generally function to stabilise identities as closed systems that seal in energies and intensities.[62] Conversely, molecular becomings – unpredictable tendencies towards change – destabilise such identificatory blocks, opening them up to new and unforeseen possibilities. In Deleuze and Guattari's formulation, all becomings begin with a process of becoming-woman, a movement that 'intends to fragment, not reinforce, essentialist gender binaries'.[63] Becomings do not entail a linear process of maturation, and 'becoming-woman' merely alludes to a movement away from a conventionally male mode of being – concerned with unity, discrete embodiment and fixity – towards a more fluid, less dualistic feminine mode.[64]

Merricat's witchery effects precisely this kind of movement away from the fixity of dualistic logic and towards a fluid multiplicity. When she first employs *veneficium*, she does so to punish her family after she is sent to bed without her supper and ultimately succeeds in disrupting the gender-based hierarchy that governs the conservative, aristocratic Blackwood home. The dinner table, with its carefully stratified seating plan, encapsulates the rigidity of the familial structure. Uncle Julian explains that before the poisoning 'My brother, as head of the family, sat naturally at the head of the table' (*WHALC*, p. 31), while the remainder of the family assumed positions that indicated their role and rank in the Blackwood clan. Likewise, the Blackwood women had traditionally been assigned an unambiguous position within the family, being charged with the provision of food and the stocking of the cellar with preserves made from various fruits and vegetables. However, when Merricat poisons the sugar bowl, she upsets the patriarchal authority that had previously regulated the family unit and creates a space for more complex relationships and identities to flourish. Without the organising force of her father's authority, Merricat can flee the molar binarism of man/woman and carve out a line of flight towards a new identity that is variegated and kinetic. Consequently, her initial act of violence can be read as a becoming-woman, not because it sets Merricat on a linear path towards maturity, but rather because it frees her from the hierarchies and binary divisions that previously governed her existence.

Throughout the novel, Merricat frequently troubles the boundaries that separate the natural from the cultural and the human from the animal. Her nickname, Merricat, although an obvious portmanteau of the more formal Mary Katherine, suggests an animalistic, feline nature. She brings dirt from the countryside into the clean, ordered bourgeois home, and at the same time, she transforms natural spaces – sheltered groves and riverside banks – into grassy bedrooms and verdant dining rooms. She also shares an extremely, almost supernaturally, close relationship with her cat, Jonas. Their intense connection recalls early modern ideas about the relationship between the witch and her familiar. As Diane Purkiss explains, the 'witch's body was thought to be coextensive with that of her familiar; if the later was hurt, the former suffered'.[65] Merricat and Jonas are similarly co-dependent, and they often appear to mirror one another's actions and emotions: 'When I ran Jonas ran and when I stopped and stood still he stopped and glanced at me and then went off briskly in another direction, as though we were not acquainted, and then he sat down and waited for me to run again' (*WHALC*, p. 52). These parallels suggest that Merricat has embarked on a line of flight that has brought her into a dynamic, generative becoming-animal, a desubjectification that will ultimately dismantle human-animal divisions and initiate an increasingly protean mode of being.

In their work on becoming-animal, Deleuze and Guattari stress that one does not become animal simply by taking on the appearance of animal or by mimicking its behaviour. Instead, one becomes animal by entering into an alliance with an animal multiplicity or pack. The individual is drawn into proximity with the pack through their engagement with an abnormal or anomalous entity. This abnormal entity is designated as such not because it exists outside of the pack, but because it forms a porous border between the pack and the world beyond.[66] The creature with which one enters such as an alliance cannot, however, be a mere household pet, which Deleuze and Guattari claim is sentimentalised and merely replicates stagnant Oedipal patterns. Becoming-animal must proceed instead through the establishment of a meaningful connection with a demonic animal. These are 'pack or affect animals that form a multiplicity, a becoming, a population, a tale'.[67] The examples Deleuze and Guattari employ to illustrate the metamorphic power of the demonic animal are *Moby Dick*'s eponymous white whale – the exceptional creature that effects Ahab's monstrous becoming-whale – and Ben, the dominant rodent in the 1971 film *Willard* who brings about the title character's becoming-rat. In *Castle*, it is Jonas, Merricat's faithful companion, who plays the part of the demonic animal. Although it may be tempting to read the cat as a pet, Jonas is a far more diabolical creature. Merricat speaks with him, and he draws her into an increasingly intense relationship with the natural world, guiding her through the fields and woodlands that surround their home. Moreover, while Jonas is the sole feline in the story, he can be understood as the visible representative of an unseen band of cats. Merricat believes that he tells her stories drawn from his own family (a pack of sorts) because he prefaces all such tales with a reminder that his mother was 'the first cat' (*WHALC*, p. 53). Thus, as Jonas draws Merricat to him, he also draws her into a relationship with a multiplicity of cats.

Jonas serves as the conduit for Merricat's becoming-animal, a process that is alluded to from the very first lines of the novel, when Merricat tells us that she would like to have been born a werewolf. As mentioned in the previous chapter, the werewolf – along with the vampire – is a creature used by Deleuze and Guattari to explain that becoming-animal is not merely a process of imitation but an exchange of particles, an adoption of new relations of speeds and slowness. One does not merely become wolf, and thereby move from one side of the human-animal binary to the other, but in the act of becoming the individual collapses these boundaries, just as the werewolf effaces the line between man and wolf. The werewolf is also important because of its tendency to overlap with the figure of the witch, and as such, its presence in the novel indicates that Merricat's witchcraft is bound up with her ability to traverse the human-animal divide. Accusations of lycanthropy often attended or were intertwined with witchcraft trials. Yet, while most European regions witnessed a preponderance of women executed for the crime of witchcraft, the lycanthrope was more likely to be male, largely due to ingrained cultural associations between aggressiveness and masculine identity positions.[68] Nevertheless, these categories often overlapped. Rolf Schulte delineates how from the 1550s onwards lycanthropy was increasingly defined as an especially violent form of *maleficium* and so was integrated into witchcraft trials.[69] Considering her interest in early modern witchcraft texts, it seems likely that Jackson would have been aware of the close relationship between witches and were-wolves during this period.

In the case of Merricat Blackwood, her affiliation with the werewolf suggests a fundamentally hybrid nature, an eternal becoming that shatters the division between human and non-human life. Analysing the female werewolf as a cultural trope, Jazmina Cininas argues that lupine women resist binary classification because they exceed 'the categories of male or female, woman or wolf, human of animal'.[70] Imagining herself as a were-wolf, Merricat embraces wildness and actively shapes her own identity by refusing the cultural norms associated with femininity and mature wom-anhood. She bristles at the domestic, playing outdoors, in the fields and forest, and, like Jonas, only returning home for food and rest. Imaging a wedding ring as a tight, suffocating metal band, she appears repulsed by heteronormative, adult relationships. When Constance suggests to Mer-ricat that 'We should have been living like other people . . . You should have boy friends', both sisters laugh at the inherent ridiculousness of the idea (*WHALC*, p. 82). Merricat even reinforces her fundamentally animal nature by implying that she doesn't need a boyfriend because 'I have Jonas' (*WHALC*, p. 82). Merricat's becoming-animal is not contingent upon a surface-level transformation, but instead occurs through inventive con-junctions that enable her to enter into new relations of motility that are essentially feline or lupine. She moves, plays and sleeps in shaded groves – much like Jonas – while her capacity for violence and love of filth align her with the werewolf.

Merricat's hybrid nature – her position between human and animal, woman and child – is also suggestive of her stubborn refusal to grow up. Although she is eighteen years old, she plays imaginative games, desir-ing a winged horse on whose back she and Constance could fly to the moon (*WHALC*, p. 22). Indeed, while Merricat's she-wolf identity might initially suggest a hypersexual nature, there is also a well-worn fictional tradition, particularly prominent in the latter half of the twentieth cen-tury, that frames the female werewolf as an indicator of anxieties about sexual maturity. Although the female werewolf can be read as hyperfem-inine, especially in light of her often-exaggerated feminine corporeality, she simultaneously displays typically masculine traits such as excessive hir-suteness and aggression.[71] Consequently, the she-wolf often represents a resistance to conventional modes of femininity or an ambivalence about linear processes of maturation. In Suzy McKee Charnas's 1989 short story

'Boobs', teenage protagonist Kelsey actively desires a lycanthropic transformation, hoping it will allow her to control her increasingly unruly body.[72] Hannah Priest argues that, 'Kelsey's lycanthropy is thus presented as an avoidance of puberty – likened more to anorexia than adolescence – and the body she inhabits as a wolf is closer to that of her "normal-looking, thin and strong" child-body than her "cartoon" woman body'.[73] Merricat's feral nature, her wish to have been born a werewolf, indicates an equally potent attachment to childhood. She revels in dirt and disorder, rejecting cleanliness, maturity and the conventions of adult society. Indeed, for Merricat, the greatest tragedy to befall the Blackwood family is not the mass-poisoning of its members, but the threat posed by heterosexual romance and the possibility that Constance may take on the more traditionally feminine roles of wife and mother. When their estranged cousin Charles expresses romantic interest in Constance, Merricat sets fire to the Blackwood house, destroying the conventional domestic space and reconfiguring it as a fairy-tale castle.

This final act of violence is liberating for Merricat. It frees her from the demands of home and domesticity, creating an eternal fantasy land in which she and Constance can play. Here, Merricat enacts her most volatile, explosive becoming, as her rejection of normative, heterosexual womanhood – a process that began with the poisoning of her family – enables her to occupy a position that Deleuze and Guattari single out as the most privileged mode of resistance: the little girl.[74] For them, the girl is not an idealised embodiment of innocence: 'The girl is certainly not defined by virginity; she is defined by a relation of movement and rest, speed and slowness, by a combination of atoms, an emission of particles: haecceity'.[75] She is a line of flight, a figure who passes through the molecular binaries of sex, gender, race and class. Girls generate multiplicities, 'they produce n molecular sexes on the line of flight in relation to the dualism machines they cross right through'.[76] When the house burns, hastened by the unwillingness of the townspeople to help salvage it or its contents, Merricat and Constance lose all conventional markers of gender and class. Even their clothing is lost, and while Constance resolves to wear old shirts and trousers belonging to their recently deceased uncle Julian, feral Merricat dons a robe fashioned from an old tablecloth and bound with a gold cord pilfered from the living room drapes. In this way, both girls – Constance in her androgynous garb of men's suits and Merricat in her makeshift robe – reject mature femininity and binary gender. Likewise, their home is left a smoking ruin, 'a castle, turreted and open to the sky' (*WHALC*, p. 120). With the boundary between inside and outside, nature and culture demolished, the sisters are left to experience abstraction, continuity and connection. Their home opens out to the world beyond, and dynamic connections between seemingly discrete entities are established.

In the novel's final pages, the sisters fully embrace the witchy identity that has hovered around Merricat since the introductory paragraph. Alone in their castle, they become objects of fear and reverence, as the villagers leave offerings of food for 'the ladies' (*WHALC*, p. 141). They gain a reputation as witches, with parents telling their children that 'They never come out except at night . . . and then when it's dark they go hunting little children' (*WHALC*, p. 141). In the final lines of the book, the pair glory in their new mythic status, with Merricat wondering aloud if she could eat a child given the chance and Constance pragmatically responding, 'I doubt if I could cook one' (*WHALC*, p. 146). 'Oh, Constance,' Merricat exclaims as the narrative draws to a close, 'we are so happy' (*WHALC*, p. 146). There is power, a subversive freedom, in this happiness and in the identity of the witch. By embracing the oppositional character of the witch – her capacity to act as a dark reflection of normative femininity – Merricat resists the demands that she grow up and settle into mature, docile womanhood.

Merricat's ability to move between binaries and her propensity to undertake dynamic, protean becomings, cast her as an invitingly transgressive figure. She refuses the static identity of woman, but engages instead in a generative, liberatory process of becoming-women. In doing so, she effects a series of decisive movements towards the animal, the natural and the hybrid. She cuts a path through the dualist thought that separates the natural from the cultural, the masculine from the feminine. At the same time, however, Merricat's freedom to engage in these radical becomings depends on violent acts: first, the mass poisoning of her family, and second, her burning of their home. Indeed, it is this second act of destruction that ultimately banishes the last vestige of constraining patriarchal power from their home, ridding the sisters of Cousin Charles forever:

> Then Constance laughed, and I laughed, and for a minute I saw Charles in the car turn his head quickly as though he had heard us laughing, but the car started, and drove off down the driveway, and we held each other in the dark hall and laughed, with tears running down our cheeks and echoes of our laughter going up the ruined stairway to the sky. (*WHALC*, p. 144)

There is a manic joy in this moment of freedom. The girls laugh, cackling like mad hags, the peals of laughter echoing up the staircase and seeping out into the world beyond. Both the initial murder and the destruction of the house rescue Merricat and Constance from patriarchal power, freeing up a line of flight through which Merricat may undertake myriad productive becomings.

Merricat's actions encourage us to enter into a complex relationship with violent or taboo acts, one in which they are both liberating and revolting. The schematics of violence that pervade *Castle* therefore recall not only the previously discussed notion of perverse readership, but they also echo Isabel Cristina Pinedo's work on recreational terror. Pinedo claims that horror cinema facilitates a 'pleasurable encounter with violence and danger'.[77] She argues that the slasher subgenre in particular stages a 'fantasy in which humiliation is transformed into unbridled female rage'.[78] Creating an imaginative scenario in which the protagonist, or final girl, is forced to dispatch a dangerous killer in order to save herself, slasher films provide an opportunity for women to experience taboo emotions (i.e., anger) and vicariously act out violent impulses in a guilt-free fantasy. In this way, Pinedo maintains that horror films:

> create an *opening* for feminist discourse by restaging the relationship between women and violence as not only one of danger in which women are the objects of violence but as a pleasurable one in which women retaliate to become the agents of violence and defeat the aggressors.[79]

Extending this analysis into the literary realm, works like Castle also facilitate a subversively pleasurable encounter with violence. Merricat presents herself to the readers as hemmed in by the authority of men like her father and, later, Cousin Charles. Although these men may not be aggressors in the same manner as the slasher villain, they nevertheless attempt to curtail Merricat's freedom and consign her to rigid, binary modes of being. Merricat's violent retaliation against these men is thus framed as liberating and pleasurable. The way in which the reader identifies with Merricat can therefore be understood as subversive, and the adolescent identity she models is one that runs counter to social norms. Yet, coming to her character as perverse readers, Merricat offers a vision of adolescent selfhood divorced from consumerism, social integration and heteronormative coupling. She is, instead, a character who embraces witchery as a path to freedom and finds in the feral, filthy werewolf a means of demolishing binaries and opening up new identificatory possibilities.

Published just over a decade after *Castle*, Stephen King's debut novel *Carrie* also invites the reader to take a perverse pleasure in the violent retribution enacted by its titular character and articulates a subversive model for the construction of adolescent identity. Like *Castle*, *Carrie* invites the reader to identify both with the violent catharsis of its protagonist's actions and with the transformative acts of becoming that allow her to explode restrictive binary structures. Although not written specifically for an adolescent audience, *Carrie*, like much of King's oeuvre, is particularly alluring to teenagers. As Gary Hoppenstand and Ray B. Browne explain: 'The teenager loves to read King. His novels are parked alongside sticker-ridden notebooks on high school students' desks. Dogeared copies of *Carrie*, *The Shining* and *The Stand* are crammed into lockers and backpacks.'[80] Moreover, King's work is often concerned with the experiences and transformations of youth, with many of his protagonists being either teenagers or young children. Although many of King's child and adolescent characters ultimately find themselves cast in the role of hero, there are others who come to embody something more sinister.

In the case of *Carrie*, the protagonist, sixteen-year-old Carrietta White, has generally been read as a monstrous figure, a grotesque incarnation of masculine fears about uncontainable female corporeality. Carrie is also repeatedly aligned with the figure of the witch, a textual motif that appears to simultaneously denigrate and empower the character. Although Carrie possesses the power of telekinesis, defined in the novel as an 'empiric function of the mind, possibly electrochemical in nature' (*Ca*, p. 50), her abilities are understood by the girl herself and those around her in terms of witchcraft. Carrie's fanatically religious mother, Margaret, describes both her daughter and her own grandmother, from whom Carrie inherited her powers, as witches, recalling that the old woman 'had been able to light the fireplace without even stirring from her rocker by the window. It made her eyes glow with . . . a kind of witch's light' (*Ca*, p. 175). Yet, while Carrie is often the passive receptacle of the label witch, an identity foisted onto her by her mother, she also engages in a process of self-fashioning whereby she consciously adopts the identity of the sorceress. On the night after her first period signals the arrival of both her psychic powers and mature femininity, Carrie lies in bed and fantasises about the subversive power of the sorceress:

> She thought of imps and families and witches. (am i a witch momma
> the devil's whore) riding through the night, souring milk, overturn-
> ing butter churns, blighting crops while They huddled inside their
> houses with hex signs scrawled on their doors. (*Ca*, p. 93)

Carrie's fantasies chime with historical beliefs in the witch's power to spoil crops and food products, but they also provide an imaginative space where she can find release and empowerment through violence.

The ambivalent nature of Carrie's witch identity is echoed in King's own complex attitude towards the character. In his literary memoir *Danse Macabre*, the author explains that when he was 'writing the book in 1973 and only out of college three years, I was fully aware of what Women's Liberation implied for me and others of my sex'.[81] At the same time, King describes Carrie as 'a woman, feeling her powers for the first time, and like Samson, pulling down the temple on everyone in sight'.[82] These remarks suggest that the novel can be approached as a multiplicity, with its heroine serving as both a reification of conservative fears regarding the women's rights movement of the 1960s and 1970s and as a liberating symbol of righteous anger.[83] King's comments about *Carrie* can also be seen as indicative of the book's interpretive fluidity. The novel itself and Brian De Palma's 1976 cinematic adaption have been read as both regressively misogynistic and progressively empowering. Returning to previously discussed theories of perverse readership/spectatorship, the reception of *Carrie* suggests that audiences are more than willing to interpret the text through the lens of their own experiences, deriving meaning from it on their terms.

An example of *Carrie*'s pliability can be seen in the work of Darren Elliott-Smith, who has written extensively about queer appropriations of the text. Elliott-Smith points out that alongside a 1988 musical adapta-tion, *Carrie – The Musical*, there have been numerous drag parodies that engage in a more explicit queering of the source text. These include *Scarrie – The Musical* (2005) and *Carrie – A Period Piece* (2006). Such parodic reimaginings of *Carrie* exist because 'Read by gay men as a variation on the "coming-out" tale, Carrie's plight as a ridiculed, bullied and self-hating adolescent offers a strong focus of identification for gay spectators'.[84] What is significant here, beyond the specifics of queer identifications with *Carrie*, is the fact that such appropriations are grounded in a view of the source text as malleable. The text is, as noted above, a multiplicity whose meaning is neither fixed nor singular. Audiences/readers can project their desires, experiences and feelings into any gaps in meaning that occur. Thus, just as queer spectators might find parallels between the book/film's treatment of marginalisation and their own experiences, so too might adolescent readers – a surprisingly large portion of King's readership – find meaningful, albeit subversive, identificatory possibilities in the character of Carrie herself. Moreover, as I argue below, such identification hinges upon how the materiality of Carrie's body, initially portrayed as grotesque, leads to a (temporarily) liberating explosion of binaries.

In her book *The Monstrous Feminine*, Barbara Creed explores Carrie's representation as both a 'witch and menstrual monster',[85] arguing that, in the case of De Palma's film adaptation, the text designates female reproductive functions as abject, a threat to the symbolic order. However, Creed is careful to acknowledge that the girl's monstrosity is a 'construct of patriarchal ideology' rather than an inherent property, noting that her abject qualities are symptomatic of misogynistic anxieties surrounding female difference.[86] While Creed's analysis of *Carrie*'s menstrual horror remains both incisive and massively influential, I want to bring the present reading of the text – specifically King's original novel – beyond the familiar terrain of psychoanalysis to consider questions of materiality. I argue that the novel's initial representation of female corporeality, as well the menstrual trauma from which Carrie's powers ostensibly derive, is less beholden to psychoanalytic notions of lack, repression and the Oedipal psychodrama, and more bound up with anxious visualisations of the body and its processes. It is, to borrow a phrase from Kelly Hurley, the very 'Thing-ness of the all-too-embodied woman' that arouses anxiety within the context of novel.[87] Rather than merely serving as a manifestation of sexual difference, Carrie's unruly body – its seepages and flows – attests to the 'grossness of the material world'.[88] As such, menstruation emerges as the locus of horror because it speaks to the clamorous vitality of the material, illustrating that neither the body nor nature are passive instruments of the human will.

In *Carrie*, the terrible chain of events that will result in the protagonist's destruction of her hometown begins with the arrival of her menstrual period in the public space of a high school locker room. The sudden advent of Carrie's menarche repulses her classmates because the appearance of menstrual blood in the clean, ordered space of a locker-room shower is a reminder of what Jack Morgan terms 'our neglected, marginalized organic life'.[89] The other teenage girls who occupy the locker room alongside Carrie are associated with cleanliness: 'Showers turning off one by one, girls stepping out, removing pastel bathing caps, towelling, spraying deodorant

. . . Bras were hooked, underpants stepped into' (*Ca*, p. 5). They engage in elaborate cleansing rituals and careful corporeal monitoring to ensure the biological systems that underpin all social reality remain invisible. They present themselves as purely cultural creatures, disentangled from the seething chaos of materiality. When they turn on Carrie, furious at the public spectacle of her bleeding, they do so because her menstrual flow attests to the discomfiting reality that the cultural cannot, in fact, be separated from nature and that matter, whether environmental or corporeal, is not inert but agentic. Kevin Trumpeter draws attention to the fact that 'the bodily systems in which we exert little or no choice – respiration, circulation, digestion, the immune system – are of far more consequence to our day-to-day survival than many of the ostensibly conscious decisions we make in a given day'.[90] Consequently, he goes on to argue that 'the body itself has an agency that extends beyond the wishes of the thinking subject that body happens to be attached to'.[91] In a similar manner, the internal systems that govern the degradation of the endometrium and the elimination of clots, secretions and mucous during the menstrual cycle bespeak the complex vitality of the material. It is for this reason that when the other girls turn to taunt Carrie, they do so by bombarding her with sanitary products and chanting 'Plug it *up*. Plug it *up*' (*Ca*, p. 9, emphasis in original). They do not wish to acknowledge that the body is simply organic matter, that all of our cultural constructions and performances are firmly imbricated within a labyrinth of complex, agentic materiality. They hope, instead, to redraw the imaginary line that separates the cultural from the biological.

Although Carrie is ostracised as a result of her inability to conceal her clamorous, vital materiality, her traumatic menarche can also be understood as a productive experience in that it marks the beginning of a dynamic becoming-woman. Distinct from the cultural clichés that position menarche as the beginning of normative womanhood, Carrie's violent puberty allows her to enter the more creative Deleuzian process of becoming-woman. Like Merricat Blackwood, she does not undertake a linear path towards mature femininity, but rather commences a movement towards multiplicity and the demolition of structuring binaries. Carrie's becoming-woman enables her to destabilise molar blocks of gender, subjectivity and identity. Moreover, her radical becomings enable her to disrupt subject/object binaries in a manner that opens up productive sites of interaction between self and other, inside and outside, animate and inanimate.

The claim that Carrie challenges mind/body dualisms may at first seem perplexing. Her traumatic puberty ignites dormant telekinesis, and the ability to move objects with one's mind is conventionally understood as a psychic ability. However, in King's novel, Carrie's powers are framed primarily in biological terms. While her abilities are mental in nature, it is made clear throughout the text that the neurological systems that facilitate them are not distinct from corporeality more broadly conceived. Indeed, it is Carrie's body that fuels and responds to the strain of her mental actions. When she levitates a hairbrush, the narrator explains that her 'Respiration had fallen to sixteen breaths per minute. Blood pressure up to 190/100. Heartbeat up to 140 – higher than astronauts under the heavy g-load of lift off' (*Ca*, p. 92). In this way, the mind is not separated from or privileged at the expense of the body. Carrie's telekinesis is not a sign that she has subordinated or transcended corporeality; rather, it is a compelling exploration of what the body can do. As she employs telekinesis to manipulate entities and objects in the external world, her powers attest to the multitude of connections that the body can make.

The connective power of Carrie's body is at its fullest during the novel's climactic prom-night sequence. Having been invited to attend the dance with the popular and charismatic Tommy Ross, Carrie adorns herself in the regalia of the feminine masquerade: make-up and a fashionable dress. She tries to create the illusion of a clean, unified body – a cohesive surface bearing no signs of its organicity. She chats confidently with her peers and even charms her date. Yet, when she is elected prom queen, Carrie becomes the victim of a cruel prank played by school bully Chris Hargensen. When Chris and her cohorts dump a bucket of pig blood on the unsuspecting Carrie, it is not only a public humiliation but a reminder of her earlier failure to properly suppress her body's unruly materiality. Chris's prank is centred around the premise of 'Pig blood for a pig' (*Ca*, p. 136), as though Carrie must be punished for her animality, for the disturbing manner in which she allowed the hidden biological process of menstruation to be rendered disturbingly visible. As the pigs' blood falls on Carrie, it is described in terms evocative of menstrual blood:

> she was red and dripping with it, they had drenched her in the very secretness of blood, in front of all of them and her thought (oh . . . I . . . *COVERED* . . . with it) was coloured a ghastly purple with her revulsion and shame. She could smell herself and it was the *stink* of blood, the awful wet, coppery smell. (*Ca*, p. 216, emphasis in original)

The language used to describe the pig blood that covers Carrie's body clearly echoes the language of menstrual blood: 'the very secretness of blood', 'revulsion and shame', 'the *stink* of blood'. Yet, if Carrie's humiliation serves to punish her for exposing the visceral biological realm that underpins the social order, her revenge is also reflective of corporeal disorder. Indeed, the manner in which she sets out to punish her peers for their cruelty towards her is contingent upon embracing her disorderly body,[92] glorying in its riotous materiality and bringing it into meaningful connection with other configurations of matter.

For much of the novel, Carrie embodies notions of gross materiality. She is repeatedly framed as unable to control her body or its process. Her fluids (menstrual blood, sweat) seep outwards, problematising the very concept of a boundary between inside and outside, subject and object. When she uses her telekinetic powers, she enacts a similar dissolution of the 'threshold' between the body's interior and exterior, while also troubling the apparent divide between subject and object. Indeed, her abilities show that the boundaries that *appear* to separate bodies are merely temporary linkages. Consumed by rage and humiliation, Carrie uses her powers to turn on the school sprinkler system to first soak and then electrocute her mocking classmates. As she does so, she merges with these inanimate objects, physically experiencing their metallic taste: 'She reached up with her mind, felt the pipes, traced them. Cold; full of water. She tasted iron in her mouth' (*Ca*, p. 222). Like the early modern witch, Carrie is able to unfix her selfhood and transcend the apparent boundaries of corporeality. Her body and her subjectivity are 'figured as plurally extensive with or diffused through a variety of objects', and her form therefore mimics 'the boundlessness of the witch's body'.[93] However, Carrie's ability to merge with the water pipes also bespeaks a continuity of materiality that engenders productive connections between all permutations of matter, whether animate or inanimate. In directing her mind outward into the pipes, Carrie recalls Deleuze and Guattari's assertion that subject and object cannot be conceptualised as discrete entities or binary opposites.[94] Within this schema, material and psychical entities can no longer be understood either in terms of boundaries, nor, conversely, can they be viewed as inherently united or singular.[95] As Elizabeth Grosz elucidates, the Deleuzian perspective imagines subject and object as a 'series of flows, energies, movements, strata, segments, organs, intensities – fragments capable of being linked together or severed in potentially infinite ways other than those which congeal them into identities'.[96] Carrie's telekinesis is thus a productive power in its capacity to blow apart dualistic divisions between self and Other, inside and outside, subject and object. Her psychic manoeuvrings constitute a series of flows and intensities that move freely and make myriad innovative connections with other bodies.

Carrie's abilities also enable her to resist attempts to classify or schematise her body, to reduce it to a hierarchy governed by her troublesome reproductive organs. In the first volume of *The History of Sexuality*, Foucault describes the 'hysterization of women's bodies', a process beginning in the late eighteenth century, 'whereby the feminine body was analyzed – qualified and disqualified – as being thoroughly saturated with sexuality'.[97] While this process is an infinitely complex one, involving the surveillance and pathologisation of the female body, it also gestures towards a broader tendency to reduce the female body to its sex organs and hormones, to create a hierarchy in which all other processes are subordinate to the uterus. It is for this reason, Ussher explains, that even in the twentieth and twenty-first centuries women's complex emotional and medical experiences are often diagnosed as *solely* uterine in nature.[98] Although Carrie's telekinetic powers stem from her menarche, the manner in which these powers use, and circulate through, her entire body means that she ultimately resists this kind of hierarchisation. When she uses her powers, her body no longer functions as 'unified or unifying organism'; it is no longer organised by an overarching consciousness, but instead becomes a mobile series of destratified intensities and flows.[99] When Carrie's telekinesis manifests following her humiliation at the prom, her entire body experiences its flexes and motions: 'She leaned against the doors, her heart pumping wildly, yet her body as cold as ice cubes. Her face was livid, but dull red fever spots stood on each cheek. Her head throbbed thickly, and conscious thought was lost' (*Ca*, p. 223). Circulating telekinetic energies, Carrie's body becomes what Deleuze and Guattari term a 'body without organs'. This is not a body opposed to organs but rather to the *organisation* of the organs. They explain that 'The body without organs is not a dead body but a living body all the more alive and teeming once it has blown apart the organism and its organization'.[100] As such, Carrie's body ceases to be a fixed, biological entity and instead becomes a series of speeds, affects and intensities.

Despite the generative potential of the new connections Carrie forges, her intensive becomings and the dismantling of her body's organisational schemata ultimately lead to her death. The circulation of psychic intensities across Carrie's body may enable her to resist organisation or hierarchisation, yet these intensities also weaken her body, straining her cardiovascular system so that even before she is stabbed by her mother, she begins to wither: 'Her body seemed to have become twisted, shrunken, cronelike.' (*Ca*, p. 247.) Her corporeality exceeds its limits too soon. Her stripping away of binary divisions between self and Other, subject and object happens too quickly; she destratifies her entire body simultaneously. This is in line with Deleuze and Guattari's belief that it is possible to create a defective body without organs: 'you can botch it. Or it can be terrifying, and lead you to your death. It is nondesire as well as desire.'[101] One common way in which this occurs is through the creation of an 'empty body without organs', a self-destructive body that 'destratifies all the strata at once'.[102] This is precisely what happens to Carrie. Her body destratifies too rapidly and nothing is preserved. She opens herself up to new connections, but hastily, all at once, and so her body dissolves into chaos and nothingness.

While Carrie's ultimate fate is tragic rather than triumphant, she nevertheless remains the reader's primary point of identification. Throughout the novel, the narrative is routinely wrenched away from Carrie by the regular insertion of fictional secondary sources: scholarly discourses, biographies, newspaper accounts. Yet, the parts of the narrative focalised through her perspective bring us into uncomfortable proximity with her. Her Otherness is undercut by the manner in which King allows us to feel Carrie's 'tears of shame . . . as hot and as heavy as that first flow of menstrual blood had been' (*Ca*, p. 220). This proximity enables us to take pleasure in Carrie's becomings and in the unexpected connections that she forges with other entities. Likewise, Carrie has been denigrated and abused so much that brutal revenge becomes her only option, and in a perverse manner, we as readers identify with her urge to punish those who have bullied her so cruelly. Returning Pinedo's analysis of the slasher film, it is clear that *Carrie* is a text that opens up space for a 'pleasurable encounter with violence and terror'.[103] Although Carrie, like all monsters, must die to restore social order, her rampage constitutes a brief, excessively violent window of subversive pleasure for many viewers.

As a violent adolescent Carrie can also be situated within Scahill's schema of 'the violent child' because of her capacity to open up 'a phantasmagoric space for spectators to *become* perverse and to wallow in perversity'.[104] Carrie herself offers myriad perverse identificatory positions that can be rejected or co-opted by the perverse reader/spectator. Although much has been made of her appeal to a queer audience, Carrie also offers new identificatory possibilities for adolescent readers, a significant demographic amongst King's fans. She echoes the adolescent's girl's anxiety about her body and its dreaded excesses, while at the same time enacting a fantasy of rage and revenge in which all of those processes and fluids are unleashed in spectacular fashion. Her menstrual flow and related telekinesis, although arousing disgust in her peers, attest to the vital agentic powers of matter. Likewise, her telekinesis, as it is mobilised for revenge on prom night, opens up new avenues for connection, transformation and becoming while allowing Carrie to resist the kind of bodily organisation that would see her reduced to her unruly womb.

Conclusion

This chapter has explored some of the ways in which teen witches might illuminate new identificatory possibilities for adolescent readers. Encompassing overtly pedagogical works, such as *The Witch of Blackbird Pond* and the early *Sabrina* comics, alongside more subversive texts, such as *We Have Always Lived in the Castle* and *Carrie*, teen witch texts of the long 1960s allow readers to project themselves into the imaginative space of the text and confront unfamiliar scenarios and modes of being. They provide fertile spaces in which young people can play with their identities. In the case, of *The Witch of Blackbird Pond* and *Sabrina*, such play is directed towards the formation of positive, or at least, socially useful identities, with the former advocating social responsibility and altruism and the latter espousing a normative femininity grounded in beauty, popularity and consumerism. At the same time, it is important to understand that the young people who consumed these works did not do so passively and would likely have used the texts as a framework through which to negotiate questions of identity formation, embodiment, authenticity and social power. In the case of the more transgressive visions of teenage girlhood presented in *Castle* and *Carrie*, violence is presented as a liberatory act that opens up lines of flight and enables radical, often subversive, becomings. In these novels, adolescent girls – through witchcraft, psychic abilities and violence – are empowered to resist molar identities, or categories, and explode the binary divisions that separate self from Other, nature from culture and subject from object.

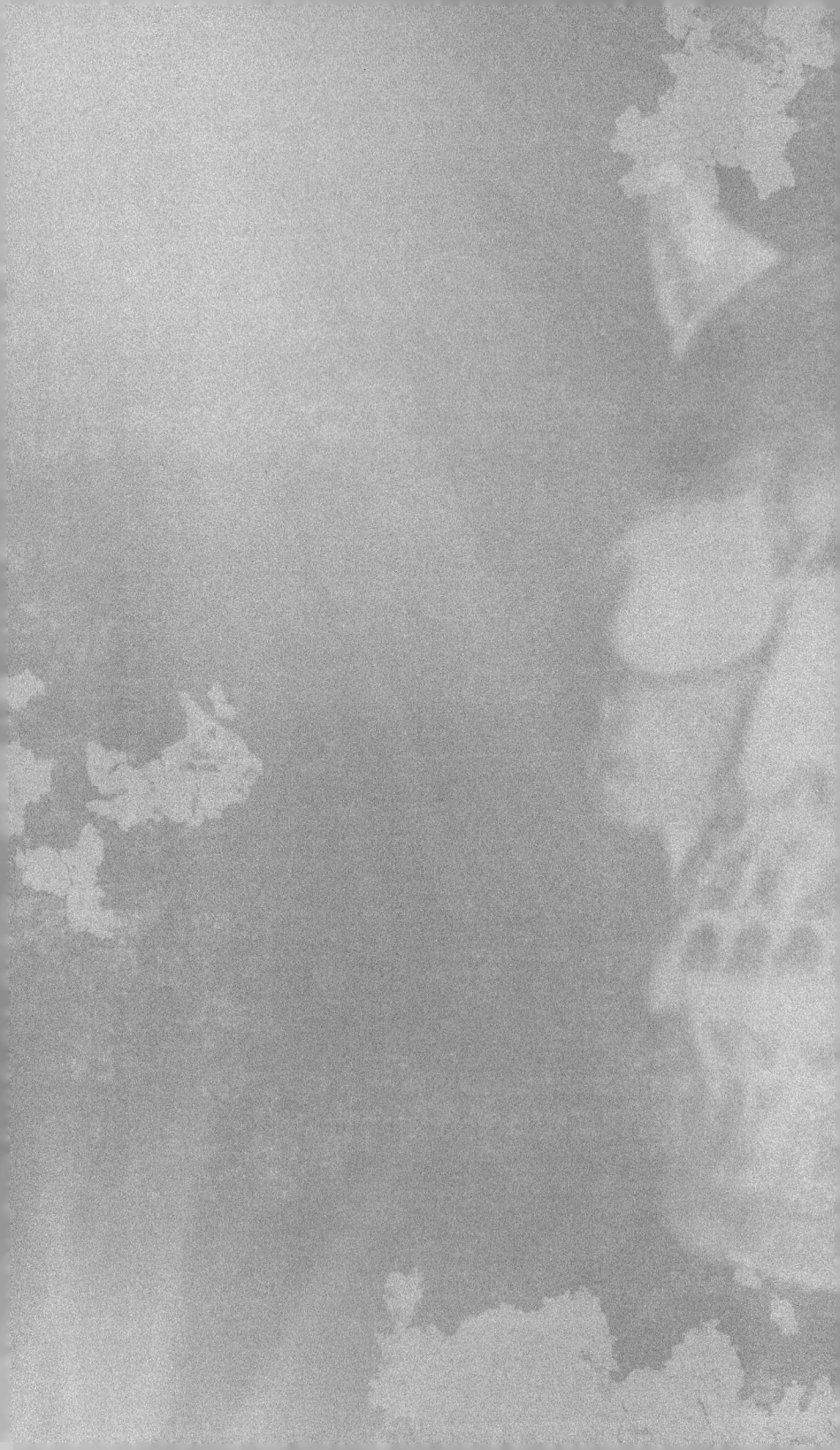

4

Becoming-Witch

Makeover Narratives and Glamourous Transformations

THIS CHAPTER represents a departure from the concerns of the previous two. Where Chapters 2 and 3 discussed the function of the teen witch – her role as either a trope through which adult authors could conceptualise adolescent femininity or an identificatory template through which teenage girls themselves could explore their identities – this chapter focuses on a key characteristic of the teenage witch: her powers of transformation. Although this facet of adolescent witchcraft has been touched on in earlier accounts of the teen witch's materiality, this chapter is wholly centred on themes of glamour and metamorphosis. In the pages that follow, I argue that teen witch texts produced between the late 1980s and the early 2000s employ the motif of the makeover as a means through which to explore the process of maturation as well as to render visible the adolescent sorceress's capacity to enact dynamic, rhizomatic becomings. I argue that the makeovers and metamorphoses depicted in these texts can be both liberating and constraining. While some transformations mark a linear movement towards a singular mode of being, thus reproducing static identities and hierarchies, others serve as productive sites of multidirectional, non-linear becoming.

I begin this chapter by contextualising the explosion of makeover narratives between the 1980s and the early 2000s in the emergence of a 'postfeminist sensibility' defined by themes of choice, responsibility, bodily surveillance and discipline.[1] I then move on to discuss the 1989 film *Teen Witch*, a text that espouses a hegemonic vision of normative femininity and utilises the trope of the magical makeover to lock its central character into an irreversible molar womanhood characterised by hierarchical stratification and the solidification of gender binaries. In the next section of the chapter, I explore three texts from the 1990s and early 2000s – *Sabrina the Teenage Witch*, *The Craft* and *Buffy the Vampire Slayer* – that present the adolescent witch's powers of transformation in a more liberating fashion. In each of these works, such metamorphoses open a space for play and facilitate molecular becomings that destabilise rigid hierarchies and binaries.

Post-feminist Sensibilities: Makeovers and Hegemonic Femininity

The witch is a figure long associated with metamorphic powers. In her study of the witch in early modern and contemporary culture, Diane Purkiss stresses the sorceress's 'ability to transform herself into other bodies, to shift shape'.[2] Themes of metamorphosis have, naturally, appeared at various points throughout this book, but up until now, they have remained peripheral or have formed part of a much broader discussion. This chapter, however, foregrounds transformations (glamours, makeovers, shapeshifting) and attributes the ubiquity of these tropes in late twentieth- and early twenty-first-century teen witch texts to an increasing cultural investment in issues of self-determination, choice, bodily surveillance and vague notions of empowerment. The four texts discussed in this chapter – *Teen Witch*, *The Craft*, *Sabrina the Teenage Witch* and *Buffy the Vampire Slayer* – were all produced during a period (1989–2004) when then the neoliberal economic model – inaugurated under US President Ronald Reagan in the 1980s and expanded throughout the 1990s – developed into a widespread culture of individualism and personal responsibility. Concomitantly, popular conceptions of feminism shifted away from notions of widescale political or structural change and towards what Catherine Rottenberg describes as 'the nurturing of each individual woman's desire to reach the top of the power pyramid'.[3] This change in mainstream articulations of women's empowerment has been labelled, not unproblematically, post-feminism.

Post-feminism has been defined variously as a reaction against the second-wave feminism of the 1960s and 1970s, a continuation of this movement and an expansion of its aims. In the context of late twentieth-century

American popular culture, post-feminism is regularly understood in terms of 'self-goals like "confidence", "independence" and "empowerment", linked to consumerist and neoliberal imperatives that demand that we work on the self as the means to achieve these aims'.[4] However, in contrast to these definitions, which frame post-feminism as either a historical or an epistemological shift, Rosalind Gill maintains that it is best understood as a sensibility.[5] In a 2007 article, Gill argues that rather than a static concept, post-feminism can be more productively apprehended through a consideration of the distinctive features of (then) contemporary articulations of gender in the media.[6] She goes on to explain that such a perspective accounts for the often contradictory nature of post-feminism as well as its connection to both feminist and anti-feminist positions.[7] Moreover, reconfiguring post-feminism as a sensibility rather than a cohesive movement or cultural shift opens up space in which to explore some of the key features of post-feminism – the view of femininity as a bodily property, emphasis on bodily discipline and self-surveillance, interest in individualism and choice, ubiquitous makeover narratives – while remaining alert to their imbrication within systems of class, gender and race inequality.[8]

Using this conception of post-feminism as a series of interrelated themes, it is possible to argue, as Gill does, that the 'makeover paradigm constitutes postfeminist media culture', offering physical transformations as quasi-magical solutions to problems that are always framed as individual, as opposed to structural or political.[9] Yet, while Gill focuses predominantly on the ubiquity of makeover narratives on television shows aimed at adult viewers, these tropes are also present in popular culture aimed at adolescents. Indeed, writing in 2002, Rachel Moseley observes that:

> Recent teen films and television shows have been profoundly engaged in the policing of difference and the construction and validation of hegemonic femininities, in the correcting of 'aberrant' femininity. The central way in which they have done this is through the trope of the 'glamour' makeover.[10]

Although Moseley cites an array of teen texts – *She's All That* (1999), *Cruel Intentions* (1999), *Never Been Kissed* (1999) – where makeovers are performed through mundane cosmetic practices, she nevertheless maintains that the adolescent witch is a dominant figure within the post-feminist makeover paradigm because of her associations with magical metamorphoses. Indeed, Moseley maintains that the onscreen teen witch of the 1990s and early 2000s embodies the lexical transformation of the word 'glamour' from its original meaning – 'magic, enchantment, spell' – to its contemporary usage as a synonym for physical feminine allure.[11] In these texts, the sorceress's powers of transformation take centre stage, and in keeping with the post-feminist sensibility of the period, they are framed as pathways to self-empowerment through the adoption of normative femininity.

The ubiquity of the teen witch and her association with makeover narratives can also be connected to profound shifts in media culture and consumption that occurred in the 1990s and early 2000s. Where teen films and television programmes had previously catered to a mixed-gender or even largely male demographic, this began to change in the final decades of the twentieth century. Frances Gateward and Murray Pomerance, writing in 2002, note that teen girls and young women are 'now the most sought after demographic of the entertainment industry'.[12] In contrast to young men, who were found to spend most of their disposable income on video games and sports activities, teenage girls at the turn of the millennium were spending almost $100 per week on two main activities: shopping and attending the cinema.[13] Gateward and Pomerance identify 1995 as a transitional year, arguing that the film industry began to shift its focus from teenage boys to their female peers following the success of Amy Heckerling's *Clueless*.[14] At the same time, major television networks also began to target a young female demographic with a host of new programmes centred on the experiences of young women (i.e., *Moesha*, *Felicity*, *Dark Angel*). It is for this reason, then, that while teen witches primarily existed within the pages of novels and comics between the 1940s and the 1970s,[15] by the 1980s and 1990s, they had colonised cinema and television screens as well.

'I want to look like her': The Molar Woman in *Teen Witch* (1989)

According Gateward and Pomerance, the majority of cinematic (and, by extension, televisual) texts aimed at young women espouse hegemonic values about femininity and can be understood as 'instructive texts rather than documents of revolution'.[16] While the later sections of this chapter complicate this reading through an exploration of texts that present – or allow the viewer to imagine – the transformations of the teen witch as liberatory, multiple and even subversive, I want to begin by discussing a work that employs the magical makeover as a means to reinforce normative femininity, reassert gender binaries and bolster hierarchical structures. Here, I argue that the 1989 film *Teen Witch* functions as a molar assemblage and that its conception of femininity is equally ground in notions of molar being, linearity and stratification. A molar mode of being is one that 'fixes everything into hierarchical categories and produces identities and subjectivities', whereas molecularity 'favours change, movement and processes'.[17] Molarity produces hierarchies and binaries, while molecularity stimulates rhizomatic connections and becomings. Likewise, molar woman is hemmed in by biology and subjectivity, while molecular woman – engaged in a dynamic becoming-woman – fragments gender binaries.[18] Although, as Sunny Hawkins points out, most texts will incorporate elements of both molecularity and molarity, 'hegemonic content [tends] to be more closely associated with molar than molecular expressions'.[19] As a hegemonic text, *Teen Witch* presents the magical makeover – itself an analogue for the process of maturation – as a linear process towards a fixed molar womanhood.

Teen Witch is a musical comedy created specifically for an adolescent audience. The narrative follows an awkward, unpopular fifteen-year-old girl named Louise Miller (Robyn Lively), who discovers that she possesses magical powers. As with many teen witch texts, Louise's entrance into witchcraft parallels the process of puberty. Shortly before her sixteenth birthday, Louise encounters the fortune-teller Madame Serena Alcott (Zelda Rubinstein), who tells her that after she turns sixteen, 'strange things will start to happen'. However, *Teen Witch* diverges from earlier works such as *Carrie* and *The Devil in Massachusetts* in its presentation of Louise's magical menarche. Rather than representing the onset of a leaky, uncontainable corporeality, Louise's maturation signifies her growing mastery of her body and her emerging powers of bodily discipline. In keeping with the narrative conventions of the post-feminist makeover paradigm, when Louise comes into her powers as a witch, she uses them to recreate herself as molar woman, reifying gender binaries in her newly feminised body.

Louise uses her magical abilities to acquire the signifiers of 1980s consumerist excess and to achieve empowerment through self-transformation (the magical makeover). When the film opens, Louise is an unpopular, clumsy fifteen-year-old girl. In many early scenes, she expresses frustration with her status as a girl and articulates a desire to become a woman. On her sixteenth birthday, Louise's mother (Caren Kaye) presents her with a gift, a brightly coloured, stripy sweater and proudly informs her daughter that she bought it in 'the young miss department'. Later, in a somewhat baffling sequence, a teacher (Shelley Berman) discovers a packet of birth control pills in Louise's bag. Holding them up for the entire class to see, he announces that the pack is *unopened*. Again, the implication seems to be that Louise is curious about, even desirous of, normative adult femininity, but she remains perennially on the threshold of this state, unable to enter. Upon gaining her magical powers on her sixteenth birthday, Louise first uses them to play mischievous tricks on her peers. However, once Madame Serena begins to instruct her in the use of magic, Louise turns towards a project of self-transformation. Gesturing towards a magazine cover featuring a famous supermodel, Louise exclaims, 'I want to look like her', and vows to make herself 'the most popular girl'. She employs magic to transmogrify the surface of her body so that it mirrors the appearance of the magazine model, and she comes to embody the norms of female beauty dominant in her unique social moment.

Louise's magical makeover is reflective of the notion of the body as project, a concept that is, as I will discuss below, closely imbricated with molar hierarchies and rigid gender binaries. According to Anthony Giddens, the conditions of late modernity are such that the body is increasingly available for human intervention and, consequently, has become subject to constant revision and re-inscription.[20] In her deconstruction of Giddens's theories, Shelley Budgeon explains that the conception of body as project derives from the view that advances in cosmetic practices, plastic surgery and exercise/diet regimes have meant that 'bodies not only become objects for human management and reconfiguration but are increasingly central to one's identity'.[21] The figuration of body as project can also be linked to post-feminist and neoliberal constructions of the body that advance a notion of 'self-actualisation' in which corporeal forms can be remade through rigorous discipline and diligent consumerism. Within this framework, one's consumer practices are reflective of selfhood and signifiers of status, while the manner in which the individual displays their body to the world is viewed as an indicator of personal success or the lack thereof.

In his study of consumption and weight in 1980s horror cinema, Thomas Fahy identifies a key contradiction of the Reagan era that was just drawing to a close when *Teen Witch* was released: 'Conspicuous consumption may have communicated personal and financial success in the eighties, but only if it did not become visible on the body.'[22] While the ability to consume with ease and discernment may have emerged as the primary barometer of personal and professional achievement, excessive consumption was balanced by the imperative to discipline the body and conceal any evidence of such excess. Exercise in particular became increasingly fashionable, and aerobics – a regimen pioneered by air force physician Dr Kenneth Cooper in the 1960s – was ubiquitous in gyms and on televisions during the 1980s. Exercise in this context was understood not just as a means of losing weight or improving health, but as a mode of shaping and reconfiguring the body. Writing on the explosion of strenuous exercise regimes in the 1970s and 1980s, Benjamin G. Rader outlines how a specific body type – either sinewy or muscular – gained new prominence as a means of self-presentation.[23] This physical ideal signified vigour and self-discipline, denoting both the dedication and, perhaps most importantly in the consumer-driven 1980s, the resources to cultivate such a sculpted physique.

In *Teen Witch*, the protagonist deploys magic to create this illusion of a carefully cultivated self. Louise is svelte, even prior to her supernatural makeover. Yet, in the early scenes her body is hidden by physical or sartorial excess. Her slim figure is engulfed by layers of fabric – voluminous skirts and sweaters that dwarf her slender body – and long, un-styled hair. When Louise uses a spell to make herself over in the image of a magazine model, she whittles down this excess, restyling her hair into a fashionable perm and replacing her wardrobe with figure-hugging garments that reveal her toned physique. Yet while such transformative practices were, in the context of 1980s post-feminism, couched in a rhetoric of personal choice and self-determination, they can also be understood as caught up in more complex processes of production and domination. In his later work, Michel Foucault distinguished techniques of the self from techniques of production or domination, based on his belief that techniques of the self permitted individuals to enact 'by their own means, a certain number of operations on their own bodies, their own souls, their own thoughts, their own conduct . . . so as to transform themselves'.[24] However, techniques of the self do not replace those of production/domination; indeed, all are present simultaneously.[25] Thus, while Foucault is careful to identify those instances where technologies of domination over individuals are counteracted by processes where the individual may act upon themselves, he also notes that there are 'points where the techniques of the self are integrated into structures of coercion'.[26] This kind of co-option frequently occurs in the case of the post-feminist rhetoric of choice and bodily discipline, as well as in the makeover paradigm that emerges as a key theme within this sensibility. Louise's magical transformations, although presented as empowering, ultimately result in her being produced as a particular kind of normative feminine subject.

In her feminist redeployment of Foucault's theories Sandra Lee Bartky extends his analysis of power, production and discipline into the realm of cosmetics. Bartky argues that techniques such as make-up, hairstyling, fashion and dieting all function as 'disciplinary practices that produce a body which in gesture and appearance is recognizably feminine'.[27] She goes on to explain that just as the modern era has deployed increasingly invasive apparatuses of power to produce docile bodies, so too do beauty practices reconstruct women as pliant subjectivities.[28] Bartky notes that while fashion magazines and popular culture may portray cosmetic practices as aesthetic activities through which each woman can 'express her individuality', this self-expression is limited and culturally circumscribed.[29] Thus, the technologies of the self that enable individuals to manipulate and transform their own bodies are integrated into systems of coercion and domination. Although the power relations implicit in this process do also have the potential to be constitutive, producing pleasure and desire as well as complicit subjectivity, such possibilities are occluded in *Teen Witch*. Louise's magical makeover, although framed in terms of self-discovery and self-actualisation, functions instead to bring her in line with normative modes of femininity that are dependent on rigid gender binaries.

The conception of the body as a project of self-identity – an idea that is easily assimilable into the post-feminist rhetoric of individualism, choice and bodily discipline – is, as Budgeon points out, heavily dependent on an inflexible mind/body dualism.[30] Within this framework 'the mind is privileged over a body which, by its denaturalization in late modern conditions . . . becomes an object of choice'.[31] Moreover, not only does the notion of body as project split the individual into mind and body, it also reconfigures the body as an object subordinated to a related, but ultimately distinct, thinking subject. Binary logic thrives as a result of this kind of stratification. In *Teen Witch* a rigid dualism is inherent in Louise's conception of her body as an object to be modified, but also in the film's representation of gender and femininity. Louise is eager to grow up and enter adult womanhood, but the kind of womanhood she desires is presented as a closed system, bounded and separated out from girlhood, as well as from masculine identities. This kind of molar segmentation is clearly expressed in an awkward musical number performed early in the film. Prior to developing her powers, Louise watches from the behind a row of lockers as a group cheerleaders dance through the girls' changing room singing, 'I'm throwing out my doll house/I'm giving up my toys/I realized this morning: I like boys'. The song not only celebrates an explicitly (hetero)normative model of femininity, but it separates the figure of the woman (associated with make-up, feminine dress and cleanliness) from the child and the man (associated with dirt, mud and immaturity):

> I'm putting on some lipstick
> To attract some boys . . .
> I'm making no more mud pies
> I'm staying out of the dirt
> I'm gonna buy some nylons
> And a leather mini skirt

In this context, entering womanhood is a linear process, a unidirectional and irreversible movement towards proper adult femininity.

As Louise moves towards womanhood, the kind of woman that she transforms into is the molar woman. In contrast to the molecular woman, who is characterised by multiplicity and the fragmentation of binaries, the molar woman is 'the woman as defined by her form, endowed with organs and functions and assigned as a subject'.[32] Louise as molar woman calcifies gendered hierarchies as her transformation severs her from both the elderly, diminutive Madame Serena and her childlike best friend, Polly (Amanda Ingber), while simultaneously locking her into a static identity as a beautiful, glamorous cheerleader. The film ends with her dancing with her crush, the handsome football-player Brad (Dan Gauthier), at the high school prom. Although she has abandoned witchcraft, fearing the excesses of unrestrained power, she retains her glamorous new look. The triumphant music that plays as she sways slowly in Brad's arms suggests that this is the end point of her transformation, she is fixed within the structures of binary gender and remains committed to a static mode of normative femininity.

Teen Witch ends with a reaffirmation of molar being. Subjectivities are hierarchically organised and 'individuals [are] fixed or frozen into subjects as a means of categorizing and conceptualizing them'.[33] This state of molarity breeds divisions and binaries, so that male is separated from female, subject from object, mind from body. However, this static molarity is not the only possibility for the post-feminist teen witch, nor is it the only outcome of the magical makeover narrative. Rather, as I demonstrate in the remainder of this chapter, there are a number of makeover texts in which the body is figured not as a passive surface, or object, to be inscribed by systems of signification or cultural norms, but as an event, an unfolding multiplicity that resists fixity and binary thinking. In the sections that follow, I discuss a number of teen witch texts – *Sabrina the Teenage Witch*, *The Craft*, *Buffy the Vampire Slayer* – where the body of the adolescent sorceress is framed as an ongoing process rather than a static, bounded entity. In contrast to Giddens's notion of the body as a project of self-identity, these works imagine cosmetic practices as an active engagement with an embodied identity that emerges from the individual's interaction with and through her body.[34] The texts discussed in the latter part of this chapter celebrate states of in-betweenness and flux. They posit makeovers and transformations not as a unidirectional movement towards molar womanhood, but as part of a series of flows, processes and connections.

'Since you got your powers, all I've seen you do is change your clothes and make brussels sprouts disappear': Playful Makeovers in *Sabrina the Teenage Witch*

The vision of the teen witch as defined by process and transformation is perhaps most clearly realised in the opening credits of the ABC sitcom *Sabrina the Teenage Witch*. Airing from 1996–2003, the series plays with the concept of adolescence as a fundamentality transformative experience, with many of its episodes hinging on magical metamorphoses. Although based on the popular Archie Comics character (see Chapter 3), the sitcom is far less prescriptive than its source material, often relying on absurd humour (Sabrina, played by Melissa Joan Hart, turns a popular cheerleader into a pineapple) and gross-out gags (Sabrina gains an unrealistic amount of weight after becoming addicted to pancakes). While moving away from the rigidly hegemonic construction of adolescent femininity espoused in the original comics, much of the series' appeal resides in Sabrina's 'glamour', both in the magical sense and as it relates to fashion. During the first three seasons, the opening credits consistently position her in front of a mirror using magic to change her outfit. This sequence, which always ends with Sabrina in a new outfit, not only sums up the basic premise of the show, but it also signals the pleasure that young, predominantly female, viewers might take in Sabrina's combination of beauty and power.

In both the first episode of *Sabrina the Teenage Witch* and the 1996 television movie that preceded the series, the protagonist awakens into her powers on the morning of her sixteenth birthday. As in the earlier *Teen Witch*, the parallels between witchcraft and puberty are explicit. The television movie, like the series, sees Sabrina use her powers for the first time to give herself a makeover. In both versions, she tries out numerous possible looks, from a 1930s-style bathing beauty to a hyper-feminine 1950s girl. Sabrina appears visibly pleased with both of these possibilities, but in the next moment, her magic transforms her style yet again. This time she appears clad in goth fashion, complete with a leather jacket and heavy make-up. Where she had previously nodded approvingly at her changing looks, the goth outfit causes Sabrina to shake her head in dissatisfaction. As Moseley notes, this sequence makes clear what kinds of femininity are and are not acceptable.[35] Moreover, as Sabrina attempts to add some height, and presumably glamour, to her high heels, her magical abilities supersede her capacity to control them and the shoes grow absurdly, comically, tall. This sequence, in which her shoes cause Sabrina to stretch towards the ceiling in an *Alice in Wonderland*-fashion, gestures towards a recurring motif, one that runs throughout the entire series, whereby Sabrina is empowered to play with her identity, but is invariably punished for excess in both her behaviour and desires. Sabrina's powers are not unlimited. As a sitcom, the status quo must be maintained, and the show ensures that the characters return to their 'normal' selves at the end of each episode. Sarah Projansky and Leah R. Vande Berg even go so far as to maintain that the show is defined by 'a *tension* between feminism and containment'.[36] Sabrina may use her powers to erode boundaries associated with gender, class and culture. However, such subversive acts always take place within a heteronormative, middle-class framework whose equilibrium is invariably restored, even as the fantasy elements of the series allow for the temporary subversion of such norms. Likewise, Sabrina's desires are always carefully reined in, her more serious transgressions punished through the application of Byzantine magical rules.

While critics such as Moseley argue that Sabrina's engagement with the magical makeover motif reduces the teen witch's power to a surface-level glamour, it is possible to read such acts of self-transformation as infinitely more complex experiments with identity. Sabrina's feline familiar Salem (Nick Bakay) chastises her by observing that 'Since you got your powers, all I've seen you do is change your clothes and make brussels sprouts disappear'.[37] Yet, Sabrina's makeovers can be read as sustained attempts to explore and revise her own identity. Over the course of the series, Sabrina's ability to transform physically, as well as her power to travel in time and space, enables her to inhabit a host of different identities. Over the seven seasons of *Sabrina the Teenage Witch* the title character is transformed into a doll (Season 2, Episode 5), a 1960s teen movie starlet (Season 5, Episode 17) and a Wild West sheriff (Season 4, Episode 19). She even swaps personalities with her nemesis, the selfish cheerleader Libby, (Season 2, Episode19) and literally vanishes after imbibing too many magical diet shakes (Season 4, Episode 13). Sabrina's shifting identity is one of the most intriguing facets of the series, as she often transforms her appearance and/ or personality in a decidedly playful manner.

Although the sequences in which Sabrina is punished for excess or explicitly refuses to adopt modes of femininity that fall outside the hegemonic ideal (i.e., the goth look) might suggest her co-option into binaristic molar gender structures, I would argue that the character's engagement with the makeover paradigm suggests a move towards more playful, even subversive, metamorphoses. Certainly, Sabrina's transformations indicate an adherence to external norms of gender presentation. Yet, they can nevertheless be read as productive techniques of the self. As noted above, techniques of the self can never be fully disentangled from those of production and domination. Moreover, Foucault explains that although 'practices of the self' enable the subject to constitute itself 'in active fashion', these techniques are 'not something invented by the individual himself. They are models that he finds in his culture and are proposed, suggested, imposed upon him by his culture, his society, and his social group'.[38] The imbrication of Sabrina's transformations within broader cultural mores does not, therefore, prevent them from being productive, liberating and even occasionally subversive. Indeed, Kaja Silverman argues that playing with sartorial norms and engaging in acts of self-fashioning invariably opens up space for play. She maintains that the constant shifting of women's fashions – from the voluminous skirts of the nineteenth century to the svelte flapper style of the 1920s, from the conservative 'New Look' of the 1950s to the jeans and t-shirts of the 1990s – allows for a degree of creativity and subversion. Silverman explains that 'The endless transformations within female clothing construct female sexuality and subjectivity in ways that are at least potentially disruptive, both of gender and of the symbolic order, which is predicated upon continuity and coherence'.[39] In *Sabrina the Teenage Witch*, Sabrina uses her magic to cycle through styles associated with various occupations, historical periods and gender presentations. In the opening credits alone, she appears variously as a traditional Halloween witch, a beatnik, a soldier in camouflage, a scientist in a lab coat, a nineteenth-century lady and a masculine construction worker. None of these outfits or personas represent a real, authentic Sabrina, nor are they a final transformation, an endpoint in a teleological process of maturation. Instead, they are playful opportunities to explore new identities and possibilities.

In contrast to more conventional makeover narratives, such as Louise's transition from dowdy geek to popular cheerleader in *Teen Witch*, Sabrina's makeovers do not follow a linear pattern. She does not move from a place of unacceptable femininity to one of socially legitimate womanhood. Instead, she simply cycles through new looks and new identities, with no indication that she seeks to uncover an authentic version of herself through these metamorphoses. Sabrina's magic often sends her back in time – to the 1960s or the nineteenth-century frontier – where she is forced to adopt vintage styles to blend in with her surroundings. In other episodes, or during the mirror sequence in the opening credits, Sabrina dons a poodle skirt or a nineteenth-century bustle. Such transformations do not signal the adoption of a permanent 'retro' identity, nor do they suggest any affinity with the values of the era represented by the outfit. Instead, they merely signal a playfully postmodern engagement with past visions of femininity. As Silverman writes:

> By recontextualizing objects from earlier periods within the frame of the present, retro is able to 'reread' them in ways that maximize their radical and transformative potential – to chart the affinities, for instance, between fashions of the forties and feminism in the eighties, or between fashions of the twenties and the 'unisex look' of the late sixties.[40]

Moreover, Silverman asserts that 'Vintage clothing is also a mechanism for crossing vestimentary, sexual and historical boundaries'.[41] These styles allow the wearer to inhabit different sexed, historicised or gendered identities without committing to any fixed mode of being. In constantly shifting between potential selfhoods, Sabrina constructs a version of adolescence that is not contingent upon a unidirectional movement towards a stable adult identity. Instead, Sabrina repeatedly crosses and recrosses boundaries associated with gender and class as she conjures herself into numerous occupations, time periods and realities.

In the sixth episode of the second series, Sabrina, wondering about the inner workings of the male mind, transforms into a boy named Jack.

Her goal is to discover what her crush, Harvey (Nate Richert), does while spending time with his male friends. However, what she ultimately achieves is a destabilisation of binary modes of being, an unsettling of the molar structures that attempt to fix subjectivities according to dualistic conceptions of gender. When Sabrina first transforms into her male equivalent, she unthinkingly reaches for a bottle of perfume and is just about to spray some on herself when Salem stops her: 'Freeze! Don't squirt that perfume unless you want to be a boy who gets beaten up.'[42] Following her transformation into Jack, Sabrina becomes acutely aware that masculinity (associated with behaviours like belching, scratching, an interest in sports) is – at least under normal circumstances – carefully separated out from femininity (associated with the wearing of cosmetics, overt sexual attraction to men, crying). However, Sabrina's metamorphosis enables her to embody both of these positions at once, destabilising dualistic constructions of gender.

This episode in particular exemplifies a pattern that Projansky and Vande Berg view as characteristic of *Sabrina the Teenage Witch*: 'Any number of episodes upend heterosexuality and gender binaries, using humor and irony to suggest lesbian, gay, and transgender experiences'.[43] When the episode ends, Sabrina and her aunt Hilda (Caroline Rhea),who had morphed into a man in order to discourage an unwanted suitor, watch a football game and yell at the television set. Even after reverting to their feminine forms, both women retain aspects of their now discarded masculine personas. This conclusion not only confuses the gender binaries established earlier in the episode, but it also suggests that individual identity is multifaceted, encompassing elements of both masculinity and femininity. Other episodes also stress this complexity, as 'the series often associates traditionally masculine things with Sabrina'.[44] Significantly, she is portrayed as excelling in maths and science, even going so far as to join her all-male high school science club. At the same time, she is shown to possess numerous stereotypically feminine interests: make-up, fashion and dating. Sabrina therefore encompasses both masculine and feminine traits, shifting comfortably between these aspects of her personality.

Sabrina is afforded the freedom to play with and derive enjoyment from her powers. Her makeovers allow her to develop a selfhood that is expansive, complex and metamorphic. She repeatedly transforms herself, resisting fixed modes of being and investing herself in a number of distinct identificatory positions. Sabrina's adolescence is a site of play and experimentation: she tries out different identities, discarding what does not satisfy her and keeping what does. In contrast to *Teen Witch*'s Louise, Sabrina does not mature towards the fixed position of molar woman. She remains continuously in process and challenges dichotomous notions of subjectivity. Through her makeovers and transformations, Sabrina models a vision of 'subjectivity that is mobile and connective'.[45] Like the Deleuzian girl, she manifests and enacts the process of becoming (molecular) woman.[46] She calls into question 'the coagulations, rigidifications, and impositions required by patriarchal . . . power relations',[47] and in doing so, remakes herself as an agent of multiplicity. Encompassing masculinity and femininity, child and woman, mature and immature, Sabrina is never fixed within a single identity or final mode of being. Instead, she remains open, fluid, connective and eternally becoming.

'Loving and cruel, all at the same time': Multiplicity and Becoming in *The Craft*

Released at the same time as *Sabrina the Teenage Witch*, in a concurrence that led writer Sinead Stubbins to dub 1996 'the year of the teen witch',[48] *The Craft* is a film that explicitly deploys witchcraft as a metaphor for female adolescence. In a 2016 interview, producer Douglas Wick claimed that *The Craft* was intended to 'explore the longings, the fears and the wants of teenage girls just as they sort of come into their power – the power of their sexuality, their power in the world'.[49] The film unfolds primarily through the perspective of Sarah (Robin Tunney), an awkward outsider who moves to Los Angeles with her family following a failed suicide attempt. Uncomfortable and displaced in her new surroundings, Sarah swiftly forges an intense bond with three other social pariahs: 'white trash' goth Nancy (Fairuza Balk), shy and scarred Bonnie (Neve Campbell) and Rochelle (Rachel True), a Black girl who is subjected to relentless racist abuse by her peers. Together, the four girls discover an affinity for witchcraft and realise that by combining their powers they can command tremendous supernatural forces. Since its release in the summer of 1996, *The Craft* has been unfailingly popular with teenage girls, garnering a cult following that has seen its aesthetic imitated in music videos and fashion magazine spreads, as well as by girls themselves. Media critic and practising witch Peg Aloi has even argued that *The Craft* directly contributed to real-world explosion of adolescent interest in witchcraft and Wicca during the late 1990s and early 2000s.[50]

The Craft is a film that pays close, intimate attention to the rituals and paraphernalia of teenage girlhood. Numerous scenes linger on the secret moments of bonding shared between the four protagonists: eating junk food together at a sleepover, laughing over wine in a secluded park, gently teasing each other about crushes. Witchcraft, with its attendant texts and tinctures, is subsumed within these panoramas of adolescent girlhood: candle-laden shrines abut posters of rock stars torn from magazines, slumber parties play host to experiments in levitation, and shopping trips invariably entail a visit to the local magic store. Considering *The Craft*'s focus on the minutiae of female adolescence, it is unsurprising that as the teenage witches at the heart of the story come into their powers, their growing confidence and facility for magic is visually encoded in their dress and self-presentation. More than a superficial transformation, these aesthetic shifts also reflect a process of becoming that destabilises the boundaries between discrete identities, unsettles human/non-human binaries and charts a line of flight away from unitary identity and towards a dynamic multiplicity.

When the movie begins, the girls lack unity in their individual styles, each of which – aside from Nancy's enduring goth look – appears either dowdy or unremarkable. Sarah, the new girl, lacks the appropriate attire for her new school, not having had time to purchase a uniform. Instead, she appears on her first day wearing a dull, ill-fitting dress and a bulky sweater wrapped around her waist. Rochelle, anxious about how her race distinguishes her from her overwhelmingly white peers, is eager to fit in and wears her uniform strictly in accordance with school guidelines. Bonnie, self-conscious about her extensive bodily scarring is shrouded in a large, baggy coat. In the case of all three, their garments indicate a desire to hide, blend in or conceal aspects of themselves that they consider undesirable. When the girls embrace the craft, the other three begin to adopt elements of Nancy's goth style so that the group's coherence is underscored by their corresponding fashions. This unity is reinforced in a scene where the foursome stride in slow motion through the schoolyard. Clad in contrasting shades of black and white, the girls appear newly confident in their form-fitting blouses, short skirts, spiked-collars, repurposed rosary beads and dark make-up. As Emily Chandler explains, 'Audiences with knowledge of the codes and conventions of feminine transformation narratives will read these fashion changes as meaning that the members of the coven have become more socially powerful'.[51] However, while the girls' various makeovers – for there are many transformations over the course of the film – are in keeping with the generic conventions of teen cinema, their physical and sartorial changes also reflect their changing conceptions of self.

The gothic makeovers undertaken by Bonnie, Rochelle and Sarah not only cleave them to the domineering figure of their *de facto* leader Nancy – whose goth style is conspicuous from the very start of the film – they also enable the girls to reposition themselves in relation to the wider social order and reimagine their own identities. As Vincent B. Leitch maintains:

> Dress is, in part, frequently in large part, about cultural capital; it often serves political designs; it consorts with hegemonic norms and domination; its regulating force incites mainly conformity but some-times resistance. To adopt a style (or uniform) is to choose a socioeconomic milieu and a future.[52]

In *The Craft* the teenage protagonists utilise fashion and self-presentation to alternately integrate into the social order and to oppose it. Initially, the girls' affinity for goth-style fashions indicates an oppositional attitude to the hegemonic norms of their peer group. However, gothic fashion, which may include 'dyed hair (usually black but sometimes in bright and unusual colors, such as blue or fire engine red), black eye makeup, black lipstick, and black clothing',[53] often suggests an ambivalent engagement with normative femininity. Chandler delineates how, by 'contrasting traditionally feminine items (like corsets and skirts) with accessories (such as spiked collars) designed to communicate toughness, remoteness, and deviant forms of sexuality' gothic fashions empower women to simultaneously critique and indulge in traditional forms of femininity.[54] Similarly calling attention to gothic fashion's potential for ambivalence and multiplicity, Catherine Spooner claims that:

> Goth deliberately appropriates transgression in a variety of coded forms (focused around the taboos of sex and death) as part of its internal iconography. To enjoy a discourse of transgression, however, is not necessarily the same thing as being transgressive. These codings are frequently formulaic and repetitive, deliberately reanimating (and often revelling in) literary and cinematic cliché.[55]

In this way, gothic fashion can be both liberating and constraining, subversive and conformist, excessively and insufficiently feminine.

In as much as *The Craft*'s misfit protagonists assume identities reflective of their witchy status – a position at once hyper-feminine and inappropriately feminine – they also reconfigure their self-presentation in accordance with prevailing social norms. Bonnie and Rochelle are visually coded as outsiders from the beginning of the film. Rochelle is figured as a racial Other, her Blackness rendered highly conspicuous in the predominantly white private school she attends, while Bonnie's difference is grounded in her extensive bodily scarring. Rochelle's racial difference is repeatedly reduced to her physical appearance and her inability to attain dominant Eurocentric beauty standards. In one scene, the racism that that informs Rochelle's daily life is metonymically distilled into ridicule of her curly hair. As Rochelle dresses after swimming practice, she overhears her classmate, the blonde and popular Laura Lizzie (Christine Taylor), expressing disgust upon finding a 'pubic hair' in her brush. After loudly announcing her horror at the discovery, Laura then corrects herself, performatively revising the incident: 'Oh no wait, wait. That's just one of Rochelle's little nappy hairs.' The term 'nappy' has a complex and contentious history. Adaeze Enekwechi and Opal Moore note that nappy 'is an inside reference and joke within the African American community. Like the word "black," it was employed as a derogatory term until the revolutionary decade of the 1960s'.[56] Referring to hair that is thick, frizzy, kinky or unruly, 'nappy hair' is often understood to be in opposition to 'good hair', or hair that is fine, straight and silky in texture. 'Nappy hair' is denigrated because it is associated with Blackness and an African aesthetic, while 'good hair' is valued for its ability to approximate a white European aesthetic. Tracy Owens Patton argues that it is for this reason that under the US system of slavery, women who possessed stereotypically European features – straight or loose wavy hair, light skin – were more likely to be used as house slaves, while women with more explicitly African traits – kinky hair, darker skin – were relegated to the fields.[57] The legacy of this racist aesthetic endures into the present day, with lighter skin being viewed as more conducive to social mobility and European features framed as the apex of physical beauty. Laura Lizzie's decision to loudly and publicly mock Rochelle's hair is not an incidental piece of adolescent bullying; rather, it is an act of cruelty intertwined with a long, racist history in which African features were cast as inferior and inhuman.

When the girls begin to experiment with magic, one of the first spells they try out is the glamour, an illusion that allows the witch to change her physical features. After Sarah playfully changes both her hair and eye colour, the other three witches beg her to let them try. Significantly, Rochelle asks Sarah to 'make me blonde'. More than just a desire to experiment with her look, Rochelle's request signals her deeper awareness of the power attached to whiteness and European features. While the scene cuts there, and we never get to see Rochelle's makeover, her desire for blonde hair is emblematic of how makeovers might be used within the fictive world of *The Craft* to reconfigure one's social position. Rochelle is painfully aware of the social capital associated with blonde hair and European features. This is also in keeping with the often-troubling role of the makeover paradigm in post-feminist discourse, as it is a narrative convention frequently bound up with misogynistic, classist, ablest and racist ideals. After all, fictional versions of the makeover paradigm tend to portray working-class women and women of colour being brought in line with hegemonic (white, middle-class, able-bodied) constructions of femininity.

In contrast to Rochelle's off-screen transformation, Bonnie is more explicit in her use of the glamour as a means of transforming her social role. When the film begins, we are told that Bonnie has scars covering her back and shoulders. Initially, her scars are not seen by the viewer, but they do seem to be the subject of schoolyard rumour, as Chris (Skeet Ulrich) informs Sarah on her first day that Bonnie 'has these weird scars all over her body'. Bonnie's scars construct her as different, and her body is understood as inferior or deviant by virtue of its diversion from the norm. Bonnie's disfigurement, and the social stigma it accrues, echoes Rosemarie Garland-Thomson's claim that 'Corporal departures from dominant expectations never go uninterpreted or unpunished, and conformities are almost always rewarded'.[58] Bonnie is conspicuous. Her body attracts rumour, speculation and gossip, its Otherness pushing her corporeality into the public domain. For this reason, Bonnie hides behind baggy clothing, concealing her body from the gaze of others. It is also due to this uncomfortable visibility that Bonnie uses her powers to restore her body to a state of 'normality' by removing her disfiguring scars.

When Bonnie's spell is successful and her scars are miraculously stripped away in the course of an ordinarily painful medical procedure, she follows Rochelle and Sarah by adopting a dramatic new look. She wears short skirts and lowcut tops intended to reveal her new, blemish-free body. Her personality also changes, and she becomes infinitely more confident. She is flirtatious and explicitly sexual in her dealings with men. Moreover, Bonnie's new promiscuous persona is an identity that she adopts with pleasure. Her desire fuels her transformation. Having previously been marginalised due to her disfigurement and inability to embody normative femininity, Bonnie is aware of the social power embedded in female beauty and sexuality. Banishing her scars, Bonnie self-consciously adopts a confident, overtly sexual and feminine persona. When she returns to school for the first time without her scars, Bonnie responds to being chastised for her tardiness with a flippant 'Sorry, my pedicure ran late'. Her reply, although sarcastic in tone, is self-conscious in its allusion to typically feminine beauty treatments. Without her disfigurement, Bonnie can inhabit and embrace such markers of conventional femininity. Bonnie here dons a masque of excessive femininity and uses it to her advantage. Her actions and appearance do not reveal a true self uncovered by her magical makeover; rather, they speak to a new, temporary, identity that she slips into and uses as powerful guise. Indeed, Bonnie moves back and forth between her old shy, awkward self and her new, highly sexual, persona. Neither of these identities are stable, nor do they seem to reflect any inherent truth about who Bonnie might be. They are simply temporary configurations of identity that enable Bonnie to move through and across social boundaries or hierarchies.

In a similar vein, Nancy also cycles through a host of different identities. Although initially appearing as the dominant personality – after all, it is her goth look that the other girls imitate – she too appropriates numerous diverse guises over the course of the film. Nancy first appears as a disaffected working-class teenager. Her anger and frustration at her socio-economic marginality and the abuse she endures at the hands of her stepfather are apparent in both her oppositional attitude and her manner of dress. Clad primarily in black, with raven hair and pallid make-up, Nancy is prone to wearing leather jackets, heavy boots and spiked collars. Her style reflects her hostility towards the world around her. Later, when she begins to bond with her sister witches, she wears more toned-down, diaphanous clothing that suggests an affinity with both her coven and the natural world. After her spells start to work and her stepfather is magically dispatched, Nancy and her mother inherit a large sum of money through his life insurance policy. They move from their decrepit trailer into a penthouse apartment in a large, light-filled skyscraper. Here, again, Nancy's look changes. Her clothes, though still dark, are now tailored, form-fitting and stylish. During the film's climax, Nancy invokes the spirit of the film's fictional deity Manon and is imbued with his power. Again, her style changes to reflect her new identity as a powerful witch, and she wears pointy-toed black boots and long black dresses.

Despite these sartorial transformations, Nancy's style remains essentially gothic, her palate primarily black. However, as she moves through different identificatory positions – white-trash waif, earthy witch, wealthy young woman, powerful sorceress – facets of the style metamorphosise to reflect Nancy's shifting persona. The mutability of her core gothic aesthetic accords with the essential playfulness of gothic fashion. Richard Davenport-Hines observes that:

> Goths reject the bourgeois sense of human identity as a serious business, stable, abiding and continuous, requiring the assertion of one true cohesive inner self as proof of health and good citizenry. Instead, goths celebrate human identity as improvised performance, discontinuous and incessantly re-devised by stylised acts.[59]

Nancy's changing yet fundamentally gothic style suggests a rejection of the notion that identity should be stable and continuous. Rather, she inhabits a series of diverse personae: the rebellious teen, the svelte socialite and the powerful witch. While each of these identities mirrors elements of Nancy's personality, none of them reflect an essential or static selfhood. Through her repeated makeovers, Nancy constructs and reconstructs her body as a site of multivalent meaning.

As the film progresses Nancy's transformations become increasingly disturbing, suggesting that such identificatory play should not be unlimited. When Sarah comes to her sister witches, dishevelled and bruised after her love interest Chris attempts to rape her, Nancy responds furiously. She follows Chris to a party and tries to seduce him. He rebuffs her advances, so Nancy employs a glamour to transform her features into Sarah's. Convinced that Nancy is Sarah, Chris embraces her, and they have sex. While this scene evokes troubling questions about consent and deception, it also constitutes an intriguing inversion of gender dynamics, as Nancy usurps Chris's (stereotypically male) role as the sexual aggressor. Just as Nancy's earlier makeover signified her capacity to cross class boundaries – moving from her trailer to a penthouse, swapping chaotic layers of fabric for streamlined tailoring – this glamour enables her to cross gender lines. Nancy's aggressive and forceful behaviour is disturbing both because it negates Chris's capacity to consent and because Nancy's abuse of power places her in a dominant, masculine position.

That such violence emerges from Nancy's metamorphic abilities ultimately renders the makeover motif disturbing. Her shapeshifting powers become troublesome and even unsettling, as in the scene where Sarah walks in to find Nancy – now her double – sexually assaulting the drunken Chris. It is for this reason that Nancy must be destroyed at the end of the film. Her transformations go too far, and her power becomes too much. Indeed, the metamorphoses enacted by Bonnie, Rochelle and especially Nancy are framed as disturbing not only because they threaten social boundaries, but also because of their instability. While *The Craft* draws on the ubiquitous teen movie trope of the feminine makeover, it rejects the finality ordinarily associated with such transformations. In hegemonic texts like *Teen Witch*, makeovers are framed as facilitating self-discovery, the excavation of the true self. They also tend to pivot on the 'recuperation of alienated characters, usually through clothing, in order to become socially acceptable in the eyes of the peer group'.[60] In *The Craft* such transformations are never final or fixed. Instead, they are multiple, continuous and unstable.

Nancy's transformations, in particular, go beyond the aesthetic and even extend into the non-human world. Not only does she assume Sarah's appearance, but she also merges with the deity Manon. She takes him into her and adopts his preternatural abilities: she walks on water and causes whales to beach themselves on the seashore. Later, when Sarah and Nancy engage in a magical battle, Sarah transforms Nancy – through a glamour – so that her fingers and hair become writhing snakes. Medusa-like, Nancy represents a transitional state between human and animal, yet she also inhabits a state somewhere between her own identity and Sarah's. *The Craft* repeatedly stresses that snakes are a source of fear for Sarah. She even tells the other girls that, prior to her suicide attempt, she hallucinated seething masses of snakes. Nancy's transformation suggests that on some level she has adopted both Sarah's phobia and facets of her identity. Her identificatory instability therefore echoes the previously discussed notion of becoming as an ongoing process of movement and flux.

In contrast to *Teen Witch*'s Louise, who effects a linear movement towards a static, rigidly delineated molar womanhood, Nancy's transformations – crossing the divide between seemingly distinct bodies – enable her to move towards a molecular womanhood, a becoming-woman that empowers her to pass beyond unitary conceptions of identity and subjectivity. Nancy frees up unexpected lines of flight, '"liberating" multiplicities, corporeal and otherwise, that identity subsumes under the one'.[61] Nancy not only shifts between class affiliations and gender roles, but she also moves between human and inhuman, mortal and divine, woman and animal. Early in the film, magic is described by an older witch named Lirio (Assumpta Serna) as being 'neither black, nor white – it's both because nature is both. Loving and cruel, all at the same time'. Echoing the multiplicity of magic and the natural world, Nancy is multiple and constantly changing: she is good and evil, loving and cruel, all the same time.

Nancy's multiplicity also brings her in line with another Deleuzian concept: the 'schizo' or 'schizoid subjectivity'. The schizo is the subject 'already fractured', a complex entity opposed to the ordered, explicable self of Freudian psychoanalysis.[62] A literal, and simplistic, connection between Nancy and the schizo subject could be applied to *The Craft*'s closing scene where we see Nancy strapped to a hospital bed, screaming that she can fly. Viewers are encouraged to read this scene as a punishment where Nancy is, in Spooner's words, 'stripped of her Goth glamour and transported to another kind of Gothic scenario altogether'.[63] However, Deleuze and Guattari caution throughout their work that we should avoid conflating schizophrenia, a real and traumatic mental illness, with the philosophical schizoid subject.[64] For them, the schizo is not a romantic figuration of clinical illness, but instead, a term that describes the:

> free man, irresponsible, solitary, and joyous, finally able to say and do something simple in his own name, without asking permission, a desire lacking nothing, a flux that overcomes barriers and codes, a name that no longer designates any ego whatever.[65]

Nancy, then, does not embody the schizo because her final moments onscreen suggest madness, but because those final moments find her still in a state of multiplicity. She overcomes barriers and codes, shattering binaries as she becomes something entirely new. She is at once free and imprisoned, powerful and powerless. Her claims of flight bring the film full circle, as the opening credits played out over a disembodied camera floating through a blue and cloudy sky. Nancy's proclamation that she is 'flying' even as she lies in hospital bed recalls this opening sequence and suggests that the witch's confinement may not be as final or as complete as it appears; she may still be caught in the process of becoming.[66] After all, 'becoming' is understood by Deleuze and Guattari as a 'process of osmosis (not metaphor) with de-anthropologized and de-identitized entities – women, infants, animals, foreigners, the insane – in order to resist the dominant mode of representation represented by any majority'.[67] Consequently, the final shot of Nancy hews closely to this understanding of becoming as a move towards minority, de-identitised entities. Over the course of the film, Nancy has moved towards the position of woman and animal, and now, lying in her hospital bed, she enacts a movement towards insanity. Nancy, then, is never confined to a single monolithic identity. She remains multiple and everchanging to the end.

'I'm cookie dough . . . I'm not done baking': Transformation and Becoming in *Buffy the Vampire Slayer*

Although states of becoming manifest in *The Craft* as threatening disso-lutions of identificatory categories, *Buffy the Vampire Slayer* – a series that went into production in the same year that *The Craft* was released – rep-resents the instability of becoming as a site of generative, though poten-tially limited, transformation. Airing originally on the youth-orientated WB network, *Buffy* is preoccupied with transformation and change. Over the course of the show's seven-season run, characters morph from human to demon and back again. Other characters are turned into monsters and animals or rendered incorporeal. As a show about teenagers and young adults, *Buffy*'s protagonists also undergo more mundane transformations as part of the process of growing up. Significantly, the series suggests that this transformative process is endless and ongoing. In the final episode of the series, the titular vampire slayer (Sarah Michelle Gellar) explains to a former lover that even at what should be the end of her journey, she is still becoming:

> I'm cookie dough . . . I'm not done baking. I'm not finished *becoming* whoever the hell it is I'm gonna turn out to be. I make it through this, and the next thing, and the next thing, and maybe one day, I turn around and realize I'm ready. I'm cookies.[68]

Buffy the Vampire Slayer can be understood as a show that resists notions of identificatory stability. Its characters exist in a state of flux. Buffy's discus-sion of her own ongoing metamorphosis is but one example of a selfhood that is constantly shifting. Indeed, while the 'cookie dough' analogy might stand as the show's most explicit articulation of its thematic concern with the instability of self, the rhizomatic identity in flight is perhaps most fully embodied in the character of the adolescent witch Willow Rosenberg (Aly-son Hannigan).

Willow is the character who transforms in the most dynamic and exciting ways. She consistently embarks on new lines of flight, new becomings, while remaining open to multiple identities at the same time. Jes Battis claims that while all of *Buffy*'s characters exist within a state of evolution, Willow's 'growing pains are of particular importance, for they identify her as a hybrid site upon which several of the show's most resounding ambivalences converge, overlap and shadow each other'.[69] Willow not only embraces magic as a conduit for power and self-expression, but, as the seasons progress, she occupies a host of distinct identificatory categories. Moving from shy high school 'geek' to trainee witch, from empowered sorceress to dark avenger, Willow regularly makes herself over in accordance with her fluctuating selfhood. Like the four witches at the centre of *The Craft*, Willow's mutability is expressed through the interlinking of witchcraft and sartorial self-fashioning. Willow, however, diverges from the model of adolescent witchcraft portrayed in *The Craft* in that while her fluidity is occasionally portrayed as dangerous or disturbing, it is also presented as a generative process that evokes new possibilities and productive becomings.

Willow first encounters witchcraft during the season 1 episode 'Witch'. Yet, her engagement with the craft is minimal, as the episode's titular 'witch' is framed as a villain and swiftly dispatched before the closing credits. It is not until the second season, in a two-part episode, appropriately entitled 'Becoming', that Willow begins her initiation into witchcraft. Her initial dalliances with magic come about when she discovers that, due to her pre-established computer skills, she is the only person capable of translating an ancient Romanian spell that will restore the soul of Buffy's vampire lover, Angel (David Boreanaz). Willow's initial proclivity for magic is linked to her role as a 'science geek': she uses a software program to translate a spell, she regularly carries out rituals in the school science lab and later explains that chemistry is 'like witchcraft, but with less newt'.[70] Willow's capacity to shift seamlessly between the ostensibly distinct worlds of science and magic, alongside her insights on the relationship between the two disciplines, harkens back to an early modern world view in which natural philosophy and emerging medical sciences were often deployed to explain the existence of witchcraft. At the same time, Willow's dual affinity for witchcraft and science serves as a bridge between her shifting identities, connecting these apparently distinct selves and allowing her to inhabit diverse positions simultaneously.

In Willow's earliest appearances, during the first and second seasons of *Buffy*, she is presented as academically minded, shy and lacking in confidence. When we first encounter her:

> Willow is conventionally gendered in most dimensions of her character: She is an excellent student, nonassertive, and concerned with the feelings and perspectives of others. She is the moral voice of the group, although she stutters and stammers much of her dialogue. Her mode of dress and grooming is more childlike than any of the teen characters.[71]

In her early appearances, Willow wears oversized pinafore dresses with crisp white blouses, baggy dungarees and brightly coloured, often fuzzy, sweaters adorned with saccharine images of flowers, love-hearts or smiley faces. Her hair is long, straight and always parted in the middle. Essentially, Willow dresses and behaves like a little girl. Yet, as Deleuze and Guattari are careful to point out, the little girl is an eternally mobile figure, capable of passing between and unsettling binaries. She is multiple, incorporating a plethora of identities, sexes and genders, what Deleuze and Guattari term '*n* sexes'.[72] Once she begins to practise witchcraft, this multiplicity becomes increasingly apparent as her physical appearance starts to change in line with each new subjectivity she inhabits. By the third season, her baggy dungarees and fluffy sweaters are interspersed with more stream-lined outfits, occasionally featuring visual references to the occult. In episode 19 of season 3, Willow wears a figure-hugging velvet dress emblazoned with a celestial pattern, an outfit that suggests a growing comfort with both her burgeoning womanhood and her increasing power as a witch. By season 4, when Willow and her friends start college, her look changes yet again: her red hair is brighter and styled in a short, spikey cut; she also wears long skirts and bold patterns suggestive of a New-Age aesthetic.

Willow's changing style and its connection to her increasing self-confidence at first seems to reflect the conventional makeover narrative found in many popular teen films and television programmes. According to Sarah Gilligan, the makeover narrative is 'structured around three key components – namely the make-under, the makeover, and the final revelation/affirmation'.[73] Gilligan explains that this narrative 'implies that through the processes of consumption and feminization, the female protagonist will achieve social mobility, popularity, and the "prize" of (a new or rekindled) heterosexual romance'.[74] Essentially, the standard makeover narrative suggests a move towards molar womanhood, a space where identities are fixed and binaries upheld. A superficial reading of Willow's arc would suggest that her character hews closely to this narrative template. Like *Teen Witch*'s Louise, Willow comes into her powers as an adolescent, and as her proficiency with witchcraft grows, she becomes more confident, both socially and sexually. However, rather than enacting a linear transformation, moving from frumpy geek to confident, sexual woman, Willow moves back and forth across this spectrum. She never fully sheds her early girlish persona, rather she merely incorporates it into the complex, multi-faceted individual that she is becoming.

In the second and third seasons of *Buffy*, Willow undergoes makeovers that reconfigure her as more confident, sexualised versions of herself. In the season 2 episode 'Halloween', Buffy gives Willow a sexy, feminine makeover. At first Willow is uncomfortable with the makeover and hides her revealing outfit beneath an oversized ghost costume. When she is later forced to reveal her sexy outfit, she quickly moves beyond her discomfort, becoming confident and even assertive. At the end of the episode, Willow discards the ghost costume and strides away confidently in her short skirt and heels. This, however, does not mean that Willow has permanently advanced to a more dominant, sexualised identity. In the next episode, she returns to her fuzzy sweaters. Yet, some of the confidence she gained whilst made-over remains, informing her behaviour and leaving her with a stronger sense of self. Similarly, in the season 3 episode 'Doppelgangland', Willow briefly assumes the appearance of her vampire double, a leather-clad, 'kinda gay' villain whom she accidently conjures from an alternate dimension. Again, Willow takes part in a makeover that renders her more sexual and assertive, only to discard her new look at the end of the episode. Echoing 'Halloween', Willow nevertheless retains some of the confidence she accrued while masquerading as her own doppelganger.

Willow does not undergo a single makeover designed to correct her 'inadequate' femininity, nor do any of her transformations propel her, irrevocably, across the boundary that separates girl from woman. Rather, Willow occupies different modes of femininity over the course of the series, learning from them and gaining new powers and skills. Hers is not a teleological progression from dowdy, overly intellectual girlchild to sexual, confident woman. Instead, Willow's many physical transformations enable her to inhabit multiple, seemingly contradictory, identificatory categories. Likewise, Willow's transformations are rarely, if ever, permanent.

Her varying metamorphoses instead 'normalize the non-linear, reversible transition from girl to woman/woman to girl'.[75] Significantly, she rarely arrives at any single, unified identity, but instead moves between them. Battis observes that:

> Throughout the course of seven seasons, Willow has occupied many personas: shy academic; computer expert; budding witch ('budding' being a signifier commonly ascribed to Willow's magical studies, which holds all kinds of double-voiced meaning when connected to her name) . . . ingénue; agent of the apocalypse; and, finally, a guilt-stricken 'reformed' addict, whose self-imposed embargo on magic is all that prevents her from reverting to primal destruction once again.[76]

However, Willow is constantly portrayed as caught within the vicissitudes of major transformation.

Her primary identity as a geeky computer expert – the reliable, smart member of the group whose main contribution is her ability to hack into an array of ill-defined databases – holds firm only until late in season 2 when she begins to study witchcraft. During her first successful attempt at spellcasting, carried out in desperation from a hospital bed, Willow is almost consumed by the power she wields: her shy, uncertain personality is evacuated and she is taken over by something infinitely more powerful. To the surprise of her friends, who have come to assist her with the ritual, her body becomes rigid and she speaks confidently in a foreign language that should be alien to her. In practising magic, she takes on a new identity. Yet, Willow only touches upon this new potential selfhood; she never actually arrives at the identity of a fully fledged witch. The next time we encounter Willow, she has largely resumed her previous role in the group, and she is once again the shy computer nerd. A few episodes later, when catching up with Buffy after a summer apart, she explains to her friend that her life has become more complex during the intervening months because she is studying witchcraft and dating a boy. The lexical proximity of these statements suggests an analogue between exploring witchcraft and Willow's tentative entrance into her first romantic relationship, as if both were adolescent rites of passage. Later, Willow informs Buffy that 'I'm not a full-fledged witch. That takes years!'.[77] Here, Willow stresses her transitional nature. She is not a witch. That is not an identity that she fully and firmly occupies. Rather, she is caught in the process of *becoming* a witch.

Subsequent episodes also allude to Willow's status as a witch in training whose powers resist her attempts to control them. In the season 4 episode 'Fear Itself', Buffy tells Willow that her spells are only 'fifty-fifty' at best.[78] Willow's inexperience as a witch is regularly emphasised throughout the first few seasons of *Buffy*. Moreover, it is repeatedly linked to Willow's maturation, a process in which she is continuously engaged in but never fully completes. In season 4, Willow begins to explore her sexuality more fully. Having previously only engaged in romantic relationships with men, she falls in love with fellow witch Tara (Amber Benson) during her freshman year of college. The budding relationship between the women and Willow's increasing comfort with her own queerness is repeatedly framed in the context of her growing power as a witch. At one point, Tara tells Willow that she 'couldn't stop thinking about that last spell we did all day',[79] a statement that explicitly conflates magic and sex. A few episodes later, Willow's and Tara's attempt to cast a spell to reach the nether realm is filmed and performed as though it were sex scene.[80] As the ritual reaches its zenith Willow begins to breathe heavily and the non-diegetic score swells. When the spell ends, Willow falls backwards, gasping in ecstasy. The parallels drawn between Willow's developing identity as a witch and her burgeoning sexuality again suggest that she exists in a state of becoming. She is moving towards adult womanhood, just as she is straining towards an identity as a fully fledged witch, but she never fully occupies either position.

Furthermore, the womanhood she moves towards is not bounded or molar. It is molecular womanhood, defined by openness and change. Willow's identity remains in flux, rhizomatic and restless, throughout the remainder of the series. Battis observes that the unstable nature of Willow's selfhood is made manifest during an erotic dream sequence in the season 4 episode 'Restless'.[81] In this scene, Willow imagines herself painting Sappho's poem 'Aphrodite Ode' in Greek letters on Tara's naked body while they discuss naming their recently adopted kitten.[82] When Tara laments that the tiny cat does not yet have a name, Willow explains that this is because 'she's not all grown yet'.[83] The kitten is still maturing, still becoming a cat, and Willow is uncomfortable with hemming the creature in by labelling it and assigning it a definitive identity. Willow's claim that the cat cannot be named due to her not being fully grown, 'only further emphasizes her lack of positioning. Willow, unlike Tara, is not all grown yet. Her corporeality is as fluid as her dream world'.[84] In contrast to Tara, who has practised the craft since childhood and is an accomplished witch, Willow is still in the midst of becoming a witch and of becoming a woman.

As the seasons progress, it becomes clear that Willow's becoming is an ongoing process, it is an endless process of destabilisation, connection and transformation. There is no final position or state of being at which Willow will finally arrive because that would entail being frozen into a molar identity. She is forever in flux, shifting between identities that she never fully claims as her own. The thematic preoccupation with Willow's multiple, ceaselessly transforming selfhood reaches its apex at the end of season 6 where, after witnessing Tara's accidental death at the hands of a trio of human villains, she embarks on a quest for vengeance. In these climactic episodes, Willow moves between myriad possible identities: powerful avenger, agent of apocalyptic chaos, the living incarnation of dark magic and the shy, loving Willow we met in the first season. Willow touches upon all these identities, but she never settles on any of them. In numerous scenes she manages to occupy a number of these distinct positions at once, while also, momentarily, claiming a host of other identities, ostensibly removed from her own. In the episode 'Villains', Willow has a brief conversation with Warren (Adam Busch), the man who shot Tara. As he tries to reason with her, Willow looks at him with disinterest and mutters 'Bored now', before skinning him alive.[85] Significantly, the phrase 'Bored now' was also uttered by Willow's vampire double in the season 3 episodes 'The Wish' and 'Doppelgangland'. By employing her doppelganger's catchphrase Willow briefly encroaches upon her identity. Likewise, in the follow-up episode, 'Two to Go', Willow stakes a claim to Buffy's identity. Using magic to imbue herself with preternatural strength, Willow engages in a physical fight with Buffy, boasting that 'Six years as a sideman; now I get to be the slayer'.[86] In these moments, Willow's proximity to others allows her to absorb facets of their identities and incorporate them into her own process of becoming.

Yet, in as much as Willow's multiplicity is portrayed as dangerous and destructive in these episodes, her capacity to contain multiple, often contradictory selves is also what saves both Willow and her friends in the season finale, 'Grave'. Just as Willow is about to unleash apocalyptic destruction on the world, her childhood friend Xander (Nicholas Brendon) pleads with her and reminds her of his love for her. He explains that despite her many acts of violence, he still cares for her. Although Willow now seeks to disavow her previous selfhood, telling Xander 'Don't call me that' when he addresses her by name,[87] her friend reminds her of her ability to occupy numerous identity positions at once. Xander relays to Willow a story from their childhood: 'the first day of kindergarten you cried because you broke the yellow crayon, and you were too afraid to tell anyone.' In recalling this event, Xander links the shy child that Willow was to the furious dark-haired witch whose overabundance of siphoned power has been etched, in dark veins, on her face: 'But the thing is, yeah, I love you. I love crayon-breaky Willow and I love scary-veiny Willow.' As Battis notes, Xander succinctly encapsulates Willow's capacity to 'reconcile the oppositional binaries of her character', which he 'so aptly terms as "crayon-breaky Willow" and "scary-veiny Willow?"':[88] 'It is thus made clear that "bad" Willow is shaped and informed by "good" Willow, and vice versa. Fittingly, then, Willow is not a static body, but rather a system of good and evil, capable of being dominated by either force.'[89] Willow, in her endless becomings, collapses binaries and unsettles dualistic modes of thought that seek to separate out identities, bodies and moral positions. She contains within her a host of distinct identificatory possibilities and positions, shifting between them without ever resting in any one potential self.

According to Battis one of the most intriguing facets of *Buffy the Vampire Slayer* is the fact that the show's characters 'change, evolve, and most often, flow between varying identities'.[90] Although all the show's characters evolve over the course of its seven seasons – by the final episode not one of them is recognisable as their season 1 persona – Willow's identity is especially fluid. The metamorphic power of the witch, her capacity to take flight and alter her corporeal form at will, empowers Willow, perhaps more than any other character, to engage in transformative, dynamic, and occasionally disruptive, acts of becoming. Although Willow's identificatory instability is not quite as destructive as Nancy's, the series does maintain a certain degree of ambivalence regarding her multivalent selfhood. Consequently, while Xander saves Willow (and the world) by appealing to the witch's capacity to contain both good and evil, destruction and healing, hate and love, in other episodes *Buffy* does attempt to rein in Willow's expansive selfhood. In the latter part of the series, after her failed attempt to bring about the apocalypse, Willow and her friends worry about the possibility that she might once again lose control. In season 7, Willow frets that if she uses magic, even for benevolent purposes, she will be consumed by the power that she wields. In the penultimate episode of *Buffy*, Willow worries that if she attempts to cast a particularly challenging spell, she might 'change, and then it's all black hair and veins and lightening bolts'.[91] Willow fears that the darker facets of her identity, her capacity for destruction, might become dominant if she relinquishes control, even momentarily.

Considering the parallels drawn throughout the series between Willow's sexuality and her magical abilities, the show also attempts to confine and contain Willow's sexuality in several significant ways. In the season 7 episode 'Touched', Willow confesses to her new love interest, Kennedy (Iyari Limon), that if they were to sleep together, she might once again lose control. This exchange implies that if Willow were to give in to sexual pleasure, she might also be tempted by the excesses of magic. Yet, when she does finally sleep with Kennedy, her loss of strict control is liberating and facilitates her realisation that she might be able to utilise magic without being consumed by it. Indeed, in the last episode, Willow does wield powerful magical forces to aid her friends in their final battle. When she performs the spell, she changes, but this time she is engulfed in a brilliant light and her hair momentarily turns white. Kennedy, who is with her throughout the spell, watches in awe and states, 'You're a goddess'.[92] Willow does not, however, retain this divine identity – it is merely one of the many selfhoods she touches upon – and is soon returned to her every-day, awkward persona.

Buffy the Vampire Slayer evinces a dual ambivalence about Willow's powers and her sexuality. Her magical abilities are awesome but always threatening to slip beyond her capacity to control them. The series simultaneously desires the spectacular force of Willow's magic and strains to confine it. In a similar manner, the show and its characters support Willow's queerness and attempt to contain it. Although Willow's friends are portrayed as accepting of her relationships with women, with the series being viewed as progressive within the context of early 2000s popular television, there is also a clear textual desire to hem in, or confine, Willow's sexuality to a single, stable category. In the first three seasons of *Buffy*, Willow is involved in a number of meaningful relationships with men. She has a long-term relationship with her high school boyfriend Oz (Seth Green) and a brief affair with her best friend Xander, whom she had been in love with since childhood. However, once she commences her relationship with Tara, Willow begins to identify as gay. In one season 5 episode, Willow responds to another character's fear that Willow will steal her boyfriend with a curt, 'Hello? Gay now'.[93] The temporal nature of this comment, 'Gay *now*', suggests that there was a time when Willow was straight, but since then, she has simply shifted to another, monolithic sexual category. As Ana Carolina De Barros argues, Willow's effusive 'Gay now' constitutes a clear instance of bisexual erasure: 'This form of bisexual erasure also appears in queer theory and media studies, where both potentially and explicitly bisexual people and characters are referred to as "gay" or "lesbian"'.[94] Em McAvan observes a similarly problematic desire to contain Willow's sexual identity, noting how her apparent movement from the category of straight to the category of gay effaces much of the character's complexity.[95]

Buffy's need to classify Willow's sexuality as either gay or straight also represents a need to contain Willow's metamorphic selfhood, to assign her an identificatory category through which she can be understood and interpolated. In actuality, Willow's sexuality is far more complex than this. In the season 5 premiere, 'Buffy vs. Dracula', Willow explicitly refers to the legendary vampire as 'sexy', while in the season 7 episode 'Him', a male football player in an enchanted letterman jacket attracts Willow's attention as well as that of the other female characters. In this way, Willow's sexuality is far more nuanced than the gay/straight binary established by the show. Despite the show's myriad attempts to remind us that Willow is 'Gay now', the division refuses to hold, as Willow repeatedly flows between sexual and identificatory positions. This fluidity is, of course, in keeping with Willow's pre-established role as an avatar of becoming and metamorphosis. She is a dynamic, restless and eternally in flux, and while this instability opens Willow up to new possibilities, it also unsettles her friends, and indeed the audience, through its potential for chaotic disruption.

Yet, if we look at Willow's mobility – her flights between natural and supernatural, good and evil, gay and straight – through the lens of the Deleuzian becoming, it ultimately presents itself as a liberating movement. Becoming destabilises 'binary machines' like masculine and feminine, opening up space for 'more amorphous forms of sexuality'.[96] Certainly, Willow undermines these 'binary machines'. She moves across existential categories, desiring both men and women, and in one instance, occupying a masculine subject position when she takes the form of a man that she had killed in a previous episode.[97] Likewise, McAvan suggests that Willow's sexuality is indeed best read in terms of the Deleuzian becoming:

> Rather than simply oscillating between a straight/lesbian binary, to register the appearance of bisexuality in *Buffy* as a supplemental excess is to begin to think through sexuality as transitive, as 'becoming' (to steal a phrase from Deleuze and Guattari) rather than being.[98]

Just as Willow never fully settles into the identity of the witch – she is never fully fledged, always in training, always learning – her sexuality is also part of a fluid identity, one that shifts between and touches on a diverse range of positions without ever definitively occupying any one role. Yet, for as much as this mutability is empowering, dismantling binary conceptions of identity, subjectivity and sexuality, it also causes immense anxiety both diegetically and amongst the show's creators. The language used by Willow and her friends, to discuss both her magic and sexuality betrays a desire to control and rein in these facets of her identity. She is labelled, and labels herself, as gay once she falls in love with Tara. Her sexuality is, at least linguistically, reduced from dangerous multiplicity to a safer singularity. Concomitantly, Willow and her friends regularly express anxiety about the excessive nature of her powers, their ability to propel her beyond the Willow they know and towards a selfhood that is infinitely more numinous and threatening.

Conclusion

Although emerging out of a post-feminist sensibility in which self-transformation was regularly bound up with bodily surveillance, consumerism and notions of individual empowerment, teen witch texts that engage with the makeover paradigm approach this motif in a variety of complex ways. Works like *Teen Witch*, hegemonic texts that view the makeover as a path towards rigidly defined mature womanhood, frame these transformations as linear processes that lock the individual into static molar identities, reflective of social norms and values. Conversely, more playful, even subversive, texts such as *Sabrina the Teenage Witch*, *The Craft* and *Buffy the Vampire Slayer* present makeovers and metamorphoses as part of rhizomatic, reversible movement between girl and woman. In these works, teen witches are enabled to inhabit a range of identities, moving back and forth between various positions in a manner that allows them to destabilise boundaries associated with class, gender, sexuality and subjectivity. Although *Sabrina*, *The Craft* and *Buffy* present the teen witch's powers of transformation as limited – they are often framed as destructive or reined in by the text's commitment to clearly defined modes of being – such texts do not imagine transformation, embodied in the makeover, as a unidirectional movement towards a final, fixed identity. Rather, they imagine makeovers as becomings that enable characters to move towards and touch upon new identities without ever becoming calcified within a single, bounded mode of being.

5

'How could there not be a choice?'

Agency and Power in Fourth-Wave Teen Witch Texts[1]

IN THE PREVIOUS chapter, I discussed one of the key characteristics of the teenage witch: her capacity for transformation, shapeshifting and metamorphosis. The present chapter continues this thematic focus through a consideration of agency and power as they are represented in post-millennial teen witch texts. Historically, witches have had a fraught relationship with agency because of the centrality of the Devil's pact – the exchange of one's soul for supernatural powers – to early modern witch trials. Although the pact has been alternately interpreted as a product of credulity, coercion and even 'heartfelt' consent,[2] it remains a narrative and historical trope around which myriad questions about agency, power and autonomy have accrued. Moreover, with the emergence of fourth-wave feminism, the Devil's pact and the related concept of *choosing* witchcraft have been reappropriated as empowering narrative conceits.

In the pages that follow, I explore a number of texts produced during the 2010s that feature the Devil's pact. These include Archie Comic's *The Chilling Adventures of Sabrina* (2014) and its Netflix adaptation of the same name (2018–20), as well as the 2015 film *The Witch*. However, I also explore other works – the television series *American Horror Story: Coven* (2013–14) and Afia Atakora's novel *Conjure Women* (2020) – where the pact is absent, but questions of agency and power nevertheless remain central. In keeping with the theoretical framework utilised throughout this book, I employ the theories of Michel Foucault and new materialist thinkers such as Karen Barad to illuminate power and agency not as individual attributes but as relational networks. Likewise, my discussion of agency includes not only human agencies but more-than-human agencies, extending the concept to environmental objects, bodies and matter in general.

I begin with a discussion of active materiality and agentic bodily matter in *American Horror Story: Coven* and *The Chilling Adventures of Sabrina*. I explore how their unruly pubertal bodies force the young witches at the heart of these texts to reconceptualise their corporeality, transforming their vision of the body from a silent, passive object into a dynamic, univocal event. I also analyse how the protagonists in these texts enact agency through intra-actions with other materials and discourses, as well as through the performance of agential cuts that 'hold together the disparate' to form temporary stabilisations, or boundaries, of phenomena.[3] I then move on to explore the Devil's pact in greater detail and discuss its centrality in *The Witch*. Utilising Foucault's work on witchcraft and power, I illuminate how the pact not only restructures prevailing networks of power and agency, but also enables the film's protagonist to assume the role of what Deleuze and Guattari term the 'sorcerer', a figure capable of discerning unexpected connections between organisms and uncovering a productive continuity of materiality.

In the final part of this chapter, I argue that while teen witch texts of the fourth wave create a space where white teenage witches can enact agency, resist power and unsettle binary dualisms, Black teen witches are rarely afforded this kind of freedom. Indeed, the Black witches who appear in *American Horror Story: Coven* and the *Chilling Adventures* television series are defined by their difference from normative white identities. Moreover, where their white counterparts are free to embark on generative becomings that allow them to explode regressive forms of mind/body dualism, Black teenage witches remain bound to corporealities that are objectified and rendered mute. I close this chapter with an exploration of one of the few texts that allows a Black teen witch to navigate systems of power and agency in a meaningful way: *Conjure Women*. In my analysis of this text, I argue that the novel creates an imaginative space where witches of colour can enact agency, resist oppressive power and inhabit complex bodies whose agentic capacities refuse objectification.

Positioning Power and Agency in Fourth-Wave Feminism

The four texts explored in this chapter – *American Horror Story: Coven*, *The Chilling Adventures of Sabrina*, *The Witch* and *Conjure Women* – were all produced during a seven-year period between 2013 and 2020. Although these works occupy a broad range of generic categories (television, comics, film and literary fiction), they were all produced at a time when feminist activism experienced heightened visibility in the media. Consequently, these works are united by a shared interest in the ideologies of fourth-wave feminism and a consideration of how these ideals are imbricated in the lived experiences of young women. Although a somewhat nebulous term, 'fourth-wave feminism' is considered to encompass the post-millennial resurgence of feminist activism, extending up to recent movements like #MeToo. Nicola Rivers traces the first mainstream discussions of the fourth wave to articles published in 2013 and 2011; although these publications themselves date the origins of the movement to 2008.[4] Rivers goes on to describe how, 'Much like the third wave before it, fourth-wave feminism is fractured and complex, frequently reinforcing the advancement of the individual and centring the seductive notions of "choice," "empowerment," and "agency".'[5] Because of the fragmented nature of fourth-wave feminism, its capacity to encompass multiple, often contradictory positions, Rivers maintains that like post-feminism, contemporary feminism may be most fully apprehended as a 'sensibility' and understood through a consideration of its key themes.[6] Viewed in these terms, it is possible to identify a number of recurrent concerns central to fourth-wave feminism. These include rape culture, victim blaming, intersectionality, gender identity, 'everyday' sexism and consent.

Yet while the fourth wave may be understood through its entanglement with certain prevailing themes and concerns, it is also defined by its colonisation of popular culture and its use of new media technologies, particularly social media, for both education and activism. Although online technologies played a large part in the dissemination of feminist discourse during the third wave of the 1990s, contemporary feminism has been more visibly linked to online activism, with numerous high-profile campaigns such as the Everyday Sexism project and #MeToo beginning on the web.[7] For this reason, commentators such as Ealasaid Munro have claimed that the fourth wave is defined by its use of the internet and the efficacy of social media in facilitating call-out culture.[8] Most crucially for this project, however, the primacy of social media and online discourse in fourth-wave feminism has enabled greater numbers of young women to participate in campaigns and create new, empowering identities for themselves as activists. Recent studies have found that while young women and girls often feel marginalised by mainstream politics, online activism has allowed them to engage with feminism in unprecedented ways.[9] From ambitious campaigns dedicated to ending sexist school dress codes to the more subtle practice of embedding political content in Tweets and Instagram posts, young women are increasingly harnessing online resources to make their voices heard.

Moreover, many young women, while first encountering feminism in online spaces, frequently extend their activism into non-digital spaces. Girls take part in protests and boycotts, attend talks and agitate for change at local and national levels. Likewise, student-led feminist clubs have recently begun to appear in second-level institutions, offering girls the opportunity to explore feminism in a safe environment.[10] Sue Jackson observes that young women and girls have historically been 'the excluded outsiders to feminism', often framed as insufficiently mature or serious to be considered viable political subjects.[11] The girl has frequently been denigrated as a frivolous figure who must be jettisoned in order to make way for the fully realised feminist woman. However, while the political actions of young women and girls are often limited by their youth – they cannot vote or run for office – many have reclaimed that very youthfulness, positioning it as the driving force behind their activism. In her study of youth activism in the Americas, Jessica K. Taft points out that in constructing their political identities 'girl activists' define themselves in relation to their status as adolescents or students.[12] These young women frequently describe themselves as 'open-minded' and 'still learning', fuelled by optimism, 'youthful energy' and 'girlish hopefulness'.[13] Like the metamorphic teen witches explored in this and previous chapters, these girl activists position themselves as becoming. Rather than being locked into a single, static identity, they are defined by their mobility, fluidity and possibility.

It is within this context of newly politicised girlhood, where the girl is less an of indicator social change and more an agent of change in her own right, that a new, explicitly political permutation of the teen witch text emerges. This is not to say that the teen witch texts discussed in earlier chapters lacked a political dimension. Many of them actively intervened in contemporary debates about the nature of adolescence (*The Devil in Massachusetts*), challenged social panics about juvenile delinquency (*The Witch of Blackbird Pond*) or commented on Women's Liberation (*Carrie*). However, it is only with the advent of the post-millennial 'girl activist' that teenage witch texts began to engage with feminist discourse in a self-conscious and explicit manner.[14] All of the texts explored in this chapter engage with the real-world campaigns, movements and discourses around which fourth-wave feminism has coalesced. These include the victim blaming and online harassment that occurred in the wake of the high-profile 2012 Steubenville and 2013 Vanderbilt rape cases (*American Horror Story: Coven*); #MeToo, sex education, trans identities (Netflix's *Chilling Adventures of Sabrina*); intersectionality and structural racism (*Conjure Women*).

As noted above, each of these texts also explores questions of agency and consent. Echoing the concerns of fourth-wave feminism, these works imagine how girls might perform agency or claim power over their lives and/or bodies. However, the manner in which they depict agency differs significantly from both third-wave and post-feminist engagements with the concept. Where third-wave feminism frequently placed the individual at the heart of the feminist project, valuing the individual capacity to choose over wider structural analysis,[15] the fourth-wave texts discussed in this chapter imagine both power and agency as complex networks of force relations. *American Horror Story: Coven, Chilling Adventures, The Witch* and *Conjure Women* do not present power as a mode of oppression enacted from above or without. Instead, they present it as pervasive and immanent in the lives of their young female characters. Such domains of power reflect the writings of Foucault, whose works described:

> the omnipresence of power: not because it has the privilege of consolidating everything under its invincible unity, but because it is produced from one moment to the next, at every point, or rather in every relation from one point to another. Power is everywhere; not because it embraces everything, but because it comes from everywhere.[16]

The teenage girls at the centre of these texts are presented as existing in a world where power is produced by and inherent in all relations. Controlling or dominant institutions (the state, law, patriarchal authorities, etc.) are not the locus of power, but rather its terminal forms.[17] Within this context, power is not, as Foucault explains 'something that is acquired, seized, or shared', but rather a multiplicity of forces 'exercised from innumerable points, in the interplay of nonegalitarian and mobile relations'.[18]

In a similar vein, agency – as imagined in these works – is not something that can be possessed, taken or given. Instead, it emerges through relations. Karen Barad's concept of agential realism not only accounts for non-human agency, but elucidates how intra-actions between the discursive, the material and the technological produce new configurations with agency. For Barad, the world is a 'process of intra-activity in the ongoing reconfiguring of locally determinate causal structures with determinate boundaries, properties, meanings, and patterns of marks on bodies'.[19] Phenomena are not 'things', but rather reconfigurings, relationalities or (re)articulations whose boundaries are constituted through material-discursive practices. Agency, then, 'is not an attribute but the ongoing reconfigurings of the world'.[20] Consequently, in this chapter, teen witches do not seize power or agency, but navigate or participate in the relations, connections and intra-actions around which these forces crystalise.

'Killer vagina': Active Corporeality and Relational Agency in *American Horror Story: Coven*

The third season of the FX anthology series *American Horror Story* is centred around a school for witches who trace their lineage back to the Salem witch trials of 1692. Like many entries in the *American Horror Story* series, *Coven* explores a wide array of themes, from ageing to religious intolerance and societal prejudice. However, a central concern that emerges in this particular season is the complex relationship between young women and their bodies as well as how this relationship is circumscribed by ongoing rearticulations of power and agency. This theme permeates every episode and manifests through a number of characters and motifs. However, it is in the figure of novice witch Zoe Benson (Taissa Farmiga) and her fraught relationship with her body that the issue of agency is most fully explored. Zoe is introduced in the season premiere when she accidentally kills her boyfriend during their first sexual encounter. Reversing the standard image of the penetrated, bleeding maidenhead, Zoe's partner Charlie begins to haemorrhage and convulse as the pair consummate their relationship. Zoe's status as a witch has gifted her with what she terms 'a killer vagina', and although never explicitly stated, her unique anatomy is emblematic of that most potent symbol of misogynistic anxiety, the *vagina dentata*, or toothed vagina. Zoe's navigation of the challenges posed by her unique anatomy forms the crux of the show's meditation on bodies and agencies, as the girl learns to view her corporeality not as Other but as part of a complex, unfolding self whose boundaries she negotiates and renegotiates over the course of the season.

The *vagina dentata* is a mythic motif that appears in numerous cultures around the globe, embodying – quite literally – what Creed terms the 'threatening aspect of the female genital'.[21] A truly pancultural mode of monstrosity, the *vagina dentata* has manifested in the creation myths of the Amazonian Yanomamo tribe, who believed that the first woman on earth possessed a vagina that could transform into a toothed mouth and devour her lover's penis, as well as on the other side of the globe, in the figure of the Melanesian goddess Le-hev-hev.[22] Existing across cultures and epochs, the *vagina dentata* has emerged as a powerful figuration of anxieties about the female body. Although historically associated with the fear of mature female sexuality, by the early twenty-first century the toothed vagina was also utilised in fictive constructions of adolescent embodiment. The 2007 horror film *Teeth*, which features a teenage abstinence advocate who discovers her own toothed, castrating genitalia in the wake of a sexual assault, is probably the best-known example of the postmodern *vagina dentata*. In this film, as Casey Ryan Kelly observes, the devouring vagina is reimagined in order to challenge 'both the cinematic and cultural discourses that subject women to masculine violence'.[23] In *American Horror Story*, Zoe's deadly anatomy similarly functions to highlight and subvert masculinist narratives about embodied femininity. At the same time, although Zoe's genitalia are 'less toothy' than previous iterations of the mythic *vagina dentata*,[24] they nevertheless suggest that she is uneasy about the gross, active materiality of her body. Zoe's *vagina dentata* is initially framed as beyond her control. She kills her boyfriend unintentionally during her first sexual experience, and her claim that she has a 'killer vagina' suggests that her anatomy possesses a discomfiting agency all its own.

This view of the body as endowed with an intentionality removed from the consciousness of the subject recalls a number of texts explored in the early chapters of this book. In particular, it echoes works such as *The Devil in Massachusetts* and *The Crucible* where the agentic capacity of the adolescent body, its flows and seepages, disrupts the binary logic that seeks to separate mind from body, nature from culture. Zoe's terror thus emerges out of the disturbing manner in which the materiality of her body appears to unsettle deeply ingrained dualisms. In the dominant philosophical modes of Western thought, mind and body are understood as separate entities, each with its own gendered significance. The mind – traditionally associated with masculine rationality – is understood as active, while the body – linked to femininity– is read as passive and pre-cultural. This position is one that has been much explored in the context of second-wave feminism. Thinkers such as Simone de Beauvoir, Sherry Ortner and Dorothy Dinnerstein have all investigated how women's subjectivity is constructed through and conflated with the physical body and, by extension, the natural world.[25] However, if either the body or nature is understood as active or agentic in its own right, this binary is problematised.

Zoe's trauma following her boyfriend's death appears to stem less from her own complicity in his demise and more from a growing anxiety about the uncontrollable nature of her body. Influenced by dualistic, phallo-centric modes of thought, Zoe initially imagines her body as an object: pre-representational, silent, negated, passive in the face of an active male reason.[26] When her corporeality refuses this silence, she is disturbed precisely because its excessive organicity troubles such binary divisions. However, as she learns about her identity as a witch, Zoe comes to understand her powers and how they relate to her body. She is given the freedom to decide how she will use her abilities, and in doing so, she comes to discover that her body and its materiality are not Other to subjectivity. As she learns about magic, apprehending its ability to transgress the ostensibly fixed boundaries between subjects and objects, minds and bodies, she comes to reconceptualise her own corporeality. No longer reducing her body to an inert vehicle for consciousness, Zoe learns to perceive her selfhood as 'a univocality whereby bodies, consciousness, actions, events, signs, and entities are specific intensities – each with its own modality and difference'.[27] This univocal self is a mode of desire, which in Deleuzian terms is figured not as a primary lack, but rather as a productive power that engenders new transformations, connections and becomings.

Zoe's reconceptualisation of her corporeality also enables her to discover the full potential of what her body can do. At the end of the first episode of *Coven*,[28] as Zoe begins to overcome her trauma, she employs her *vagina dentata* to seek revenge on a fraternity brother who raped her fellow witch Madison Montgomery (Emma Roberts) at a college party. In doing so, Zoe does not interact with or rein in her unruly body, bending it to her will. Instead, she engages in a complex series of what Karen Barad terms 'intra-actions' that stabilise the differential boundaries of her selfhood. Barad claims that humans are 'not independent entities with inherent properties but rather beings in their differential becoming, particular material (re)configurings of the world with shifting boundaries and properties that stabilize and destabilize'.[29] Zoe's identificatory boundaries thus shift over the course of the episode to encompass not only her consciousness but also her body and its active materiality, so that her corporeality no longer seems alien to her. According to Barad, such boundary shifting is not a passive experience. Rather, they argue that it is possible to intervene in the 'material-discursive boundary-making practices that produce "objects" and "subjects", and other differences out of, and in terms of, a changing relationality'.[30] Within such a framework, the binary divisions associated with Cartesian dualism are undone in favour of agential cuts, which 'do not mark some absolute separation but a cutting-together/apart – a "holding together" of the *disparate* itself'.[31] As Ann K. Brooks elaborates, 'the "agential cut" each of us makes, whether it is a tree cut, a Tweet sent, or one research variable selected over another, matters to the whole, in that it both includes and excludes'.[32] In this way, Zoe's evolving relationship with her body enables her to perform an agential cut that holds together, or entangles, the disparate components of her selfhood in a manner that extends to and encompasses her unruly corporeality.

By cutting together her selfhood in this way, Zoe is also empowered to forge new connections and create dynamic assemblages. Drawn from the work of Deleuze and Guattari, an assemblage is created from the connections forged between previously discrete entities; it 'acts on semiotic flows, material flows, and social flows simultaneously'.[33] Zoe enters a number of such assemblages over the course of the season, but the most creative of these is the sexual relationship she forges with Kyle (Evan Peters), a young man brought back from the dead and reanimated using an array of stitched-together body parts. Himself an assemblage of body parts called into being through a (re)articulation of boundaries, Kyle's relationship with Zoe transgresses heteronormative coupling to become a far more complex assemblage. Afraid that her *vagina dentata* might harm Kyle in the act of intercourse, Zoe assents to a three-way relationship with Madison and Kyle. This arrangement would presumably allow Madison to fulfil the sexual components that Zoe is unwilling or unable to perform. Zoe thus consents to an unconventional sexual configuration that would empower her to find pleasure through novel connections and fluid relations. Here, however, her enactment of agency does not reduce the concept of agency to a simple act of choosing. Instead, agency remains imbricated within a process of intra-action and agential cutting. Zoe rearticulates the boundaries and reshapes the meaning of sexual union, moving it away from the heteronormative paradigm that had guided her first traumatic sexual encounter to produce a new assemblage imbued with multiple desires, pleasures and potentialities.

172 • Witchcraft and Adolescence in American Popular Culture

(Re)articulations of Agency and Identity in *The Chilling Adventures of Sabrina*

Roberto Aguirre-Sacasa and Robert Hack's comic book series *Chilling Adventures of Sabrina* is a complex, and often ambiguous, exploration of girlhood and agency. The series is an ongoing saga, but this chapter will focus primarily on the first trade paperback collection, aptly entitled *The Crucible*, as well as on some selected scenes from its Netflix adaption. A single link in an increasingly convoluted chain of adaptation and appropriation, Aguirre-Sacasa and Hack's comic book has its origins in the Archie Comics publications discussed in Chapter 3 of this book and the television sitcom explored in Chapter 4. *Chilling Adventures* draws on the diverse figurations of Sabrina that have appeared in comics, films and television series from the 1960s through to the early 2000s, as well as from popular post-war horror comics and the occult cinema of the 1960s and 1970s. The first trade paperback collection centres on Sabrina's 'baptism' as a witch and her ambivalence about dedicating herself to Satan. According to Sabrina's principal guardians, her aunts Hilda and Zelda, witches undertake their diabolic baptism at the age of sixteen, and while for male witches the ceremony is merely a formality, for women it is a powerful moment of transition in which they are pledged to Satan and officially become witches, with all the attendant powers and responsibilities.

Throughout *Chilling Adventures* Sabrina's baptism is both subtly and explicitly conflated with puberty and entry into womanhood. When preparing Sabrina for the experience, her aunt Zelda informs her that:

> As discussed, the ceremony would customarily take place on the first full moon after your sixteenth birthday . . . but I've already had your astral chart prepared . . . and your sixteenth birthday falls not just on any full moon, but on the best kind of full moon . . . a blood-moon . . . the same night as a lunar eclipse . . . on Samhain. (*CAS*, n.p.)

That Sabrina's initiation into the craft is set to take place on a blood moon is significant. Blood is a recurring motif throughout the series, and the blood moon links this particular rite of passage to a host of cultural discourses that associate menstruation with the moon. Although attempts to link menstruation to moon cycles have resulted in largely inconclusive findings,[34] popular wisdom and turns of phrase regularly designate the menstrual period as 'my time of the month/moon' or the 'red moon'.[35]

Menstrual symbolism abounds in Aguirre-Sacasa and Hack's portrayal of Sabrina's baptism. On the night of the ceremony, Sabrina wears a white dress with a red scarf or sash. Her method of transport is a goat, which she must ride through the air and then slaughter at the outset of the ceremony, ensuring that the baptism begins with the girl covered in blood. The primacy of blood imagery – the slaughtered goat, the blood moon and Sabrina's scarlet sash – all frame her baptism as a ritual, symbolic analogue to puberty.

In many ways, the ubiquity of sanguine imagery connects Sabrina to the chaotic materiality of the teen witches, or witch-like figures, discussed in earlier chapters. Like Miller's Abigail Williams and King's Carrie, the disruptive power of Sabrina's pubertal body is signalled through an excess of blood. Moreover, as with *Coven*'s Zoe, Sabrina is initially disturbed by the lack of control she seems to exert over both her future and her changing body. This sense of corporeality out of control explicitly recalls deeply embedded cultural narratives that frame puberty, menarche and menstruation as unstable biological eruptions. As noted in Chapter 2, the shift from hysteria to premenstrual syndrome as the aetiological root of feminine disturbance entailed an emphasis on PMS as a 'loss of control', a violent manifestation of how 'woman's subjectivity is tied to an unruly body, necessitating discipline and containment'.[36] As Jane M. Ussher explains:

> The positioning of PMS as lack of control, attributed by the woman, and in many cases also her partner, to the body, thus reflects hegemonic representations of woman as monstrous, closer to nature, with excess emotion or lack of control attributed to an unruly fecund body . . . The body thus becomes objectified, alien to the woman, something that is acting against her in an out of control manner.[37]

Chilling Adventures echoes this vision of the female body as excessive and out of control. The blood-drenched imagery of Sabrina's baptism alludes not only to menarche, but to an eruption of violent, seething biology. Recalling Zoe's horrified response to her body's agentic capacities, Sabrina is disturbed by this tumult of biological excess, although here it is represented metaphorically through the ceremonial goat blood that she is drenched in. Again, the vital materiality of the pubertal body disrupts dualistic figurations of the body as a mere object or vehicle for consciousness. Sabrina is thus forced to reconceptualise her body as a univocal event, a continuity of consciousness, corporeality and events. She engages in a rearticulation of her selfhood, so that her body is brought into her conception of self and becomes part of the identificatory construct for which she must bargain in the comic's climax. Where she had previously been alienated from her body – she docilely allows it to be dressed and prepared by others in advance of her baptism – by the end of the narrative it is no longer a passive object, but part of the selfhood that she seeks to preserve from the Devil's powers.

Sabrina also performs agency through the renegotiation of her body's phenomenal boundaries that takes place between her and the Devil, to whom that body has been promised. Here, Sabrina performs an agential cutting apart, differentiating herself from the satanic power that has held her for so long. However, Sabrina does not seize power from the Dark Lord, because – like agency – power cannot be possessed, 'it is a relationship, not a thing'.[38] Viewed through a Foucauldian lens, power is not 'a general system of domination exerted by one group over another', but a 'process which, through ceaseless struggles and confrontations, transforms, strengthens, or reverses' a dynamic multiplicity of force relations.[39] Sabrina's entanglements with the Devil and her desire to wrest her body from his grip, figures both power and agency as precisely this kind of relationship, where new relations and phenomena come into being between individuals. Through her intra-actions with Satan, Sabrina negotiates the phenomenal parameters of her body, closing it off from his influence, and transforms the power relations that constitute their relationship.

In *Chilling Adventures*, it is made explicit that in order to become a fully fledged witch, Sabrina is expected to give herself over to the Devil. Her familiar Salem even reminds her that no males will be allowed at her baptism because that will be her 'first night with his High Darkness' (*CAS*, n.p.). The Netflix adaptation is less overt in this respect, but it does frame Sabrina's baptism as a wedding night, with Sabrina's aunt Zelda (Miranda Otto) informing her that she must remain a virgin prior to the ritual.[40] In both versions, however, Sabrina is assured that the decision to give herself to Satan is hers alone. Nevertheless, the comic is most explicit in how it places agency at the centre of Sabrina's initiation as a witch. As Sabrina's aunt, Hilda, explains:

in the old days, witch-babies were baptized with unholy water on the first full moon after their birth. Which never quite made sense to me. How could there not be a choice? Free will? The Fall – the foundation on which our faith is based – happened because of free will. (*CAS*, n.p.)

Her other aunt, Zelda, then elaborates by explaining why the age of baptism was changed from infancy to adolescence: 'a young person, on the cusp of adulthood, is fully capable of deciding for herself – (or himself) – whether or not to accept our Dark Lord's gift and fully embrace their witchhood' (*CAS*, n.p.). Although the language here may suggest a simple act of choosing reliant of humanistic notions of free will, Sabrina's enactment of agency emerges out of her intra-action with others, the negotiations that she enters into with her family members, who urge her to embrace her witchhood, and with the Devil, who desires her as both a loyal subject and a sexual conquest. Sabrina's enactments of agency, as expressed here, 'Do not precede, but rather emerge through', her intra-actions with others.[41] That *Chilling Adventures* does not merely reduce agency to the act of choosing can be seen in Sabrina's ultimate refusal to choose. In the comic's final pages, she commits neither to witchcraft, by giving herself to the Devil, nor to a renunciation of the dark arts. Instead, Sabrina flees first to the forest and later into the welcoming arms of a more unorthodox coven. Her performance of agency thus hinges on the severance of her relationship with Satan and the establishment of new intra-actions with the agencies, both human and non-human, that she encounters during her flight from the baptism.

A similar refusal to reduce agency to choice defines the Netflix adaptation of *Chilling Adventures*. In the first episode, Sabrina (Kiernan Shipka) explains that on her sixteenth birthday she must choose between the witch world of her family and the human world of her friends.[42] Like the comic, this choice is centred around Sabrina's dark baptism and her decision to give herself over to the Devil as a sign of her new witch identity. As a teenager, Sabrina is framed as a dynamic, metamorphic character who regularly crosses and recrosses the boundaries between witch and mortal, the fantastic and the mundane. She therefore accords with Patricia Meyer Spacks's vision of the adolescent as an entity that 'rejects boundaries, blithely crosses them, refusing to stay put, to remain a child, to accept subservience, to be predictable'.[43] As an adolescent Sabrina is free to transgress cultural and existential categories, but in order to enter adulthood, she must choose a single subject position to inhabit. Spacks notes that while adolescence is popularly associated with exploration, transformation and growth, adulthood is linked to less appealing states of inertia and statis.[44] Growing up for Sabrina means choosing which state to exist in. However, as in the comic, Sabrina does not choose. She refuses to pledge herself to the Devil, but neither does she fully embrace the human world inhabited by her friends. Over the course of the show's four seasons, Sabrina never makes this choice, but instead inhabits multiple identities: she attends a mortal high school with her peers, and she attends an academy of mystical arts with other young witches. Later, when given the choice to ascend to the throne as Queen of Hell, she also refuses to choose. Instead, her identity is split in two, so that one version of Sabrina can occupy the diabolic throne while the other remains an ordinary high school student. As her aunt Zelda explains in the final episode of the series, Sabrina is 'a cheerleader by day; Queen of Hell by night'.[45] In any case, the agency Sabrina performs is relational, emerging within the context of intra-actions between the teen witch herself and other actants: her friends, family members, fellow students and, of course, the Dark Lord himself. While she never enacts agency through the seizure of power, she repeatedly engages in complex negotiations wherein that power is transformed, reversed or even strengthened. Ultimately, these negotiations (re)produce Sabrina as a multiplicity, a metamorphic, constantly shifting subjectivity who moves endlessly through different realms and realities.

The multifaceted relationality of agency represented in *Chilling Adventures* is further underscored by the centrality of the Devil's pact to both the comic and the television series. This was 'a prominent theme in early modern European theology. Central to the debate was the idea that witches and magical practitioners of all types gained their powers from selling their soul to the Devil'.[46] In his 1975 lecture on witchcraft and demonic possession, later republished in *Abnormal*, Foucault argues that demonic pacts were bound up with complex power relations. He observes that where cases of possession transform the body of the demoniac into a contested corporeal site where myriad forces – both natural and supernatural – enter into conflict, witchcraft is contingent upon negotiation and the reversal of power dynamics. As noted in Chapter 1, Foucault maintains that the witch's will is juridical in nature: 'The witch agrees to an offered exchange: You offer me pleasure and power and I give you my body and soul'.[47] In possession, 'the will is charged with all the ambiguities of desire', but witchcraft is defined by 'the great juridical bloc of heartfelt consent given once and for all by the witch when she signs the pact with the devil'.[48] The witch thus enacts agency within the context of her relationship with the Devil, but also – presumably – through intra-actions with other entities in the diabolic assemblage: the book she signs, the blood she is anointed with, the familiar who led her to Satan. In this way, neither the witch nor the Devil possesses power or agency. Rather, as demonstrated in *Chilling Adventures*, these forces emerge, relationally, through negotiation, exchange and intra-action.

'What canst thou give?': Agency, Power and the Demonic Pact in *The Witch*

The demonic pact is also central to Robert Eggers's 2015 horror film *The Witch*. However, where Sabrina refuses to enter into an alliance with the Devil, and indeed refutes all of the choices offered to her, the protagonist of *The Witch* controversially makes a bargain with Satan in the film's final moments. As in the other texts discussed in this chapter, the eponymous witch constitutes herself as an agent through a series of intra-actions. Like Zoe and Sabrina, the film's heroine, Thomasin (Anya Taylor-Joy), is confronted with the vital materiality of her pubertal body and forced to reconfigure her body, not as a passive object, but as part of a dynamic continuum of selfhood. In doing so, Thomasin is constituted as an actant through both her reconfiguration of her body's phenomenal boundaries – via the agential cut – and relationally via her intra-actions with her family, the environment and, finally, the Devil. This last relationship also initiates a dynamic becoming that empowers Thomasin to explode binary divisions and blur the lines between human and animal, nature and culture.

Eggers's film is a painstaking recreation of seventeenth-century Massachusetts. Set in 1630, the events of *The Witch* predate the Salem witch trials by more than half a century, though the film takes place only four years after the 1626 acquittal of Joan Wright in what was possibly the first witchcraft trial in the British colonies. Not only does the film strive for accuracy in its set design and costuming, *The Witch* also carefully reconstructs the social and religious systems that constrained the lives of women in colonial New England. The family at the heart of the film – father, William (Ralph Ineson); mother, Katherine (Kate Dickie); children, Thomasin, Caleb (Harvey Scrimshaw), Mercy (Ellie Grainger), Jonas (Lucas Dawson) and infant, Samuel – have been exiled from their rigid Puritan community due to Williams's blasphemous interpretation of the Bible. Settling on the remote edge of an immense forest, the family is isolated, but, in its isolation, it serves as a microcosm of Puritan social and spiritual structures. As Marilyn J. Westerkamp observes, 'Puritans were deeply concerned with familial relations, including those of husbands and wives, fathers and daughters, and mothers and sons'.[49] Likewise, Carol F. Karlsen has discussed how, for early American Puritans the family served as 'a model of relationships between God and his creatures and as a model for all social relations'.[50] Thus, the deference of a wife and children to their husband and father should reflect the obedience shown by the congregation to the minister.

Initially, this rigid familial framework appears to be upheld in *The Witch*, as even in their exile, the family defers to the wisdom of the father, William. The relations of power and agency dominant within the family constitute its members in specific ways, as the phenomenal boundaries of individuals shift, destabilise and crystalise throughout the film. Agency emerges within the constellation of the domestic unit through the intra-actions between its constituent parts. When Thomasin first appears on screen, she is quiet and submissive to the authority of both her father and God. Indeed, her first lines of dialogue are the confession of sins, and she laments that she has 'followed the desires of mine own will, and not the Holy Spirit'. Thomasin has been constructed as a silent, pious agent through a web of material and discursive factors, bound together in the entanglement of the family. These include religious discourse, the harsh new England environment and the dictates of her authoritarian father. Thomasin not only interacts (or intra-acts) with these agencies, but she is constituted through them. Likewise, the operations of power within the household – schedules of work and prayer, regimes of surveillance – fix her body in a state of docility.

However, as the film progresses, the relations of power and agency dominant within the household begin to shift. Thomasin enacts an agential cut, reconfiguring her own phenomenal boundaries to engage in more meaningful intra-actions with her body. As in *American Horror Story: Coven* and *Chilling Adventures*, Thomasin comes to view her body not as a passive object, a repository of Otherness or a negation of consciousness, but as an active, generative materiality. In the early part of the film, the agentic matter of corporeality is framed as a source of horror, as Thomasin's pubertal body emerges as a disruptive force. This portrayal of the female body as unstable, even dangerous, aligns with seventeenth-century figurations of feminine corporeality. During the early modern period, the spiritual and intellectual weakness of woman was seen to reside in her physical being. In contemporary medical discourse, influenced as it was by humoral theory, 'women were thought to be subject to the overwhelming influence and vagaries of bodily fluids'.[51] Menstrual blood was seen as responsible for both woman's excessive physicality and her remoteness from the rationality that defined masculinity. Menstruation was viewed as:

a means through which woman expelled turgid, fermented humors, necessary because her body overflowed with polluting fluids. Unfortunately, the very nature and behavior of women showed that menses itself was less than adequate. Frequently overwhelmed by excess fluids, women became emotional, enthusiastic, and ill.[52]

In *The Witch* Thomasin's body is repeatedly framed as excessive and disruptive. Although the film begins with the disappearance of their youngest child, the event that finally plunges the family into chaos, paranoia and murderous suspicion is Thomasin's menarche. Her mother whispers in hushed, and indeed frightened, tones that Thomasin 'hath begat the sign of her womanhood'. The unnatural disruptions that plague the family appear to have more to do with Thomasin's menstruation than with the presence of the forest witch, who is initially assumed to have snatched the infant. In one scene, Thomasin goes to milk one of the family's goats and discovers to her horror that the pail is filled not with fresh, white milk, but with visceral, red blood. In another, the family discovers that their corn has inexplicably rotted and their crops have failed, an allusion to the popular folk belief that a menstruating woman possesses the power to wilt crops, sour milk and rust iron.[53]

However, rather than simply suggesting a seepage of corporeal corruption, the parallels established between Thomasin's menarche and the environmental entities that surround her illuminate a dynamic enmeshment of natural and bodily matter. Thomasin acts as what Stacy Alaimo terms a 'contact zone', a point of interaction between human corporeality and non-human nature.[54] Indeed, there is an explicit parallel in how Thomasin's father attempts to exert control over the natural environment – futilely chopping wood in an attempt to hold back the dense forest, planting crops in an inhospitable wilderness – and how the family tries to rein in Thomasin's pubertal body. Both refuse passivity and exploitation, revolting against patriarchal intervention in increasingly violent ways. The continuity established between Thomasin's body and the natural world establishes a kind of 'trans-corporeality', a state 'in which the human is always intermeshed with the more-than-human world' and the 'the corporeal substance of the human is ultimately inseparable from "the environment"'.[55] This trans-corporeal flow challenges dualistic conceptions of matter (both natural and corporeal) as mute, passive and mindless – eternally remote from the realm of thought and consciousness.[56]

Thomasin's capacity to act as a contact zone between corporeal and natural matter also opens up possibilities for new and unexpected relationships. Thomasin is the only family member to develop a meaningful relationship with the monstrous he-goat and diabolic vessel Black Phillip. While her parents view the animal as a resource to be exploited, her younger siblings, Mercy and Jonas, treat the goat primarily as a pet, singing to and tormenting the beast. However, as Deleuze and Guattari note, the pet is emblematic of static, bounded Oedipal relations. Conversely, for Thomasin, Black Phillip functions as 'the demonic animal', facilitating a series of transformative becomings. Through her association with Black Phillip, Thomasin takes on the role of the Deleuzian sorcerer. The sorcerer is an anomalous figure, a point of contact between the pack and the outside world.[57] Sorcerers are overwhelmed or possessed by affects, which go beyond mundane human affects to express intensities, vibrational oscillations, that expose an unsettling interconnection whereby all organisms are composed of the same forces.[58] Thomasin's affinity with Black Phillip allows her to discover a contiguity of matter that extends from her own body to the world around her. She is able to apprehend a continuity between what Ben Woodard terms the 'exteriorized microorganic nature (the world out there)' and 'our own human interiors in terms of the molecular, cellular, and the micro-organic'.[59] In the closing moments of the film, the goat not only leads her into the dark space of the nocturnal forest, but Thomasin herself appears to become part of that forest, joyfully engulfed by its blackness in the final scene.

The ending of *The Witch* is undeniably controversial. The actress who played Thomasin, Anya Taylor-Joy, has argued that the film's denouement is empowering because Thomasin's decision to become a witch is the first choice she is ever allowed to make.[60] Conversely, the religious scholar Laurel Zwissler has argued that the conception of the film as empowering stems from an:

> anachronistic conflation of witchcraft and feminist agency, a construct at odds with the early modern world otherwise so faithfully portrayed in the film, which leads to conflicting understandings of the ultimate meaning of the protagonist, Thomasin, and her actions.[61]

Zwissler contends that Thomasin's decision to become a witch does not signify feminist agency. The film concludes with her family all dead and, as such, she has no choice but to align herself with Satan. Moreover, Zwissler argues, Thomasin is caught in a power struggle between two essentially patriarchal structures: the Christian family embodied by her father and the overtly masculine oppositional power represented by Satan.[62] While Zwissler's argument is convincing, such a position reduces agency to a choice rather than a relationality. As noted above, agency is not something that an individual can possess; rather, it is a force that emerges amongst individuals (both human and non-human). Thomasin's agency manifests through a complex set of intra-actions between materialities (again, human and more-than-human) and discourses (patriarchal norms, Christian doctrine, Black Phillip's promise of freedom). The close of the film does not see Thomasin choose either satanic liberation *or* patriarchal servitude. Instead, she constitutes herself as an agent through her engagement with these other bodies, entities and discourses.

Analogously, it cannot be said that Thomasin is empowered in the conventional sense of seizing power. Power is not something that can belong to any one individual. Power is ubiquitous and inescapable. However, as Foucault tells us, it can be resisted. Although Thomasin is not able to fully escape the phallocentric strictures of either early modern Puritanism or the misogyny inherent in popular beliefs that portrayed primarily female witches in thrall to an explicitly masculine Devil, she does resist, and even reverse, dominant power relations through the pact that she negotiates with Black Phillip. As Margaret McLaren explains in her feminist analysis of Foucauldian theory, 'Resistance comes from the struggle and contestation of competing claims of power, rather than the ability to get outside of power',[63] and it is precisely this kind of struggle that emerges between Thomasin and Black Phillip/Satan.

There is an undeniable element of coercion in Satan's tempting of Thomasin, and he does appear to her in overtly masculine forms: first, as the immense, heavy-breathing he-goat Black Phillip, and then, as a shadowy man. However, the pair struggle and negotiate for her soul as Thomasin considers signing her name in his book. When the he-goat asks her, 'What dost thou want?', her response is telling: 'What canst thou give?' Thomasin's recourse to the Devil is not born of desperation, but out of desire, which is productive, and self-interest. She agrees to serve him as a witch when he asks, 'Wouldst thou like the taste of butter? A pretty dress? Wouldst thou like to live deliciously? . . . Wouldst thou like to see the world?' Like the New England demoniac Elizabeth Knapp, described in Chapter 1, Thomasin signs the Devil's book and pledges him her soul because he promises her luxury, beauty and the chance to see the world.

Moreover, the Devil does not simply appear to Thomasin; she conjures him, commanding, 'Black Phillip, I conjure thee to speak to me'. Considering Thomasin's previous status within the household – her obedience to her father's authority, her silent docility and the exploitation of her labour – her commanding of Black Phillip and the bargain that she strikes with him is the first opportunity she has to enact agency, to perform an agential cut that differentiates her as a specific kind of entity.

Thomasin's negotiations with Black Phillip thus challenge dominant power relations. The agreement that she reaches with him signifies the enactment of 'heartfelt consent' that Foucault claims is always involved when the witch signs a pact with the devil. She may, in Foucault's terms, agree to become the 'docile servant of the devil', but she does so in exchange for myriad other gifts: power, flight, invisibility.[64] Satan does not simply seize power from her, but instead enacts a reversal of power relations, so that consent, authority, magic and pleasure all flow in new ways between the two parties. At the same time, the agreement that Thomasin enters into with Black Phillip enables her to enter into new alliances, new becomings. Deleuze and Guattari explain that the diabolical pact is not grounded in 'obligation or connection transmitted through blood', but instead it is an abstract alliance, an 'agreement "bound" through words or signs or gestures'.[65] Enabling the girl to move beyond the rigid, static systems of filiation that had frozen her into a submissive subjectivity within the domestic space, the pact allows Thomasin to embark on a line of flight that brings her into proximity with the natural, animal world. In leaving behind her family home to serve Black Phillip and dance with his witches in the forest, she disrupts binary divisions between human and animal, nature and culture. Walking naked into the woodland, Thomasin disregards the signifiers of her previous domestic life in order to enter into a new assemblage with a natural space that has, like her, refused silence and exploitation and rejected patriarchal settlement.

'I grew up on white girl shit like *Charmed* and *Sabrina the Teenage Cracker*': Black Witches and Agency

Post-millennial teen witches engage, often explicitly, with the ideals of fourth-wave feminism and interrogate questions of agency and power. In many such texts, the rhetoric of contemporary movements like #MeToo is transposed directly onto the narrative of the series. In the Netflix

adaptation of *The Chilling Adventures of Sabrina*, characters regularly articulate the guiding precepts of the fourth wave, expressing a desire for
freedom, self-determination and bodily autonomy. Sabrina and her high
school friends, a young trans man named Theo (Lachlan Watson) and
Roz (Jaz Sinclair), a Black girl with psychic abilities, even form a club 'to
topple the white patriarchy'.[66] They name the club 'WICCA' ('Women's
Intersectional Cultural and Creative Association'), presumably an hom-
age to the recently revived 1960s activist group WITCH (Women's International Terrorist Conspiracy from Hell). However, in as much as these
series engage with the language and iconography of fourth-wave feminism,
the movement's central tenets – consent, agency and empowerment – are
often inscribed onto the white witches who headline these series, while the
few Black witches afforded screen time are positioned problematically in
relation to these ideals.

The optimistic conclusion of the previous section, the claim that contemporary teen witches are empowered to unsettle dualistic binaries and
embark on novel becomings, does not always hold true for Black adolescent
witches. If the iconic teen sorceresses of the fourth wave – Zoe, Sabrina,
Thomasin – enact agency through agential cuts, the contestation of dominant power claims and the dissolution of binary divisions – such conceptions of agency do not apply to their Black sisters, who have, for centuries,
been subject to controlling images that lock them into molar subjectivity,
thwart liberatory becomings and reaffirm mind/body dualisms. In her
book *Black Feminist Thought*, Patricia Hill Collins prefaces her discussion
of Black women, labour and the body with a quotation from Zora Neale
Hurston's 1937 novel *Their Eyes Were Watching God*. In the lines borrowed
by Collins, an elderly Black woman, Nanny, tells her granddaughter that
women of colour are 'de mules uh de world'.[67] For Collins, this exchange
exemplifies how Black women have historically been removed from the
category of appropriate femininity, reduced to their bodies and capacity
for labour. Such discourses not only affirm mind/body dualisms, but they
intentionally lock women of colour into the body side of the binary.

Both before and after slavery, Black women have been imagined in
static corporeal terms. As plantation house 'mammies', Reagan-era 'wel-
fare queens' and 'strong black women', Black women have been repeatedly
reduced to strong and/or sexualised bodies and bound up with ideas of
fecundity. Collins explains that Black women, characterised by both racial
and gender difference, serve as a means through which US culture can define
the Other. This mode of Otherness 'symbolizes the oppositional difference

of mind/body and culture/nature thought to distinguish Black women from everyone else'.[68] Women of colour, then, undergo what Deleuze and Guattari term 'subjection' or 'subjectification'. As Awad Ibrahim explains, subjectification/subjection is the *'fenêtre* or the window through which the body passes only to be looked at in exactly one way'.[69] Social subjection creates subjects who are locked into molar categories of being:

> You will be organized, you will be an organism, you will articulate your body – otherwise you're just depraved. You will be signifier and signified, interpreter and interpreted – otherwise you're just a deviant. You will be a subject, nailed down as one.[70]

The subjectivity to which women of colour are 'nailed down' is, in the context of US culture, deeply intertwined with notions of excessive corporeality, sexuality and fecundity.

Moreover, for Deleuze and Guattari there exists, intertwined with the process of subjection, the phenomenon of machinic enslavement in which 'there are no subjects, just bodies, affects, and flows of energy that modulate a larger unity'.[71] While these processes may initially appear contradictory, Deleuze and Guattari maintain that they can be integrated, giving the example of television viewing where the individual is simultaneously addressed as a subject *and* reduced to 'a mere number in a larger machine of ratings and demographic data'.[72] In the case of African-American women, the legacy of slavery and the horror of ongoing exploitation ensure that these concepts are bound together in a disturbing tangle of dehumanisation: the subjectivity in which they are frozen is one rooted in embodiedness. This results in the construction and endurance of racialised binaries whereby whiteness is associated with civilisation, culture and the intellect, just as blackness is conflated with the animal, the primitive and the objectified body. In Deleuzian terms, women of colour, as they are portrayed in popular culture and political discourse, are fixed upon the molar plane, where entities are subjectified, stratified, hierarchised and locked into a congealed identity. Consequently, where white women are depicted as embarking on dynamic lines of flight or engaging in molecular becomings that unsettle restrictive binaries, Black women are frozen into explicitly embodied subjectivities. In teen witch texts, Black witches are given little or no opportunity to enact agency, engage in meaningful, boundary-shaping intra-actions or trouble the dualistic frameworks that bind them to an objectified corporeality.

The witches in *American Horror Story: Coven* are overwhelmingly white, with the sole exception of Queenie (Gabourey Sidibe), whose power – she is a 'human voodoo doll' capable of causing others pain through self-injury – is both racialised and sexualised. Her status as a voodoo *doll* connects her to African-American religio-magical practices while at the same time constructing her as an object, a doll. Moreover, where other teen witch texts discussed in this chapter challenge the tendency of mind/body dualism to reduce the body to an object, Queenie's body is consistently framed as a blank, passive negation of consciousness. The fact that her abilities not only inhere within her body but depend on her body gestures towards the historical reduction of Black women's subjectivity to corporeality. As Amanda Kay Le Blanc notes, Queenie is, from the very start of the series, differentiated from her white peers. When she is first introduced to the white witches, we see her sitting with them in Miss Robichaux's Academy for Exceptional Young Ladies:

> The camera is high in the ceiling and looks down on the young women: Queenie's dark body is contrasted to the white walls of the coven and the white couch she is sitting on. The white witches fade into the furniture. Queenie stands out as physically different immediately in *Coven*.[73]

In this sequence, as in the series as a whole, Queenie's difference is not presented as productive, generative or liberating. It exemplifies a hierarchical difference-between-identities, rather than the less stratified notion of what Deleuze and Guattari call 'difference in itself'. This latter mode of difference is one 'capable of being understood outside the dominance or regime of the one'; however, Queenie is presented in keeping with the former conception of difference, where it is understood 'only as a variation or negation of identity'.[74] In her conspicuous Blackness, accentuated by camerawork, set design and framing Queenie is a negation of and a deviation from the overwhelming, normalised whiteness of her fellow witches.

Moreover, while the white teen witches discussed in this book are empowered to enact generative becomings – becoming-woman, becoming-animal – Queenie remains locked in a dehumanising molar animality. In later episodes of *American Horror Story: Coven* Queenie is caught in a 'love triangle' with voodoo queen Marie Laveau (Angela Bassett) and a nineteenth-century slave named Bastien (Miguel Capo Viu) who has been transformed into a minotaur. When first confronted with the creature,

Queenie asks if he wants to love her because 'they called me a beast too'.[75] Here, Queenie's sexuality, like her body more broadly, is figured as aberrant and animalistic. *American Horror Story: Coven* not only normalises whiteness and white bodies by 'juxtaposing animalistic black sexuality with the more humanized, less disturbing, sexuality of the white characters',[76] but it also binds witches of colour to their bodies. Queenie's affiliation with the minotaur does not represent a liberating becoming-animal, as Thomasin's relationship with Black Phillip or Merricat's connection with Jonas might. The possibility of such molecular hybridity is occluded in Queenie's case, and she is associated instead with the molar animal. She is fixed within an animalistic state that does not promise the explosion of binaries, but instead reinforces them. In later episodes of *American Horror Story: Coven*, Queenie does display some telekinetic abilities and, in the subsequent seasons, *American Horror Story: Hotel* (2015–16) and *Apocalypse* (2018), she becomes a ghost and is rendered incorporeal, transcending her body only in death. Yet, for most of her screen time, Queenie is tethered to her body. As a character, Queenie exposes the limits of fourth-wave feminist rhetoric. While the influence of this movement may empower white adolescent witches to nullify boundaries, challenge dualistic divisions between mind and body, and enact agency through a series of boundary-(re)making intra-actions, Black witches are rarely afforded such freedom.

The character of Queenie, through her conspicuous Blackness, also highlights the sparsity of witches of colour in mainstream American media. Contrasted with her slender, white peers, Queenie embodies a discomfiting Otherness. Early in the series, Queenie explicitly addresses the cultural marginalisation of Black witches: 'I grew up on white girl shit like *Charmed* and *Sabrina the Teenage Cracker*. I didn't even know there were Black witches'.[77] In other teen witch texts of the early twenty-first century, Black witches are similarly marginal figures. Repositories of difference, they haunt the representational boundaries of the text. Kinitra D. Brooks identifies a wider trend in horror fiction whereby a racist patriarchal system allows for multiracial representations of men 'while perpetuating monoracial representations of women'.[78] Brooks's critique centres on one of Western literatures most well-known Black witches, William Shakespeare's Sycorax. In *The Tempest* (1610–11), Shakespeare offers varied representations of manhood, but the only legitimate representation of femininity is the white, upper-class Miranda. At the same time, the play's only non-white woman and the island's original inhabitant, Sycorax, is effaced. However, as Brooks explains 'Sycorax refuses to be excluded, as

her absence in erasure is subverted by her presence as an idea that produces fear and suspicion in the play's remaining characters'.[79] Analogously,
in contemporary teen witch texts, Black sorceresses, although peripheral
figures, regularly refuse their exclusion and manifest to embody disturbing
figurations of difference.

In the Netflix adaptation of *The Chilling Adventures of Sabrina*, Black
witches similarly function as unsettling avatars of hierarchised difference.
During the show's four seasons Sabrina is regularly contrasted with magical 'mean girl' Prudence Night (Tati Gabrielle). Initially hostile to Sabrina,
Prudence is at first a marginal figure, hovering on the edges of the protagonist's narrative and relatively indistinguishable from her 'sisters', two fellow
orphans who dress and speak like her. As the series progresses, Prudence
comes to embody a mode of difference that exists only in relation (or opposition) to Sabrina's normative identity. Her Blackness is contrasted with Sabrina's overwhelming whiteness (which extends not just to her skin, but to her
hair as well). Where Sabrina is associated with purity and innocence, Prudence is worldly and manipulative. Sabrina's kindness and optimism likewise
find their opposites in Prudence's cynical cruelty. Sabrina's core narrative
progression is also reflected in Prudence's story. Just as Sabrina seeks to learn
the truth about her parentage, so too does Prudence struggle to be acknowl-
edged by her father, Faustus Blackwood (Richard Coyle). Sabrina's (osten-
sible) father was the late Edward Spellman, the progressive, enlightened
former high priest of the Church of Night. Prudence's father is the current,
regressive and power-hungry high priest. Moreover, in the early part of the
series, Prudence is shown to bully Sabrina because she is not a full-blooded
witch, being half-mortal on her mother's side. Prudence refers to Sabrina
as a 'half-blood', and Sabrina herself describes the students of the magical
school that she must attend as 'snobby' and 'racist'. In this way, while Prudence's status as a Black witch leads her to be pushed to the periphery of the
narrative, the internal logic of the show (where witches value only the pure
born) allows this racism to be displaced onto the very Other it marginalises.

Chilling Adventures' other Black teen witch, Roz, is also regularly
pushed to the edges of the narrative. She is framed, like Prudence, as a
shadowy reflection of Sabrina. Sabrina's father was a Satanic high priest,
while Roz's father is a Christian preacher. Sabrina inherits her magical abilities from a long line of witches, and Roz receives her own psychic powers
from the generations of Walker women who came before her. However,
while Sabrina's witchcraft requires training and study, familiarity with
Latin and arcane tomes, Roz's powers are innately physical and born of

intuition. Roz has the power of premonition, but her gift is also an affliction. The women in her family, following a centuries-old curse, are fated
to go blind in order to develop psychic powers. Although Sabrina heals
Roz's eyes, the interlinking of sight-loss and psychic abilities suggests that
Roz's powers are deeply physical, an extra sense to replace her lost vision.
Moreover, Roz's powers are referred to by the women in her family as 'the
cunning', a term that connects them to folk magic, as opposed to the
high magic practised Sabrina and her kin. Drawn from English folk beliefs
about practitioners of counter-magic, or cunning folk, 'cunning' has been
used in some parts of the United States as a synonym for African-American
magical practices like hoodoo, tricking or Conjure. Later, in the fourth
season, Roz is revealed to have an even more deeply ingrained connection to Black religio-magical traditions when the Haitian Vodou priestess
Mambo Marie (Skye Marshall) reveals that the girl comes from a long
line of vaguely delineated 'Weird Women'. Roz is thus linked to a form
of magic that is framed throughout the series as a more physical, intuitive
parallel to the witchcraft of the Spellman family. Again, it is a mode of
difference understood simply as a negation of, or variation on, normative
'white' witchcraft. As in *American Horror Story: Coven*, *Chilling Adventures*
establishes a clear rift between the intellectual, European magic of white
witches and the more ecstatic, corporeal magic of Voodoo.

If, as Suzanne Preston Blier has argued, 'magic is . . . the religion of the
other',[80] then Voodoo is the witchcraft of the Other. In a series focused on
white adolescent witches, Black teen witches often affix themselves to historically Black magical systems. Morrow Long provides a general taxonomy of
Black religio-magical beliefs, explaining that New Orleans Voodoo, a system
that thrived with an especial vibrancy during the colonial period and the
nineteenth century – is a religion, closely related to Haitian Vodou.[81] These
religions are syncretic in nature, developed from the encounter between
European Christianity and diverse African faiths during the slave trade. On
the other hand, purely magical systems known as Conjure, tricking, goofer
and, in the twentieth century, Hoodoo or rootwork, are concerned only with
achieving tangible, real-world results. Popular media often conflates these
distinct systems, evoking an iconography of primitivism and tribal rites to
signify African-American spirituality as a whole.

In recent years, however, literature, film and television series produced
by Black creators have reclaimed these practices as both liberatory and
as a means of recentring Black femininity.[82] Afia Atakora's novel *Conjure
Women* not only foregrounds African-American folk magic, but it also

frames these practices as a means through which women of colour can engage in the kind of productive, agential intra-actions described in the previous section of this chapter. Moreover, in the context of this novel, such religio-magical practices enable Black women to contest and resist dominant power claims and reconfigure their bodies, not as passive, unthinking objects, but as vital, agentic forces.

Conjure Women follows nineteen-year-old Rue, a former slave who has learned the art of Conjure from her recently deceased mother, Miss Mae Belle. Set in the period immediately following Emancipation, the novel moves back and forth through time, showing how Rue uses Conjure in both childhood and adolescence as a means of defining her own identity and intervening in the boundary-making practices that determine her own phenomenal, ongoing becomings. Conjure can be understood in this context as an assemblage, a meeting of heterogeneous elements that challenges hierarchies and breaks down binary divisions between African and European identities, Christianity and Paganism. Historian Yvonne P. Chireau defines Conjure as a:

> magical tradition in which spiritual power is invoked for various purposes, such as healing, protection and self defense. The relationship between Conjure and African American religion – in particular, Christianity – is somewhat ambiguous . . . Yet from slavery days to the present, many African Americans have readily moved between Christianity, Conjure, and other forms of supernaturalism with little concern for their purported incompatibility.[83]

Where texts like *American Horror Story: Coven* and *Chilling Adventures* portray Voodoo and Conjure in opposition to white Euro-American witchcraft, pinning it to an identificatory position where it is defined by its difference *from* these dominant practices, in *Conjure Women* these spiritualities exist as difference in itself: They are mobile, dynamic and resist hierarchical systems of organisation.

During Rue's childhood, her mother employs Conjure primarily for healing and protection. She serves as the plantation's midwife, making herself and her daughter – a Conjure woman in training – indispensable to their master and thus ensuring that neither will be sold away. As Mae Belle expounds, 'He keeps my child in his ownership and I make her worth owning' (*CW*, p. 62). Mae Belle garners influence and respect as a result of her reputation as a Conjure woman, evinced by the fact that the other slaves always refer to her as '*Miss* Mae Belle'. While terminal forms of power are portrayed in the novel as crystallising in and around the institution of slavery and coalescing in the figure of the plantation owner, the novel presents power as relational and omnipresent. On the plantation, and later in the free Black community where Rue lives, 'Power is mobile, local, heterogeneous, and unstable. Power comes from everywhere; it is exercised from innumerable points'.[84] Slavery is of course, characterised by violence and oppression, constituting what Foucault might term a state of domination, or 'the locking together of power relations with the relations of strategy'.[85] While such ossified power relations can only be reversed through collective action,[86] they can nevertheless be resisted by individuals. Mae Belle uses the identity of Conjure woman to challenge dominant power claims and secure a future for herself and her daughter. In doing so, she enacts a number of the strategies that Foucault claims are capable of changing – sometimes only temporarily – systems of domination. Amongst these tactics, Foucault lists 'violent resistance, flight, deception, strategies capable of reversing the situation'.[87] Moreover, through her intra-actions with other individuals and the natural world (from which she draws her knowledge and potions), and her engagement with cultural discourses about Conjure, Mae Belle reconfigures herself as an influential figure within her community. Through specific agential intra-actions Mae Belle reconceptualises the boundaries of her own identity and articulates a powerful position for herself on the plantation.

Following Mae Belle's death, Rue negotiates between agencies and power relations to constitute herself as a formidable Conjure woman, cutting together disparate materialities and discourses to differentiate herself as a respected healer. She also inherits the deference afforded to her mother and is addressed as '*Miss* Rue' by other members of the community. As Chireau elucidates, 'Conjurers were highly visible figures on the cultural landscape in black America'.[88] Indeed, numerous Antebellum accounts note the presence of a conjurer on the larger Southern plantations, observing that these figures were afforded a great deal of respect by their fellow slaves. Significantly, in contrast to earlier representations of Black witches – the title character in Ann Petry's 1964 novel *Tituba of Salem Village*, for instance – the identity of witch is not a form of exoticised Otherness projected onto Rue, but rather a persona she creates for herself.

In comparison to her mother, Rue's actions appear even more closely aligned with Foucault's strategies of resistance, as her behaviour often suggests a degree of deception. For much of the novel, Rue herself appears rather sceptical about the efficacy of Conjure. Thinking about the elderly Ma Doe, Rue reflects that, 'Ma Doe had been in the habit of wearing such charms all her life, believing that they could ward off all manner of illness and evilness, and she believed her old age to be a testament to that fact, though Rue had her doubts' (*CW*, p. 43). Rue understands the power inherent in Conjure, which if not mystical, is at least social. Later in the novel, after the Civil War, Rue and Ma Doe forge correspondence from the daughter of her former master to prevent his family from seizing control of their small community of emancipated slaves. Rue describes the deception and the protection it affords as 'an act of power better than conjure' (*CW*, p. 111). By employing this deceptive strategy, Rue resists dominant power claims and brings about a shift, or at least a change, in power relations.[89] Although as a young woman of colour, living first on a slave plantation and later in the immediate aftermath of the Civil War, Rue can never escape racist systems of domination, she can – at times – resist or reverse these power relations. Similarly, while power can be a negative force – limiting, dominating and normalising – it can also be productive, creating new possibilities, ideas and relations. It is precisely this kind of productive power that enables Mae Belle and Rue to (re)configure themselves as influential Conjure women and intervene to protect their families and communities.

In *Conjure Women*, neither Black religio-magical practices nor Black women embody subordinate modes of difference *from* a dominant norm. They do not exist as overtly physical, basely corporeal mirrors of white witchcraft and its Caucasian practitioners, nor do they serve as the negation of normative white identity. Instead, *Conjure Women* represents difference in itself, difference without domination or reduction to the status of Other. By focusing on African-American folk magic without subordinating it to Euro-American magical traditions, the novel allows Conjure practitioners to emerge as vital, complex figures who constitute their identities through dynamic agentic intra-actions and use magic to contest dominant power claims. At the same time, *Conjure Women* refuses to adhere to racist mind/body binaries and does not reduce its Black witches to bodies that are figured as passive objects. For other Black teen witches, affiliation with the body is reductive (in the case of *Chilling Adventures'* Roz) and objectifying (in the case of *Coven'*s Queenie), but in *Conjure Women* the Black body is framed as agentic, vital and dynamic. Like Zoe, Sabrina and Thomasin, Rue envisions the body as a metamorphic force comprised of endless becomings, events, connections and entities.[90] Crucially, however, Rue, unlike her white sister witches, is never horrified by the body's materiality – it is not something she must learn to accept – instead she embraces its agentic capabilities from the outset. When Rue menstruates for the first time, she is neither horrified nor repulsed. The narrative voice, focalised through Rue's perspective, simply observes, 'She couldn't feel a thing but a warm damp. It was like a new-sprung well. *A thing happening without her say-so*' (*CW*, p. 203, emphasis added). Conversely, Rue's white mistress Varina is anxious and ashamed of her body, fearful of its clamorous vitality. When Varina expresses confusion about how menstruation might function, Rue tells her, 'It's natural, my mama said . . . There's no shame. It's beautiful' (*CW*, p. 202). While the novel does not romanticise or essentialise menstruation, it nevertheless presents a joyful, productive trans-corporeality, whereby the active materiality of the pubertal body is enmeshed within and connected to an equally agentic exterior nature. Her menstrual flow is linked to the whirls and eddies of a newly sprung well, and in an earlier sequence, Rue masturbates after collecting flowers, her ecstasy causing the plants she has gathered to fall to the ground where they are 'reunited with the earth' (*CW*, p. 34). Rue is associated with nature throughout the novel; it is the source from which she derives her magical ingredients, and she understands its motions and transformations, the behaviour of its flora and fauna. However, the natural world she is connected to is not a passive resource ripe for white, patriarchal exploitation; rather, it is an active, agentic and vital space. Rue appreciates the 'aroma the earth made when it sighed' (*CW*, p. 33) and wonders at the behaviours of the wild foxes believed by the locals to be her mother's familiars. For Rue, nature is not silent or stolid; it comprises a teeming multitude of agencies, both animate and inanimate.

Conclusion

Elizabeth Grosz lists six criteria for constructing a feminist approach to corporeality:

> avoiding mind/body dichotomies; avoiding the association of body with one sex or race such that they must bear the burden of corporeality; refusing singular or normative models of the body; rejecting any essentialist ontology of the body; including psychical representation of the subject's lived body; and lastly, problematizing binary pairs such as private/public, nature/culture, psychical/social, instinct/learning, genetic/environmentally determined.[91]

The first step that must be taken to approach embodiment from a feminist perspective is to reject 'dichotomous accounts of the person which divide the subject into the mutually exclusive categories of mind and body'.[92] Likewise, Grosz insists that we problematise binary pairs, such as the dualistic division between nature and culture. In *American Horror Story: Coven*, *Chilling Adventures* and *The Witch*, complex representations of agency produced through material-discursive intra-actions disrupt the dualistic positioning of the body (as a mute, passive object) in opposition to the mind (as a conscious, active force). In these texts, the discovery that the body is not simply a vehicle for consciousness, but an agentic vitality is initially framed as a source of horror, linked to disturbing, essentialist visions of female biological excess. However, in each case, the teen witches at the heart of the narrative reconceptualise their selfhoods, so that rather than being envisioned as Other, the body is incorporated – along with consciousness, events and entities – into an eternally unfolding univocality of self. Moreover, the complex relational agencies presented in these works empower teen witches to create dynamic new assemblages and multiplicities, as well as to embark on becomings that refuse fixed binary oppositions and create novel new assemblages.

Texts that feature witches of colour, however, rarely afford them such freedom. The Black witches who appear in *American Horror Story*: Coven and the *Chilling Adventures* television series are constructed through a historically racist mind/body dichotomy that binds them to a corporeality regularly figured as a mute, passive object. These texts fail to problematise binary pairs, and the generative becomings enjoyed by white teen witches are occluded. Young witches of colour often exist in these works to embody hierarchically determined modes of difference that negate the normative identities of their white peers. At the same time, though, works by authors of colour, such as Afia Atakora's *Conjure Women*, are beginning to undo the rigid molarity associated with fictional Black witches. Her novel imagines an adolescent witch who, in adopting the identity of the Conjure woman, is able to establish new relations of power and agency, all the while resisting dualistic divisions that seek to position her body (or the natural world) as a passive object.

Conclusion

'By then I might be an entirely different person'

THIS BOOK OPENED with a meditation on the strangeness of the teenage girl in the middle decades of the twentieth century. It described the lexicon of animality and otherworldliness used to capture her seemingly bizarre habits, disruptive social position and metamorphic corporeality. I argued here that within the context of post-World War II America, the teen witch emerged as a trope through which both adults and, later, teenagers themselves could conceptualise adolescent femininity. In this sense, the teenage witch, from her very inception, fulfilled a tropological function, effecting a linguistic or imaginative movement through which 'unknown or unfamiliar phenomena are provided with meanings by different kinds of metaphorical appropriations'.[1] Yet, in her earliest formulations, in the late 1940s and early 1950s, the teenage witch was a comparatively limited trope. Like the teenage girl herself, she was largely defined by her whiteness, middle-class status and heteronormative femininity. Over the seven decades since the teenage witch trope came into being, it has nevertheless evolved to encompass working-class teenagers, queer teenagers and teenagers of colour. Although these identities are often constrained or associated with subordinated modes of difference, the transformative power of the teen witch trope is such that it continues to embark on new lines of flight, new becomings.

This metamorphic capability is perhaps best expressed in a recent publication, Michael Thomas Ford's novel *Love and Other Curses* (2019), that challenges the initial limitations of the teenage witch trope and opens it up to new possibilities. Ford's book, which was published by the HarperTeen imprint of HaperCollins Publishers and aimed at the fourteen to seventeen demographic, centres on the experiences of a sixteen-year-old boy named Sam. Although Sam is not explicitly labelled a witch, he does – like Merricat in *We Have Always Lived in the Castle* – engage in forms of sympathetic magic. Under the tutelage of his grandmother, great-grandmother and great-great-grandmother, he learns to direct spirits to the afterlife, using an egg and a needle, and decipher omens in the behaviour of animals and insects. The novel is very much a coming-of-age story, focusing on Sam's unrequited love for a trans boy called Tom, as well as on his evolving sense of self and his relationship with his unconventional working-class family.

Like a number of the texts discussed in this book, *Love and Other Curses* posits a liberating vision of a molecular identity in process. As Sam learns about magic and explores his own identity, he refuses to be pinned down to a static, bounded molar subjectivity; rather, he commences a series of multi-directional, reversible and contingent lines of flight. Alongside developing his magical abilities and falling in love, Sam becomes increasingly interested in drag performance. He spends time with a group of older drag queens at a bar called the Shangri-La and comes to love drag precisely because of the identificatory fluidity it affords him. As Sam reflects early in the novel, 'when I'm at the Shangri-La I can be someone else. Even if I haven't quite decided who that someone is yet' (*LOC*, p. 4). Sam views identity not as a solid block of molar being, but as a molecular process defined by transformation and multiplicity. Indeed, Sam refuses to characterise his identity as stable or fixed. While trying to devise an appropriate drag name, he feels no need to rush because, 'it will be another year before I can even legally perform here. By then I might be an entirely different person' (*LOC*, p. 7). Moreover, when Sam finally settles on a name, it is not framed as a moment of finality, the last stop in a linear progression towards a true, authentic subjectivity. As he sits in front of the mirror and begins to apply make-up, he stresses that 'I don't think about what I'm going for, or what kind of character I want to become' (LOC, p. 322). The name he finally chooses is one that he takes in honour of his deceased friend Persephone, but when he selects the name, he is explicit that 'I'm not trying to be her, or to imitate her. I'm trying to be me' (LOC, p. 323).

Sam's journey can therefore be mapped onto the Deleuzian notion of becoming that has defined so many of the teen witches described in this book. His path, over the course of the novel, 'is a rhizome, not a classificatory or genealogical tree' and it 'is certainly not imitating, or identifying with something'.[2] Rather, what Sam engages in is a series of liberating movements that allow him to transform into someone or something entirely new. His adoption of the Persephone persona does not signify a permanent settlement within a static molar identity, but a momentary identificatory alignment. Moreover, Sam's drag persona represents a disruption of dualistic binary logic. As Patricia MacCormack explains: 'Dualistically constructed society territorialises every system, every structure and every mode of existence. This sets up all entities as analogies of proportion or series – a is not b – and relations of proportionality or structure – as a is to b so c is to d.'[3] However, queer identity, which MacCormack figures as hybrid, rejects these binaristic terms in favour of the 'gaps between the terms'.[4] MacCormack defines drag performance similarly, though not identically, as a 'hybrid, teeming with symbols belonging to one or another, but not ambiguous enough to be constructed through the spaces between the symbols'.[5] Nevertheless, drag personas confuse and thus unsettle binary modes of thought, and it is this dualistic rigidity that is troubled throughout *Love and Other Curses*. Even beyond the obvious multiplicity inherent in drag performance, Sam continually problematises dualistic conceptions of identity and unsettles rigid gender binaries. He notes with pride, 'I'm pretty sure I'm the only guy in my school who can replace a faulty kickdown switch and also create the perfect smoky eye' (*LOC*, p. 9). In this way, not only does *Love and Other Curses* celebrate multiplicity and transformation, but it also extends the parameters of the teen witch trope. By centring a queer male protagonist, the novel shows that the teen witch trope does not need to be aligned with a specific gender, sexuality, race or class. Rather, the trope, like popular conceptions of adolescence, has become increasingly more fluid since the mid-twentieth century.

Throughout this book, I have traced the development of the teen witch trope from its birth amidst the immense sociocultural and economic shifts of the post-World War II period up to its current state in the early 2020s. By closing with an analysis of a text in which the teenage witch is a queer working-class boy, I hope to elucidate not just the metamorphic potential of the trope, but to position it as a multiplicity. The teen witch is, after all, not a singular figure, and as a trope it appears fundamentally multivalent, complex and even contradictory. If, as noted previously, a multiplicity is defined 'by the abstract line' or the line of flight 'according to which they change in nature and connections with other multiplicities',[6] the teenage witch, as a trope, enacts precisely this kind of movement. Incapable of being pinned down or assigned a static bounded subjectivity, the teen witch is a figure who transforms through endless combinations with other multiplicities. The teen witch trope is never complete and never at rest, but always contingent and in process. It is continuously shaped and reshaped through its connection with different genres, cultural contexts and ideologies.

In my analysis of the teenage witch as an ever-evolving archetype, I have been interested in two key issues: the functions they serve for both authors and readers, and what they can do in the context of their own fictional worlds. In Chapters 2 and 3, I considered this first facet through an exploration of teen witch texts produced between the 1940s and the 1970s. These works, created when the teenage girl was still a novel phenomenon, deploy the teen witch as a means of conceptualising adolescent femininity and articulating a distinct teenage identity. The second aspect of the teen witch that has engaged me over the course of this book has been their immense potential, what they can do. Consequently, in Chapters 4 and 5, I moved beyond my initial consideration of teen witch's function – their role as trope through which adolescence could be considered – and towards an evaluation of their key characteristics: transformation and power. Here, I explored how the teenage witch is capable of both challenging and reinforcing social hierarchies through acts of shapeshifting and the (re)negotiation of power dynamics.

Despite the diversity of teen witches discussed in this book – they range from early modern girls entangled in historical witch trials to contemporary adolescents with the ability to alter reality with the point of a finger, a magical zap – they are united by a shared, fraught, relationship with dualistic modes of apprehension. My construction of adolescence in general is one that troubles the binaries that separate essentialism and constructivism, mind and body, biology and culture. I have argued earlier in this book that the adolescent, as a real-world everyday phenomenon, is best understood through a biocultural model. This framework insists that 'Bodies are always cultural and biological' and that cultural infrastructures respond to biological phenomena, while bodies respond to cultural and environmental factors.[7] However, as I argue in Chapter 1, the teenage witch is infinitely more vexing, more fluid, than the bioculturally constituted adolescent proper. The teen witch is constantly in process. Changing shape and taking flight, the adolescent witch manifests a sometimes unsettling continuity of matter that goes beyond biocultural intersection to suggest a univocity of materiality.

Throughout this book, I have maintained that a key feature of the teenage witch is that rather than being locked into a fixed state of being, they are (almost) always represented as existing in an ongoing state of becoming. The Deleuzian theory that has guided much of my work here is one that reworks and, indeed, refutes binary divisions through images of dynamic, surprising becomings. Adolescent witches participate in becomings through the connections they make, the alliances they forge. They enter zones of proximity and circulate new speeds, intensities and affects. Teen witches engage in spectacular displays of becoming-woman, which, rather than signalling an irreversible movement towards hierarchically organised, molar femininity, effect a dissolution of gender binaries. Likewise, in becoming-animal, teenage witches do not simply imitate or empathise with animals, they explode the dualistic structures that separate human from non-human, nature from culture, animate from inanimate. In moving between bodies and forms, or inhabiting mobile, transformative bodies, teenage witches draw attention to the 'co-extensive materiality of humans and nonhumans' and foreground the agentic capacities of both bodies and nature.[8]

The manner in which such active, mobile materiality is treated in the texts discussed throughout this book varies and is largely dependent on the author's/creator's investment in maintaining dualistic divisions (nature/culture, biology/society, body/mind) and reinforcing molar hierarchies. In Chapter 2 alone, I juxtapose two works that frame the agentic capacity of the pubertal body as a dangerous threat to the social order – Starkey's *The Devil in Massachusetts* and Miller's *The Crucible* – against a series of texts that position this same active materiality as liberatory and exciting – Ray Bradbury's Cecy stories. Indeed, Cecy's liberating, pleasurable becomings are in stark contrast to the pubertal bodies described by Starkey and Miller, whose flows and seepages suggest an 'oozing mobility' that draws attention to the body's 'gross materiality'.[9] Likewise, even within a single text, it is possible to find deep ambivalences regarding the metamorphic corporeality of the adolescent witch. In works such as *The Craft* and *Buffy the Vampire Slayer*, the teen witch's ability to undertake transgressive becomings is presented as both liberating and potentially destructive. Still, in other texts – *We Have Always Lived in the Castle* and *Carrie*, for instance – the choice to interpret the witch's becomings as both/either horrifying and/or exciting depends on the reader, their reception of the text and the experiences they bring to their interpretation.

Although the ability to undertake diverse becomings is, as noted above, a key feature of teen witch texts, these works – like the teen witch archetype itself – are not homogenous. Not all teenage witches are empowered to take flight and enter the process of becoming. Indeed, this is not something all teen witches even desire. A significant number of the texts explored in this book negate the possibility for molecular becomings, locking their protagonists into the fixed molar unities of race, class, sex and gender. In the 1989 comedy *Teen Witch*, for example, the heroine's powers of self-transformation (the magical makeover motif) do not free her to embark on exciting, disruptive becomings, but instead they calcify her identity within a molar block of normative femininity. In this film, the witch is fixed to the molar plane where subjectivities are hierarchised and stratified in a way that bolsters dualistic divisions. Similarly, in many texts explored in this book – *American Horror Story: Coven* and the Netflix adaptation of *The Chilling Adventures of Sabrina* – witches of colour are pinned to molar subjectivities that reinforce historically racist mind/body, subject/object binaries. For Black witches, the possibility of transformative becoming is often occluded, and they are frequently bound to bodies figured as passive objects.

Alongside their preoccupation with transformative becomings and dynamic lines of flight, teen witch texts participate in the negotiation and renegotiation of power and agency. Figuring both of these forces as relational, as opposed to 'things' that can be possessed, it is possible to decipher in many texts a series of confrontations, contestations, intra-actions and agential cuts that reconfigure dominant flows of power and agency. Teen witch texts also investigate some of the ways in which bodies, and by extension subjectivities, are moulded and rendered docile through various disciplinary techniques, including surveillance, regimes of work and play, social norms and even fashion. However, in novels such as *The Witch of Blackbird Pond* and the early Sabrina comics, power can also be constructive and generative. Young witches not only conform to cultural imperatives that dictate how they should present themselves to the world, they also participate in techniques of the self that enable them to transform their bodies in a host of meaningful ways. Neither the teen witches themselves nor the young readers who followed their adventures should be understood as passively imbibing social norms; rather, they actively navigate, embrace and resist the systems of power immanent within their lives. In *American Horror Story: Coven*, *Chilling Adventures* (the comic and the television series), *The Witch* and *Conjure Women*, young witches hold together and cut apart new phenomenal boundaries, remaking themselves as distinct agencies via their intra-actions with other bodies, materialities and discourses. Likewise, many of these sorceresses constitute themselves as subjects and reverse or resist prevailing power structures through the negotiation of a demonic pact.

One of the central features of Deleuze and Guattari's notion of becoming is its emphasis on continuous motion, eternal transformation. In contrast with states of being, characterised by stasis, becoming is defined by a line of flight that never arrives at a fixed destination. In becoming, there is no final identity at which one comfortably, definitively arrives. This is why Deleuze and Guattari valorise the werewolf as a figuration of becoming: a werewolf is not simply a man who has exchanged species and become molar wolf. The werewolf is a generative figure, it is a becoming characterised by 'proximities between molecules in composition, relations of movement and rest, speed and slowness between emitted particles'.[10] Analogously, I would argue that the teenage witch, as a trope or archetype, does not have a concrete destination waiting at the end of their many flights. They do not have a final identity at which they will one day arrive. Instead, they are defined by their movements between different points, locations and subjectivities. Although I have attempted to map the teen witch's evolution or journey over the course of this book, this is not to suggest that such movement is linear or teleological. It is, in fact, decidedly non-linear, reversible and contingent. As I mentioned above, the teen witch is also a multiplicity. They are not a static or bounded unity, but a dynamic multitude who enters into and severs an array of diverse combinations with other multiplicities. They transform via the emission and exchange of particles, the adoption of new motilities of speed and slowness, new affects.

The teen witch is already changing based on their interactions with different contexts, archetypes and media. In the *Fear Street* trilogy (2021) the teen witch trope merges with the final girl, the cinematic archetype of the frequently masculinised survivor who becomes the point of audience identification over the course of the typical slasher.[11] In *Fear Street: 1666*, the last entry in the series, tomboyish final girl Deena (Kiana Madeira) is transported from the early 1990s to the seventeenth century to experience the last days of accused witch Sarah Fier (played by both Maderia and Elizabeth Scopel). The two characters, although initially representing distinct cultural archetypes, merge and overlap in a host of intriguing ways:

Deena experiences magical visions (a power characteristic of the witch) and Sarah is forced to battle a knife-wielding maniac (a narrative device usually associated with the final girl). In these moments the boundaries between distinct figurations of adolescent girlhood breakdown and each character adopts new affects, exchanging particles with her opposite. In a similar vein, Kendare Blake's upcoming book *In Every Generation* (January 2022) is a continuation of *Buffy the Vampire Slayer* that features Willow Rosenberg's daughter, Frankie, as the first Slayer-Witch.[12] These texts, newly released or forthcoming at the time of writing, suggest that the teenage witch remains, even now, dynamic and metamorphic. Forging unexpected connections with other, diverse figurations of adolescent femininity, teenage witches refuse to remain still or static, nor are they bounded or discrete. Rather, the adolescent witch is always moving, always becoming and endlessly transforming.

Endnotes

Introduction

1. 'Subdebs: They Live in a Jolly World of Gangs, Games, Gadding, Movies, Malteds & Music', *Life* (27 January 1941), 75, *www.books.google.ie* (last accessed 21 December 2020).
2. *Life*, 75.
3. Jon Savage, *Teenage: The Creation of Youth, 1875–1945* (London: Chatto & Windus, 2007), p. xiii.
4. *Life*, 75. Emphasis added.
5. Carlo Ginzburg, *Ecstasies: Deciphering the Witches' Sabbath* (trans. Raymond Rosenthal) (New York: Pantheon, 1991), p. 1.
6. *Life*, 75.
7. In Ilana Nash, *American Sweethearts: Teenage Girls in Twentieth-Century Popular Culture* (Bloomington IN: Indiana University Press, 2006), p. 4.
8. Savage, *Teenage*, p. xiii.
9. Mary Celeste Kearney, 'Birds on the Wire: Troping Teenage Girlhood Through Telephony in Mid-Twentieth-Century US Media Culture', *Cultural Studies*, 19/5 (2005), 572.
10. Catherine Driscoll, *Girls: Feminine Adolescence in Popular Culture and Cultural Theory* (New York: Columbia University Press, 2002), p. 3.
11. Rikke Schubart, *Mastering Fear: Women, Emotion, and Contemporary Horror* (London: Bloomsbury, 2018), p. 273. See Chapter 3 for more on this.

12. Christine Jarvis, 'Becoming a Woman Through Wicca: Witches and Wiccans in Contemporary Teen Fiction', *Children's Literature in Education*, 39 (2008), 45.
13. Darren Elliott-Smith, *Queer Horror Film and Television: Sexuality and Masculinity at the Margins* (London: I. B. Tauris, 2016), Kindle edition, Loc. 554.
14. Karen Cushman, 'Introduction', in Elizabeth George Speare, *The Witch of Blackbird Pond* (New York: Houghton Mifflin Harcourt, [1958] 2011), p. vi.
15. Hayden White, T*ropics of Discourse: Essays in Cultural Criticism* (Baltimore MD: Johns Hopkins University Press, 1978), p. 5.
16. Nash, *American Sweethearts*, p. 3.
17. Kearney, 'Birds on the Wire', 571. Emphasis added.
18. Ronald Hutton, *The Witch: A History of Fear, from Ancient Times to the Present* (New Haven CT: Yale University Press, 2017), p. 44.
19. Anita Obermeier, 'Witches and the Myth of the Medieval Burning Times', in Stephen J. Harris and Byron L. Grigsby (eds), *Misconceptions About the Middle Ages* (Abingdon: Routledge, 2008), p. 218.
20. Brian P. Levack, *The Witch-Hunt in Early Modern Europe* (Abingdon: Routledge, [1987] 2016), Kindle edition, Loc. 951.
21. Levack, *The Witch-Hunt in Early Modern Europe*, Loc. 270, 346.
22. Exceptions to this perspective include Margaret Murray's *The Witch-Cult in Western Europe* (1921) and Carlo Ginzburg's *The Night Battles: Witchcraft and Agrarian Cults in the Sixteenth and Seventeenth Centuries* (1983).
23. Stuart Clark, *Thinking with Demons: The Idea of Witchcraft in Early Modern Europe* (Oxford: Oxford University Press, 1999), e-book, p. 7.
24. Clark, *Thinking with Demons*, p. viii.
25. Clark, *Thinking with Demons*, p. viii.
26. The Satanic Panic refers to a widespread moral panic that occurred primarily in the United States, Great Britain and Australia during the 1980s and early 1990s. It manifested in conspiracies about a clandestine network of Satanic cults kidnapping, abusing and sacrificing children. A complex phenomenon, the Satanic Panic also extended to popular fears about heavy metal music, horror films and role-playing games such as Dungeons and Dragons. It also resulted in serious miscarriages of justice such as the McMartin Preschool trial and the case of the West Memphis Three, both of which saw innocent people imprisoned for alleged Satanic crimes. For more, see Kier-La Janisse and Paul Corupe, *Satanic Panic: Pop-Cultural Paranoia in the 1980s* (Godalming: FAB Press, 2015).
27. Clark, *Thinking with Demons*, p. viii.

28. Charles Zika, *The Appearance of Witchcraft: Print and Visual Culture in Sixteenth-Century Europe* (Abingdon: Routledge, 2007), Kindle edition, p. 4.

29. Walter Stephens, *Demon Lovers: Witchcraft, Sex, and the Crisis of Belief* (Chicago IL: University of Chicago Press, 2002), p. 35.

30. Hutton, *The Witch*, p. 23.

31. Robert Thurston, *The Witch Hunts: A History of Witch Persecutions in Europe and North America* (Abingdon: Routledge, 2007), p. 10.

32. Christina Larner, 'Was Witch-Hunting Woman-Hunting', in Darren Oldridge (ed.), *The Witchcraft Reader* (2nd ed.) (Abingdon: Routledge, 2008), p. 255.

33. Clark, *Thinking with Demons*, p. 113.

34. Clark, *Thinking with Demons*, p. 113.

35. Clark, *Thinking with Demons*, pp. 120–1.

36. Clark, *Thinking with Demons*, p. 120.

37. Serenity Young, *Women Who Fly: Goddesses, Witches, Mystic, and Other Airborne Females* (Oxford: Oxford University Press, 2018), p. 154.

38. Clark, *Thinking with Demons*, p. 130.

39. Marion Gibson, *Witchcraft Myths in American Culture* (Abingdon: Routledge, 2007), Kindle edition, p. 41.

40. Gibson, *Witchcraft Myths in American Culture*, p. 41.

41. Virginia Woolf, *A Room of One's Own* (London: Wiley Blackwell, [1929] 2015), p. 36.

42. Heather Greene, *Bell, Book and Camera: A Critical History of Witches in American Film and Television* (Jefferson NC: McFarland, 2018), Kindle edition, p. 55.

43. Jack Halberstam, *Skin Shows: Gothic Horror and the Technology of Monsters* (Durham NC: Duke University Press, 1995), p. 2.

44. Halberstam, *Skin Shows*, p. 2.

45. Halberstam, *Skin Shows*, p. 88.

46. Barbara Creed, *The Monstrous Feminine: Film, Feminism, Psychoanalysis* (Abingdon: Routledge, 1993), p. 74.

47. Christopher B. Strain, *The Long Sixties: America, 1955–1973* (London: Wiley-Blackwell, 2016), e-book.

48. Driscoll, *Girls*, p. 51.

49. See Elizabeth Arveda Kissling, 'On the Rag on Screen: Menarche in Film and Television', *Sex Roles*, 46 (2002), 5–12, for a discussion of the symbolic role of menarche in screen media.

50. Although beyond the scope of this book, it is worth noting the preponderance of queer or queer-coded adult male witches: Nicky Holyrod (Jack Lemmon)

in *Bell, Book and Candle* (1958), Vincent Owens in Alice Hoffman's *The Rules of Magic* (2017) and Ambrose Spellman (Chance Perdomo) in *The Chilling Adventures of Sabrina* (Netflix, 2018–20). In the conclusion to this book, I do, however, discuss one of the few queer, male teen witches.

51. The only example of a trans girl witch encountered in my research is Lourdes (Zoey Luna) from the 2020 film *The Craft: Legacy*. However, this facet of her character is not explored in any detail and is mentioned only in passing. Conversely, Aiden Thomas's *Cemetery Boys* (2020) is a thoughtful novel about a trans boy raised in the magical tradition of *brujería*. Unfortunately, I have been unable to include this novel in my study.

52. Robin Wood, 'An Introduction to the American Horror Film', in Barry Keith Grant (ed.), *Robin Wood on the Horror Film: Collected Essays and Reviews* (Detroit MI: Wayne State University Press, 2018), p. 79.

53. Andrew Scahill, *The Revolting Child in Horror Cinema: Youth, Rebellion and Queer Spectatorship* (Basingstoke: Palgrave, 2015), p. 13.

54. Scahill, *The Revolting Child in Horror Cinema*, p. 13.

55. Nathaniel Hawthorne, The Scarlet Letter (Seattle WA: Amazon Classics, [1850] 2017), Kindle edition, p. 85.

56. Hawthorne, *The Scarlet Letter*, p. 239.

57. Kristina West, *Reading the Salem Witch Child: The Guilt of Innocent Blood* (Basingstoke: Palgrave, 2020), p. 5.

Chapter 1

1. Rosi Braidotti, 'Mothers, Monsters and Machines', in Katie Conboy, Nadia Medina and Sarah Stanbury (eds), *Writing on the Body: Female Embodiment and Feminist Theory* (New York: Columbia University Press, 1997), p. 62.

2. Catherine Driscoll, *Girls: Feminine Adolescence in Popular Culture and Cultural Theory* (New York: Columbia University Press, 2002), p. 6.

3. Michel Foucault, *The History of Sexuality, Volume 1: The Will to Knowledge* (trans. Robert Hurley) (New York: Pantheon, [1976] 1978), p. 36.

4. Foucault, *The History of Sexuality*, p. 36.

5. G. Stanley Hall, *Adolescence: Its Psychology and Its Relations to Physiology, Anthropology, Sociology, Sex, Crime, Religion and Education* (New York: D. Appleton & Co., 1904), p. 73, *https://archive.org/details/adolescenceitsp01hall-goog/page/n6/mode/2up* (last accessed 26 October 2021).

6. Jeffrey Jensen Arnett, 'G. Stanley Hall's Adolescence: Brilliance and Nonsense', *History of Psychology*, 9/3 (2006), 187.

7. Perry R. Hinton, 'The Cultural Construction of the Girl "Teen": A Cross-cultural Analysis of Feminine Adolescence Portrayed in Popular Culture', *Journal of Intercultural Communication Research*, 45/3 (2016), 234.

8. Hinton, 'The Cultural Construction of the Girl "Teen"', 235.

9. Anders Berg-Sørensen, Nils Holtug and Kasper Lippert-Rasmussen, 'Essentialism vs. Constructivism: Introduction', *Distinktion: Journal of Social Theory*, 11/1 (2010), 40.

10. Rikke Schubart, *Mastering Fear: Women, Emotion, and Contemporary Horror* (London: Bloomsbury, 2018), p. 275.

11. Elizabeth Grosz, *Volatile Bodies: Toward a Corporeal Feminism* (Bloomington IN: Indiana University Press, 1994), p. 212, n. 15.

12. Schubart, *Mastering Fear*, p. 276. Emphasis added.

13. Daniel J. Hruschka *et al.*, 'Biocultural Dialogues: Biology and Culture in Psychological Anthropology', ETHOS, 33/1 (2005), 1.

14. Torben Grodal, *Embodied Visions: Evolution, Emotion, Culture, and Film* (Oxford: Oxford University Press, 2009), p. 5.

15. Grodal, *Embodied Visions*, p. 5.

16. Grodal, *Embodied Visions*, p. 4.

17. Schubart, *Mastering Fear*, p. 32.

18. Meredith W. Reiches, 'Adolescence as a Biocultural Life History Transition', *Annual Review of Anthropology*, 48 (2019), 152.

19. Reiches, 'Adolescence as a Biocultural Life History Transition', 152.

20. Reiches, 'Adolescence as a Biocultural Life History Transition', 152.

21. Reiches, 'Adolescence as a Biocultural Life History Transition', 158.

22. Hruschka *et al.*, 'Biocultural Dialogues', 3.

23. Grodal, *Embodied Visions*, p. 5.

24. Stacy Alaimo and Susan Hekman, 'Introduction: Emerging Models of Materiality in Feminist Theory', in Stacy Alaimo and Susan Hekman (eds), *Material Feminisms* (Bloomington IN: Indiana University Press, 2008), p. 5.

25. Grosz, *Volatile Bodies*, p. vii.

26. Grosz, *Volatile Bodies*, p. ix.

27. Grosz, *Volatile Bodies*, p. x.

28. Grosz, *Volatile Bodies*, pp. ix–x.

29. Grosz, *Volatile Bodies*, p. vii

30. Grosz, *Volatile Bodies*, p. viii.

31. Grosz, *Volatile Bodies*, p. xi.

32. Grosz, *Volatile Bodies*, p. xii.

33. Brent Adkins, *Deleuze and Guattari's* A Thousand Plateaus: *A Critical Introduction and Guide* (Edinburgh: Edinburgh University Press, 2015), p. 161.

34. Adkins, *Deleuze and Guattari's A Thousand Plateaus*, p. 36.

35. Margaret A. McLaren, *Feminism, Foucault, and Embodied Subjectivity* (New York: SUNY Press, 2002), p. 3.

36. McLaren, *Feminism, Foucault, and Embodied Subjectivity*, p. 3.

37. McLaren, *Feminism, Foucault, and Embodied Subjectivity*, p. 3.

38. Michel Foucault, 'Nietzsche, Genealogy, History', in Paul Rabinow (ed.), *The Foucault Reader* (New York: Pantheon Books, 1984), p. 83.

39. McLaren, *Feminism, Foucault, and Embodied Subjectivity*, p. 85.

40. Foucault, 'Nietzsche, Genealogy, History', p. 82.

41. Schubart, *Mastering Fear*, p. 16.

42. Foucault, 'Nietzsche, Genealogy, History', p. 83.

43. McLaren, *Feminism, Foucault, and Embodied Subjectivity*, p. 103.

44. McLaren, *Feminism, Foucault, and Embodied Subjectivity*, p. 86.

45. Foucault, *The History of Sexuality*, p. 92.

46. McLaren, *Feminism, Foucault, and Embodied Subjectivity*, pp. 89–90.

47. Foucault, *The History of Sexuality*, p. 92.

48. Grosz, *Volatile Bodies*, p. 143.

49. Grosz, *Volatile Bodies*, p. 143.

50. Grosz, *Volatile Bodies*, p. 143.

51. Michel Foucault, *Abnormal: Lectures at the Collège de France, 1974–1975* (trans. Graham Burchell) (London: Verso, 2016), p. 207.

52. Foucault, *Abnormal*, p. 207.

53. Foucault, *Abnormal*, p. 211.

54. Foucault, *Abnormal*, p. 212.

55. Thomas Lemke, 'New Materialisms: Foucault and the "Government of Things"', *Theory, Culture & Society*, 32/4 (2015), 4–5.

56. Foucault in Lemke, 'New Materialisms', 9.

57. Lemke, 'New Materialisms', 13.

58. Lemke, 'New Materialisms', 9.

59. Lemke, 'New Materialisms', 9.

60. Lemke, 'New Materialisms', 9.

61. Alaimo and Hekman, 'Introduction', p. 1.

62. Alaimo and Hekman, 'Introduction', pp. 4–5.

63. Alaimo and Hekman, 'Introduction', p. 9.

64. Karen Barad, 'Posthumanist Performativity: Toward an Understanding of How Matter Comes to Matter', in *Material Feminisms*, p. 133.

65. Barad, 'Posthumanist Performativity', p. 133. Analogously, Donna Haraway has coined the term 'material-semiotic actor' to afford agency to the 'object of knowledge' while simultaneously bearing in mind that the boundaries

of such objects 'materialize in social interaction among humans and non-humans, including the machines and other instruments that mediate exchanges at crucial interfaces and that function as delegates for other actors' functions and purposes'. See Donna Haraway, 'The Promise of Monsters', in Lawrence Grossberg *et al.* (eds), *Cultural Studies* (New York: Routeledge, 1992), p. 298.

66. Rosi Braidotti, 'Teratologies', in Claire Colebrook and Ian Buchanan (eds), *Deleuze and Feminist Theory* (Edinburgh: Edinburgh University Press, 2000), p. 160.

67. Adkins, *Deleuze and Guattari's* A Thousand Plateaus, p. 24.

68. Gilles Deleuze and Félix Guattari, *A Thousand Plateaus: Capitalism and Schizophrenia* (trans. Brian Massumi) (Minneapolis MN: University of Minnesota Press, 1987), p. 239.

69. Deleuze and Guattari, *A Thousand Plateaus*, p. 7.

70. Adkins, *Deleuze and Guattari's* A Thousand Plateaus, p. 28.

71. Adkins, *Deleuze and Guattari's* A Thousand Plateaus, p. 28.

72. Deleuze and Guattari, *A Thousand Plateaus*, p. 10.

73. Deleuze and Guattari, *A Thousand Plateaus*, pp. 276–7.

74. Driscoll, *Girls*, p. 192.

75. Driscoll, *Girls*, p. 197.

76. Driscoll, *Girls*, p. 198.

77. Driscoll, *Girls*, p. 198.

78. Anna Powell, *Deleuze and Horror Film* (Edinburgh: Edinburgh University Press, 2005), e-book, p. 63.

79. Powell, *Deleuze and Horror Film*, p. 66.

80. Powell, *Deleuze and Horror Film*, p. 78.

81. Margrit Shildrick, *Embodying the Monster: Encounters with the Vulnerable Self* (London: Sage, 2002), p. 5.

82. Braidotti, 'Mothers, Monsters and Machines', p. 62.

83. Barbara Creed, 'Baby Bitches from Hell: Monstrous Little Women in Film', in J. Craw and R. Leonard (eds), *Mixed-up Childhood* (Auckland: Auckland Art Gallery, 2005), p. 36.

84. Julia Kristeva, *Powers of Horror: An Essay on Abjection* (trans. Leon Roudiez) (New York: Columbia University Press, 1982), p. 4.

85. Kristeva, *Powers of Horror*, p. 53.

86. Creed, *The Monstrous Feminine,* pp. 10–11.

87. Creed, *The Monstrous Feminine*, p. 105.

88. Creed, *The Monstrous Feminine*, p. 83.

89. Powell, *Deleuze and Horror Film*, p. 64.

90. Powell, *Deleuze and Horror Film*, p. 3.
91. Powell, *Deleuze and Horror Film*, p. 18.
92. Deleuze and Guattari, *A Thousand Plateaus*, p. 5.
93. Deleuze and Guattari, *A Thousand Plateaus*, p. 2.
94. Jack Morgan, *The Biology of Horror: Gothic Literature and Film* (Carbondale IL: Southern Illinois University Press, 2002), p. 6.
95. Morgan, *The Biology of Horror*, p. 3.
96. Morgan, *The Biology of Horror*, p. 3.
97. Nicholas Royle, *The Uncanny* (Manchester: Manchester University Press, 2003), p. 14.
98. Royle, *The Uncanny*, p. 6.
99. Larrie Dudenhoeffer, *Embodiment and Horror Cinema* (Basingstoke: Palgrave, 2014), p. 6.
100. Susan Yi Sencindiver, '"It's Alive!" New Materialism and Literary Horror', in Kevin Corstorphine and Laura R. Kremmel, *The Palgrave Handbook to Horror Literature* (London: Palgrave, 2018), p. 494.
101. Sencindiver, 'It's Alive', p. 494.
102. Kelly Hurley, *The Gothic Body: Sexuality, Materialism, and Degeneration at the Fin de Siècle* (Cambridge: Cambridge University Press, 1996), p. 33.
103. Morgan, *Biology of Horror*, p. 3.
104. Joan Jacobs Brumberg, *Fasting Girls: The History of Anorexia Nervosa* (London: Vintage, 2000), p. 43.
105. Brumberg, *Fasting Girls*, p. 43.
106. Megan Warin, *Abject Relations: Everyday Worlds of Anorexia* (New Brunswick NJ: Rutgers University Press, 2010), p. 135.
107. Ron Van Deth and Walter Vandereycken, 'What Happened to the "Fasting Girls"? A Follow-up in Retrospect', in Wolfgang Herzog, Hans Christian Deter and Walter Vandereycken, *The Course of Eating Disorders: Long-Term Follow-up Studies of Anorexia and Bulimia Nervosa* (Berlin: Springer-Verlag, 1992), p. 348.
108. Brumberg, *Fasting Girls*, p. 49.
109. Van Deth and Vandereycken, 'What Happened to the "Fasting Girls"?', p. 348.
110. Brumberg, *Fasting Girls*, p. 52.
111. H. Gethin Morgan, 'Fasting Girls – Past, Present and Future', in Raghu N. Gaind and Barbara L. Hudson (eds), *Current Themes in Psychiatry 2* (Basingstoke: MacMillan Press, 1977), pp. 302–3.
112. Brumberg, *Fasting Girls*, p. 66.
113. Brumberg, *Fasting Girls*, p.80.
114. McLaren, *Feminism, Foucault, and Embodied Subjectivity*, p. 106.
115. McLaren, *Feminism, Foucault, and Embodied Subjectivity*, p. 106.

116. McLaren, *Feminism, Foucault, and Embodied Subjectivity*, p. 99.

117. Nancy A. Gutierrez, *'Shall She Famish Then?': Female Food Refusal in Early Modern England* (Abingdon: Routledge, 2003), e-book, chapter 1.

118. See Caroline Walker Bynum, *Holy Feast and Holy Fast: The Religious Significance of Food to Medieval Women* (Berkeley CA: University of California Press, 1987).

119. Warin, *Abject Relations*, p. 11.

120. Warin, *Abject Relations*, p. 130.

121. Deleuze and Guattari, in Powell, *Deleuze and Horror Film*, p. 78.

122. Powell, *Deleuze and Horror Film*, p. 78.

123. Deleuze and Guattari, *A Thousand Plateaus*, p. 30.

124. J. A. Sharpe, 'Disruption in the Well-Ordered Household: Age, Authority and Possessed Young People', in Paul Griffiths, Adam Fox and Steve Hindle (eds), *The Experience of Authority in Early Modern England* (New York: St Martin's Press, 1996), p. 188.

125. Sharpe, 'Disruption in the Well-Ordered Household', p. 188.

126. Erika Gasser, *Vexed with Devils: Manhood and Witchcraft in Old and New England* (New York: New York University Press, 2017), p. 23.

127. Sarah Ferber, 'Possession and the Sexes', in Alison Rowlands (ed.), *Witchcraft and Masculinities in Early Modern Europe* (Basingstoke: Palgrave, 2009), p. 219.

128. Sharpe, 'Disruption in the Well-Ordered Household', p. 201.

129. Sharpe, 'Disruption in the Well-Ordered Household', p. 199.

130. Samuel Willard, 'The Possession of Elizabeth Knapp', in Elaine G. Breslaw (ed.), *Witches of the Atlantic World: A Historical Reader and Primary Source Book* (New York: New York University Press, 2000) p. 235.

131. Willard, 'The Possession of Elizabeth Knapp', p. 236.

132. Ferber, 'Possession and the Sexes', p. 217.

133. Foucault, *Abnormal*, p. 205.

134. Foucault, *Abnormal*, p. 206.

135. Foucault, *Abnormal*, p. 207.

136. Foucault, *Abnormal*, p. 207.

137. Foucault, *Abnormal*, p. 207.

138. Adkins, *Deleuze and Guattari's* A Thousand Plateaus, p. 26.

139. Adkins, *Deleuze and Guattari's* A Thousand Plateaus, p. 26.

140. Foucault, *Abnormal*, p. 207

141. Ferber, 'Possession and the Sexes', p. 217.

142. Alex Owen, *The Darkened Room: Women, Power, and Spiritualism in Late Victorian England* (London: Virago, 1989), p. 6.

143. Owen, *The Darkened Room*, p. 10.

144. Ann Braude, *Radical Spirits: Spiritualism and Women's Rights in Nineteenth-Century America* (Indianapolis IN: Indiana University Press, 2001), pp. 86–7.
145. Braude, *Radical Spirits*, p. 87.
146. Foucault, *Abnormal*, p. 212.
147. Robert Brain, 'Materialising the Medium: Ectoplasm and the Quest for Supra-Normal Biology in Fin-de-Siècle Science and Art', in Anthony Enns and Shelley Trower (eds), *Vibratory Modernism* (Basingstoke: Palgrave, 2013), p. 114.
148. Foucault, *Abnormal*, p. 212.
149. Joshua Delpech-Ramey, 'Deleuze, Guattari, and the "Politics of Sorcery"', *SubStance*, 39/1 (2010), 10.
150. Deleuze and Guattari, *A Thousand Plateaus*, p. 269.
151. Deleuze and Guattari, *A Thousand Plateaus*, p. 258.
152. Hurley, *The Gothic Body*, p. 9.
153. Brain, 'Materialising the Medium', p. 118.
154. Beth Rodgers, *Adolescent Girlhood and Literary Culture at the* Fin de Siècle: *Daughters of Today* (Basingstoke: Palgrave, 2016), p. 9.
155. Rodgers, *Adolescent Girlhood and Literary Culture at the* Fin de Siècle, p. 9.
156. Driscoll, *Girls*, p. 35.
157. Driscoll, *Girls*, p. 39.
158. Driscoll, *Girls*, p. 40.
159. Deleuze and Guattari, *A Thousand Plateaus*, p. 293.
160. Deleuze and Guattari, *A Thousand Plateaus*, p. 293.

Chapter 2

1. Sections of this article appeared in *The Irish Journal of Gothic and Horror Studies*. Reprinted with permission.
2. Hayden White, *Tropics of Discourse: Essays in Cultural Criticism* (Baltimore MD: Johns Hopkins University Press, 1978), p. 5.
3. White, *Tropics of Discourse*, p. 5.
4. Robert J. Cottrol, 'Through a Glass Diversely: The O. J. Simpson Trial as Racial Rorschach Test', *University of Colorado Law Review*, 67 (1996), 910.
5. Larry Gragg, 'Review of *Switching Sides: How a Generation of Historians Lost Sympathy for the Victims of the Salem Witch Hunt*, by Tony Fels', *Journal of American History*, 105/4 (2019), 993.
6. Marion L. Starkey, *The Devil in Massachusetts: A Modern Inquiry into the Salem Witch Trials* (New York: Knopf, 1949). Emphasis added.

7. Gibson, *Witchcraft Myths*, p. 120.

8. Ilana Nash, *American Sweethearts: Teenage Girls in Twentieth-Century Popular Culture* (Bloomington IN: Indiana University Press, 2006), p. 17.

9. Grace Palladino, *Teenagers: An American History* (New York: Basic Books, 1996), p. xii.

10. Palladino, *Teenagers*, p. 5.

11. Palladino, *Teenagers*, p. 5.

12. Palladino, *Teenagers*, p. 5.

13. Palladino, *Teenagers*, p. 5.

14. Nash, *American Sweethearts*, p. 139.

15. Nash, *American Sweethearts*, p. 139.

16. Palladino, *Teenagers*, p. xiv.

17. Palladino, *Teenagers*, p. xiv.

18. Palladino, *Teenagers*, p. 59.

19. Stacy Schiff, *The Witches: Salem, 1692: A History* (London: Weidenfeld & Nicolson, 2015), p. x.

20. Palladino, *Teenagers*, p. 51.

21. Nash, *American Sweethearts*, p. 120.

22. Nash, *American Sweethearts*, p. 2.

23. Nash, *American Sweethearts*, p. 124.

24. Nash, *American Sweethearts*, p. 124.

25. In her book *Good Wives: Image and Reality in the Lives of Women in Northern New England, 1650–1750* (London: Vintage, [1980] 1991) Laurel Thatcher Ulrich notes that this notion of youth as period of preparation for one's wifely duty also explains why many families utilised the labour of neighbours or neighbours' daughters instead of, or alongside, indentured servants. She points out that 'Families with more children than work to do exported maids; families with big houses or no children or very young children took them' (p. 57). In this way, young girls could undertake a kind of apprenticeship, whereby they could learn the kinds of domestic skills that would later be of use to them as wives and mothers.

26. Jane M. Ussher, *Managing the Monstrous Feminine: Regulating the Reproductive Body* (London: Routledge, 2006), p. 15.

27. In *Managing the Monstrous Feminine*, Ussher notes that scholars such as Nancy Oudshoorn view sex hormones as an invention of nineteenth-century endocrinology, as both men and women possess oestrogen, progesterone and testosterone in varying levels (p. 15).

28. Anne Fausto-Sterling, *Sexing the Body: Gender Politics and the Construction of Sexuality* (New York: Basic Books, 2000), p. 177.

29. Fausto-Sterling, *Sexing the Body*, p. 177.

30. Michelle H. Martin, '"No One Will Ever Know Your Secret!" Commercial Puberty Pamphlets for Girls from the 1940s to the 1990s', in Claudia Nelson and Michelle H. Martin (eds), *Sexual Pedagogies: Sex Education in Britain, Australia, and America, 1879–2000* (New York: Palgrave, 2004), p. 142.

31. *The Story of Menstruation* (Walt Disney Productions, 1946), *www.youtube.com/watch?v=vG9o9m0LsbI* (last accessed 21 December 2020).

32. See Chapter 1.

33. Kelly Hurley, *The Gothic Body: Sexuality, Materialism, and Degeneration at the Fin de Siècle* (Cambridge: Cambridge University Press, 1996), p. 32.

34. Hurley, *The Gothic Body*, p. 3.

35. Sencindiver, 'It's Alive', p. 486.

36. Hurley, *The Gothic Body*, p. 31.

37. See Cora Kaplan, 'Witchcraft: A Child's Story', *History Workshop Journal*, 41/1 (1996), for a discussion of the book's anachronistic treatment of childhood.

38. Arthur Miller, '*The Crucible* in History', in Steven R. Centola and Robert A. Martin (eds), *The Collected Essays of Arthur Miller* (London: Bloomsbury, Methuen Drama, 2015), p. 476.

39. Margo Burns, 'Arthur Miller's *The Crucible*: Fact & Fiction (or Picky, Picky, Picky . . .)', *www.17thc.us/docs/fact-fiction.shtml* (last accessed 1 April 2019).

40. Although Starkey seems to suggest that *The Devil in Massachusetts* is novel in its application of psychoanalysis and psychology to early modern history and witchcraft, the connection between witchcraft, psychology and hysteria was already well established in both medical literature and popular culture. The renowned neurologist and head of Paris's Salpêtrière clinic Jean-Martin Charcot (1825–93) analysed early modern artworks depicting demonic possession and claimed that the flailing limbs and rigid postures of the possessed were symptomatic of hysterical attacks. Another nineteenth-century physician, Paul Regnard, maintained that witches experienced seizures similar to those of hysterics. Later, in 1897, Sigmund Freud – one of Starkey's main sources – published an article drawing parallels between his female patients and historical descriptions of witches. In Sweden, towards the end of the nineteenth century, physician Anton Nyström published a book on the early modern witch trials in which he theorised that the confessions of accused witches could be attributed to women's propensity for fantasy and their susceptibility to states of 'ecstasy' or hysteria (see Per Faxneld, *Satanic Feminism: Lucifer as the Liberator of Women in Nineteenth-Century Culture* (Oxford: Oxford University Press, 2017), pp. 209–11, for a more thorough and nuanced account of the relationship between nineteenth-century psychology and witchcraft). The complex interrelation between hysteria, psychoanalysis and witchcraft

also characterises early twentieth-century films such as Benjamin Christensen's *Häxan* (1922).

41. Jonathan M. Metzl, '"Mother's Little Helper": The Crisis of Psychoanalysis and the Miltown Resolution', *Gender & History*, 15/2 (2003), 233. Metzl actually dates the origins of popular interest in psychoanalysis to 1955, so Starkey appears to be something of an innovator in this regard.
42. David B. Allison and Mark S. Roberts, 'On Constructing the Disorder of Hysteria', *The Journal of Medicine and Philosophy*, 19/3 (1994), 242.
43. Allison and Roberts, 'On Constructing the Disorder of Hysteria', 251.
44. Rachel P. Maines, *The Technology of Orgasm: 'Hysteria', the Vibrator, and Women's Sexual Satisfaction* (Baltimore MD: Johns Hopkins University Press, 1998), p. 23.
45. Sigmund Freud, 'Fragment of an Analysis of a Case of Hysteria', in James Strachey (ed.), *The Standard Edition of the Complete Psychological Works of Sigmund Freud, Volume 7 (1901–1905)*, p. 49.
46. Patricia Gherovici, '"Where Have the Hysterics Gone?" Lacan's Reinvention of Hysteria', *ESC: English Studies in Canada*, 40/1 (2014), 47.
47. Ussher, *Managing the Monstrous Feminine*, p. 24.
48. See Per Faxneld's *Satanic Feminism* for a thorough discussion of the complex interrelations between first-wave feminists, witches and hysterics in nineteenth-century culture.
49. Faxneld, *Satanic Feminism*, p. 212.
50. Michel Foucault, *Psychiatric Power: Lectures at the Collège de France, 1973–1974* (trans. Graham Burchell) (Basingstoke: Palgrave, 2006), p. 253.
51. Michel Foucault, *Abnormal: Lectures at the Collège de France, 1974–1975* (trans. Graham Burchell) (London: Verso, 2016), p. 207.
52. Hélène Cixous and Catherine Clément, *The Newly Born Woman* (trans. Betsy Wing) (London: IB Tauris, 1996), p. 85.
53. Cixous and Clément, *The Newly Born Woman*, p. 85.
54. Cixous and Clément, *The Newly Born Woman*, p. 85.
55. Thatcher Ulrich, *Good Wives*, p. 57.
56. Andrew Scull, *Hysteria: The Disturbing History* (Oxford: Oxford University Press, 2009), p. 2, p. 135.
57. Margaret A. McLaren, *Feminism, Foucault, and Embodied Subjectivity* (New York: SUNY Press, 2002), p. 15.
58. Foucault, *Psychiatric Power*, p. 253.
59. Foucault, *Psychiatric Power*, p. 254.
60. Elaine Showalter, *The Female Malady: Women, Madness and English Culture, 1830–1980* (London: Penguin, 1985), p. 5.

61. Erika Gasser, *Vexed with Devils: Manhood and Witchcraft in Old and New England* (New York: New York University Press, 2017), p. 5.

62. Foucault, *Abnormal*, p. 212.

63. Foucault, *Abnormal*, p. 213.

64. Miller's and Starkey's conceptualisation of the Salem girls as contemporary teenagers has had a major influence on twenty-first-century young-adult fiction. At least two recent novels – Katherine Howe's *Conversion* (2014) and Adriana Mather's *How to Hang a Witch* (2016) – directly transpose the dynamics of the Salem witch trials onto contemporary high school settings.

65. Schiff, *The Witches*, p. 323.

66. Diane Purkiss, *The Witch in History: Early Modern and Twentieth-Century Representations* (Abingdon: Routledge, 1996), Kindle edition, p. 134.

67. Purkiss, *The Witch in History*, p. 125.

68. Iris van der Tuin and Rick Dolphijn, 'The Transversality of New Materialism', *Women: A Cultural Review*, 21/2 (2010), 159.

69. Hurley, *The Gothic Body*, p. 31.

70. The Elliott stories were later collected in Bradbury's late career fix-up novel *From the Dust Returned*. These are the versions that I will reference throughout this chapter.

71. Jonathan R. Eller, *Becoming Ray Bradbury* (Champaign IL: University of Illinois Press, 2011), p. 202. Ray Bradbury may also have been interested in witchcraft because his ancestor, Mary Bradbury, was accused during the Salem trials. It was claimed that she transformed into a blue boar, scrambled under a horse's hooves and startled the rider (see Schiff, *The Witches*, p. 294).

72. Miranda Corcoran and Steve Gronert Ellerhoff, 'Introduction', in Miranda Corcoran and Steve Gronert Ellerhoff (eds), *Exploring the Horror of Supernatural Fiction: Ray Bradbury's Elliott Family* (Abingdon: Routledge, 2020), p. 1.

73. Hurley, *The Gothic Body*, p. 28.

74. Anna Powell, *Deleuze and Horror Film* (Edinburgh: Edinburgh University Press, 2005), e-book, p. 77.

75. In *From the Dust Returned*, the fix-up novel that I am using as a source for these stories, this particular tale has been renamed 'The Wandering Witch'. However, all previously published versions of the tale have used the title 'The April Witch', and this is how it is referred to by most readers and scholars. As such, I will use the title 'The April Witch' to avoid confusion.

76. Serenity Young, *Women Who Fly: Goddesses, Witches, Mystic, and Other Airborne Females* (Oxford: Oxford University Press, 2018), p. 156.

77. Elizabeth Grosz, *Volatile Bodies: Toward a Corporeal Feminism* (Bloomington IN: Indiana University Press, 1994), p. 75.

78. Grosz, *Volatile Bodies*, p. 75.
79. For a more detailed discussion of adolescent fantasy and embodiment in 'The April Witch', see Miranda Corcoran, '"I'll be in every living thing in the world tonight": Adolescent Femininity and the Gothic Uncanny in Bradbury's "The April Witch"', *The New Ray Bradbury Review*, 6 (2019), 121–41.
80. Brent Adkins, *Deleuze and Guattari's* A Thousand Plateaus: *A Critical Introduction and Guide* (Edinburgh: Edinburgh University Press, 2015), p. 146.
81. Powell, *Deleuze and Horror Film*, p. 67.
82. Gilles Deleuze and Félix Guattari, *A Thousand Plateaus: Capitalism and Schizophrenia* (trans. Brian Massumi) (Minneapolis MN: University of Minnesota Press, 1987), p. 272. Emphasis in original.
83. Powell, *Deleuze and Horror Film*, p. 67.
84. Peter Heymans, 'Eating Girls: Deleuze and Guattari's Becoming-Animal and the Romantic Sublime in William Blake's Lyca Poems', *Humanimalia*, 3/1 (2011), 6–7.
85. Deleuze and Guattari, *A Thousand Plateaus*, p. 275.
86. Gilles Deleuze and Félix Guattari, *Kafka: Toward a Minor Literature* (trans. Dana Polan) (Minneapolis MN: University of Minnesota Press, 1986), p. 13.
87. Fernando Gabriel Pagnoni Berns, 'Dark Ecology in *From the Dust Returned*', in *Exploring the Horror of Supernatural Fiction*, p. 121.
88. Karen Barad, 'Posthumanist Performativity: Toward an Understanding of How Matter Comes to Matter', in *Material Feminisms*, p. 139. Emphasis in original.
89. Barad, 'Posthumanist Performativity', p. 141.
90. Deleuze and Guattari, *A Thousand Plateaus*, p. 8.
91. Adkins, *Deleuze and Guattari's* A Thousand Plateaus, p. 26.

Chapter 3

1. Christopher B. Strain, *The Long Sixties: America, 1955–1973* (London: Wiley-Blackwell, 2016), e-book.
2. Grace Palladino, *Teenagers: An American History* (New York: Basic Books, 1996), p. 231.
3. Palladino, *Teenagers*, p. 231.
4. Palladino, *Teenagers*, p. 239
5. Strain, *The Long Sixties*, p. 120.
6. Jeffrey B. Russell and Brooks Alexander, *A New History of Witchcraft: Sorcerers, Heretics & Pagans* (London: Thames & Hudson, 2007), p. 172.

7. Patricia MacCormack, *The Ahuman Manifesto: Activism for the End of the Anthropocene* (London: Bloomsbury, 2020), p. 102.
8. MacCormack, *The Ahuman Manifesto*, p. 103.
9. Asbjorn Dyrendal, James R. Lewis and Jesper Aa. Petersen, *The Invention of Satanism* (Oxford: Oxford University Press, 2016), p. 3.
10. Dyrendal, Lewis and Petersen, *The Invention of Satanism*, p. 4.
11. Magus Peter H. Gilmore, 'Introduction', in Anton Szandor LaVey, *The Satanic Bible* (London: Avon, 1992), n.p.
12. Marcello Truzzi, 'The Occult Revival as Popular Culture: Some Random Observations on the Old and the Nouveau Witch', *The Sociological Quarterly*, 13/1 (1972), 18.
13. In Peter Bebergal, *Season of the Witch: How the Occult Saved Rock and Roll* (London: Tacher, 2015), p. 73.
14. Truzzi 'The Occult Revival as Popular Culture', 25.
15. Truzzi, 'The Occult Revival as Popular Culture', 29.
16. This transplantation of the witch to modern American youth culture can be seen in a range of television movies and exploitation films from this period, including *Satan's School for Girls* (David Lowell Rich, 1973), *Satan's Cheerleaders* (Greydon Clark, 1977) and *The Initiation of Sarah* (Robert Day, 1978).
17. Chloé Germaine Buckley, *Twenty-First-Century Children's Gothic: From the Wanderer to Nomadic Subject* (Edinburgh: Edinburgh University Press, 2018), p. 69.
18. Elizabeth Bullen, 'Inside Story: Product Placement and Adolescent Consumer Identity in Young Adult Fiction', *Media, Culture & Society*, 31/3 (2009), 498.
19. The Young Adult Library Services Association was only founded as a division of the American Library Association in 1957. During the post-World War II period young-adult literature became an increasingly prominent literary mode as teenagers began carving out distinct identities for themselves.
20. Jessica Kokesh and Miglena Sternadori, 'The Good, the Bad, and the Ugly: A Qualitative Study of How Young Adult Fiction Affects Identity Construction', *Atlantic Journal of Communication*, 23/3 (2015), 139.
21. Jonathan Cohen, 'Defining Identification: A Theoretical Look at the Identification of Audiences With Media Characters', *Mass Communication and Society*, 4/3 (2001), 245.
22. Kokesh and Sternadori, 'The Good, the Bad, and the Ugly', 142.
23. Kokesh and Sternadori, 'The Good, the Bad, and the Ugly', 142.
24. Ramona Caponegro, 'Where the "Bad" Girls Are (Contained): Representations of the 1950s Female Juvenile Delinquent in Children's Literature and *Ladies' Home Journal*', *Children's Literature Association Quarterly*, 34/4 (2009), 312.

25. Jules Michelet, *Satanism and Witchcraft: The Classic Study of Medieval Superstition* (London: Kensington Publishing, 1998), pp. 144–5.
26. Jane M. Ussher, *Managing the Monstrous Feminine: Regulating the Reproductive Body* (London: Routledge, 2006), p. 20.
27. Ussher, *Managing the Monstrous Feminine*, p. 38.
28. Ussher, *Managing the Monstrous Feminine*, p. 19.
29. Ussher, *Managing the Monstrous Feminine*, p. 19.
30. Susan K. Freeman, *Sex Goes to School: Girls and Sex Education before the 1960s* (Champaign IL: University of Illinois Press, 2008), p. 87.
31. Niva Piran, *Journeys of Embodiment at the Intersection of Body and Culture: The Developmental Theory of Embodiment* (Cambridge MA: Academic Press, 2017), p. 128.
32. Piran, *Journeys of Embodiment*, p. xiv.
33. Ussher, *Managing the Monstrous Feminine*, p. 56.
34. Luisa Colón, 'How Archie Got His Groove Back', *JSTOR Daily* (7 May 2018) *www.daily.jstor.org/archie-got-groove-back/* (last accessed 22 December 2020).
35. Sharon Scholl, 'The American Teenager: From *Archie* to *Funky*', *Studies in Popular Culture*, 2 (1979), 38.
36. Freeman, *Sex Goes to School*, p. 100.
37. Freeman, *Sex Goes to School*, p. 101.
38. Mark Jancovich, *American Horror in the 1950s* (Manchester: Manchester University Press, 1996), p. 123.
39. Jancovich, *American Horror in the 1950s*, p. 124.
40. Bullen, 'Inside Story', 497.
41. Jennifer Helgren, *American Girls and Global Responsibility: A New Relation to the World During the Early Cold War* (New Brunswick NJ: Rutgers University Press, 2017), p. 102.
42. Helgren, *American Girls and Global Responsibility*, p. 102.
43. Joan Ormrod, 'Endless Summer (1964): Consuming Waves and Surfing the Frontier', *Film & History: An Interdisciplinary Journal of Film and Television Studies*, 35/1 (2005), 40.
44. Ormrod, 'Endless Summer (1964)', 40.
45. Piran, *Journeys of Embodiment*, p. 180.
46. Margaret A. McLaren, *Feminism, Foucault, and Embodied Subjectivity* (New York: SUNY Press, 2002), p. 147.
47. In McLaren, *Feminism, Foucault, and Embodied Subjectivity*, p. 147.
48. In other incarnations, Sabrina Spellman is portrayed as a more complex character. It would be productive to map the evolution of Sabrina across half a century of comics, cartoons, films and live-action series, but this level of detail

is beyond scope of the present project and would require an entire book in its own right.

49. Buckley, *Twenty-First-Century Children's Gothic*, p. 76.
50. Elizabeth Grosz, *Volatile Bodies: Toward a Corporeal Feminism* (Bloomington IN: Indiana University Press, 1994), p. 167.
51. Andrew Scahill, *The Revolting Child in Horror Cinema: Youth, Rebellion and Queer Spectatorship* (Basingstoke: Palgrave, 2015), p. 61
52. Buckley, *Twenty-First-Century Children's Gothic*, p. 73.
53. Eve Kosofsky Sedgwick, *Tendencies* (London: Routledge, 1994), pp. 3–4.
54. Janet Staiger, *Perverse Spectators: The Practices of Film Reception* (New York: New York University Press, 2000), e-book, p. 37.
55. Staiger, *Perverse Spectators*, p. 37.
56. Ruth Franklin, *Shirley Jackson: A Rather Haunted Life* (New York: W. W. Norton, 2016), p. 106.
57. Franklin, *Shirley Jackson*, p. 358.
58. Bernice M. Murphy, '"The People in the Village Have Always Hated Us": Shirley Jackson's New England Gothic', in Bernice M. Murphy (ed.), *Shirley Jackson: Essays on the Literary Legacy* (Jefferson NC: McFarland, 2005), p. 119.
59. Joyce Carol Oates, 'Afterword', in *We Have Always Lived in the Castle* (London: Penguin, 2009), p. 148.
60. Malcolm Gaskill, *Witchcraft: A Very Short Introduction* (Oxford: Oxford University Press, 2010), p. 14.
61. 'Veneficus', *World of Dictionary*, www.worldofdictionary.com/dict/latin-english/meaning/veneficus (last accessed 22 December 2020).
62. Grosz, *Volatile Bodies*, p. 172.
63. Anna Powell, *Deleuze and Horror Film* (Edinburgh: Edinburgh University Press, 2005), e-book, p. 73.
64. Joshua Delpech-Ramey, 'Deleuze, Guattari, and the "Politics of Sorcery"', *SubStance*, 39/1 (2010), 10–11.
65. Diane Purkiss, *The Witch in History: Early Modern and Twentieth-Century Representations* (Abingdon: Routledge, 1996), Kindle edition, p. 122.
66. Delpech-Ramey, 'Deleuze, Guattari and the "Politics of Sorcery"', 13.
67. Gilles Deleuze and Félix Guattari, *A Thousand Plateaus: Capitalism and Schizophrenia* (trans. Brian Massumi) (Minneapolis MN: University of Minnesota Press, 1987), p. 241.
68. Hannah Priest, 'Introduction', in Hannah Priest (ed.), *She-Wolf: A Cultural History of Female Werewolves* (Manchester: Manchester University Press, 2017), p. 3.
69. Rolf Schulte, 'She Transformed into a Werewolf, Devouring and Killing Two Children', in *She-Wolf*, p. 48.

70. Jazmina Cinina, 'Fur Girls and Wolf Women', in *She-Wolf*, p. 90.

71. Priest, 'Introduction', p. 16.

72. Hannah Priest, 'I Was a Teenage She-Wolf', in *She-Wolf*, p. 131.

73. Priest, 'I Was a Teenage She-Wolf', p. 132.

74. Grosz, *Volatile Bodies*, p. 174.

75. In Grosz, *Volatile Bodies*, p. 175.

76. Deleuze and Guattari, in Grosz, *Volatile Bodies*, p. 175.

77. Isabel Cristina Pinedo, *Recreational Terror: Women and the Pleasures of Horror Film Viewing* (New York: State University of New York Press, 1997), p. 69.

78. Pinedo, *Recreational Terror*, p. 86.

79. Pinedo, *Recreational Terror*, p. 87. Emphasis in original.

80. Gary Hoppenstand and Ray B. Browne, *The Gothic World of Stephen King: Landscape of Nightmares* (Bowling Green OH: Bowling Green State University Press, 1987), p. 7.

81. Stephen King, *Danse Macabre* (London: Hodder & Stoughton, [1981] 2006), p. 198.

82. King, *Danse Macabre*, p. 198.

83. John Sears, *Stephen King's Gothic* (Cardiff: University of Wales Press, 2011), p. 29.

84. Darren Elliott-Smith, *Queer Horror Film and Television: Sexuality and Masculinity at the Margins* (London: I. B. Tauris, 2016), Kindle edition, Loc. 486.

85. Barbara Creed, *The Monstrous Feminine: Film, Feminism, Psychoanalysis* (Abingdon: Routledge, 1993), p. 78.

86. Creed, *The Monstrous Feminine*, p. 83.

87. Kelly Hurley, *The Gothic Body: Sexuality, Materialism, and Degeneration at the Fin de Siècle* (Cambridge: Cambridge University Press, 1996), p. 120.

88. Hurley, *The Gothic Body*, p. 120.

89. Jack Morgan, *The Biology of Horror: Gothic Literature and Film* (Carbondale IL: Southern Illinois University Press, 2002), p. 3.

90. Kevin Trumpeter, 'The Language of the Stones: The Agency of the Inanimate in Literary Naturalism and the New Materialism', *American Literature*, 87/2 (2015), 229.

91. Trumpeter, 'The Language of the Stones', 229.

92. For more on Carrie's embrace of her unruly corporeality, see Miranda Corcoran and Anne Mahler, '"You either ate the world or the world ate you": Gender Performance and Violence in Stephen King's Campus Shooting Trilogy', *Aeternum*, Winter 2021.

93. Purkiss, *The Witch in History*, p. 121.

94. Grosz, *Volatile Bodies*, p. 167.

95. Grosz, *Volatile Bodies*, p. 167.
96. Grosz, *Volatile Bodies*, p. 167.
97. Michel Foucault, *The History of Sexuality, Volume 1: The Will to Knowledge* (trans. Robert Hurley) (New York: Pantheon, [1976] 1978), p. 104.
98. Ussher, *Managing the Monstrous Feminine*, p. 15.
99. Grosz, *Volatile Bodies*, p. 168.
100. Deleuze and Guattari, *A Thousand Plateaus*, p. 31.
101. Deleuze and Guattari, *A Thousand Plateaus*, p. 149.
102. Adkins, *Deleuze and Guattari's* A Thousand Plateaus, p. 106.
103. Pinedo, *Recreational Terror*, p. 69.
104. Scahill, *The Revolting Child in Horror Cinema*, p. 58. Emphasis in original.

Chapter 4

1. Gill, Rosalind, 'Postfeminist Media Culture: Elements of a Sensibility', *European Journal of Cultural Studies*, 10/2 (2007), 148.
2. Diane Purkiss, *The Witch in History: Early Modern and Twentieth-Century Representations* (Abingdon: Routledge, 1996), Kindle edition, p. 125.
3. Catherine Rottenberg, *The Rise of Neoliberal Feminism* (Oxford University Press, 2018), p. 68.
4. Stéphanie Genz and Benjamin A. Brabon, *Postfeminism: Cultural Texts and Theories* (Edinburgh: Edinburgh University Press, [2009] 2018), p. 18.
5. Gill, 'Postfeminist Media Culture', 148.
6. Gill, 'Postfeminist Media Culture', 148.
7. Gill, 'Postfeminist Media Culture', 149.
8. Gill, 'Postfeminist Media Culture', 149.
9. Gill, 'Postfeminist Media Culture', 156.
10. Rachel Moseley, 'Glamorous Witchcraft: Gender and Magic in Teen Film and Television', *Screen*, 43/4 (2002), 405.
11. Moseley, 'Glamorous Witchcraft', 404.
12. Frances Gateward and Murray Pomerance, 'Introduction', in Frances Gateward and Murray Pomerance (eds), *Sugar, Spice, and Everything Nice: Cinemas of Girlhood* (Detroit MI: Wayne State University Press, 2002), p. 15.
13. Gateward and Pomerance, 'Introduction', p. 15.
14. Gateward and Pomerance, 'Introduction', p. 15.
15. There are some exceptions to this trend. Exploitation films and low-budget horror often depicted teenage witches or Satanists in sensational or exploitative ways. See the previously mentioned *Satan's School for Girls*, *Satan's Cheerleaders*, etc.

16. Gateward and Pomerance, 'Introduction', p. 14.

17. Teresa Rizzo, in Sunny Hawkins, *Deleuze and the Gynesis of Horror: From Monstrous Births to the Birth of the Monster* (London: Bloomsbury, 2020), p. 72.

18. Anna Powell, *Deleuze and Horror Film* (Edinburgh: Edinburgh University Press, 2005), e-book, p. 72.

19. Hawkins, *Deleuze and the Gynesis of Horror*, p. 73.

20. Shelley Budgeon, 'Identity as an Embodied Event', *Body & Society*, 9/1 (2003), 36.

21. Budgeon, 'Identity as an Embodied Event', 37.

22. Thomas Fahy, *Dining with Madmen: Fat, Food, and the Environment in 1980s Horror* (Jackson MS: University Press of Mississippi, 2019), 'Introduction'.

23. Benjamin G. Rader, 'The Quest for Self-Sufficiency and the New Strenuosity: Reflections on the Strenuous Life of the 1970s and the 1980s', *Journal of Sport History*, 18/2 (1991), 255.

24. Michel Foucault, 'About the Beginning of the Hermeneutics of the Self: Two Lectures at Dartmouth', *Political Theory*, 21/2 (1993), 203.

25. Foucault, 'About the Beginning of the Hermeneutics of the Self', 203.

26. Foucault, 'About the Beginning of the Hermeneutics of the Self', 203.

27. Sandra Lee Bartky, 'Foucault, Femininity and the Modernization of Patriarchal Power', in Katie Conboy, Nadia Medina and Sarah Stanbury (eds), *Writing on the Body: Female Embodiment and Feminist Theory* (New York: Columbia University Press, 1997), p. 133.

28. Bartky, 'Foucault, Femininity and the Modernization of Patriarchal Power', p. 148.

29. Bartky, 'Foucault, Femininity and the Modernization of Patriarchal Power', p. 138.

30. Budgeon, 'Identity as an Embodied Event', 41.

31. Budgeon, 'Identity as an Embodied Event', 36.

32. Gilles Deleuze and Félix Guattari, *A Thousand Plateaus: Capitalism and Schizophrenia* (trans. Brian Massumi) (Minneapolis MN: University of Minnesota Press, 1987), p. 275.

33. Hawkins, *Deleuze and the Gynesis of Horror*, p. 35.

34. Kathy Davis, in Budgeon, 'Identity as an Embodied Event', 48.

35. Moseley, 'Glamourous Witchcraft', 407.

36. Sarah Projansky and Leah R. Vande Berg, 'Sabrina, the Teenage . . .?: Girls, Witches, Mortals and the Limitations of Prime-Time Feminism', in Elyce Rae Helford (ed.), *Fantasy Girls: Gender in the New Universe of Science Fiction and Fantasy Television* (Lanham MD: Rowman & Littlefield, 2000), p. 16.

37. Season 1, Episode 4, 'Terrible Things'.

38. Foucault, in Mark G. Kelly, 'Foucault, Subjectivity, and Technologies of the Self', in Christopher Falzon *et al.* (eds), *A Companion to Foucault* (Oxford: Blackwell, 2010), p. 256.

39. Kaja Silverman, 'Fragments of a Fashionable Discourse', in Tania Modleski (ed.), *Studies in Entertainment: Critical Approaches to Mass Culture* (Bloomington IN: Indiana University Press, 1986), p. 148.

40. Silverman, 'Fragments of a Fashionable Discourse', p. 151.

41. Silverman, 'Fragments of a Fashionable Discourse', p. 151.

42. Season 2, Episode 6, 'Sabrina, the Teenage Boy'.

43. Projansky and Vande Berg, 'Sabrina, the Teenage . . .?', p. 23.

44. Projansky and Vande Berg, 'Sabrina, the Teenage . . .?', p. 25.

45. Catherine Driscoll, *Girls: Feminine Adolescence in Popular Culture and Cultural Theory* (New York: Columbia University Press, 2002), p. 192.

46. Driscoll, *Girls*, p. 193.

47. Elizabeth Grosz, *Volatile Bodies: Toward a Corporeal Feminism* (Bloomington IN: Indiana University Press, 1994), p. 176.

48. Sinead Stubbins, '"We are the weirdos, mister": *The Craft* and the Year of the Teen Witch', AV Club (3 May 2015), *www. film.avclub.com/we-are-the-weirdos-mister-the-craft-and-the-year-of-1798246863* (last accessed 22 December 2020).

49. Matthew Jacobs and Julia Brucculieri, 'Relax, It's Only Magic: An Oral History of *The Craft*' (20 May 2016), *https://www.huffingtonpost.co.uk/entry/the-craft-oral-history_n_5734f7c9e4b060aa7819d362* (last accessed 22 December 2020).

50. Peg Aloi, 'A Charming Spell: The Intentional and Unintentional Influence of Popular Media Upon Teenage Witchcraft in America', in Hannah E. Johnston and Peg Aloi, *The New Generation Witches: Teenage Witchcraft in Contemporary Culture* (Aldershot: Ashgate, 2007), p. 118.

51. Emily Chandler, '"Loving and Cruel, All at the Same Time": Girlhood Identity in *The Craft*', *Girlhood Studies*, 9/2 (2016), 114.

52. Vincent B. Leitch, 'Costly Compensations: Postmodern fashion, Politics, Identity', *Modern Fiction Studies*, 42/1 (1996), 112.

53. Brooke Ballantyne, 'Goth Girls', in Claudia A. Mitchell and Jacqueline Reid-Walsh (eds), *Girl Culture: An Encyclopedia* (Westport CT: Greenwood Press, 2008), p. 331.

54. Chandler, 'Loving and Cruel, All at the Same Time', 113.

55. Catherine Spooner, *Fashioning Gothic Bodies* (Manchester: Manchester University Press, 2004), p. 165.

56. Adaeze Enekwechi and Opal Moore, 'Children's Literature and the Politics of Hair in Books for African American Children', *Children's Literature Association Quarterly*, 24/4 (1999), 196.

57. Tracey Owens Patton, '"Hey Girl, Am I More than My Hair?": African American Women and Their Struggles with Beauty, Body Image and Hair', *NWSA Journal*, 18/2 (2006), 26.

58. Rosemarie Garland-Thomson, *Extraordinary Bodies: Figuring Physical Disability in American Culture and Literature* (New York: Columbia University Press, 1997), p. 7.

59. Richard Davenport-Hines, *Gothic: Four Hundred Years of Excess, Horror, Evil and Ruin* (New York: Northpoint Press), p. 7.

60. Spooner, *Fashioning Gothic Bodies*, p. 182.

61. Grosz, *Volatile Bodies*, p. 178.

62. Emma Renold and Jessica Ringrose, 'Schizoid subjectivities? Re-theorizing teen girls' sexual cultures in an era of "sexualization"', *Journal of Sociology*, 47/4 (2011), 393.

63. Spooner, *Fashioning Gothic Bodies*, p. 184.

64. Hawkins, *Deleuze and the Gynesis of Horror*, p. 33.

65. Deleuze and Guattari, in Powell, *Deleuze and the Horror Film*, p. 21.

66. The notion that Nancy is still becoming, or transforming, at the end of the film is reinforced by the 2020 sequel/reboot *The Craft: Legacy* (directed by Zoe Lister-Jones). In her brief cameo at the end of the film, Nancy appears to have transformed yet again. She is still curt in her manner, but now she is a mother, and it is implied that she has become a more caring person.

67. Alice Jardine, 'Woman in Limbo: Deleuze and His Br(others)', *SubStance*, 13/3/4 (1984), 52.

68. Season 7, Episode 22, 'Chosen'. Emphasis added.

69. Jes Battis, '"She's Not All Grown Yet": Willow as Hybrid/Hero in *Buffy the Vampire Slayer*', *Slayage: The Journal of Whedon Studies*, 2.1/5 (2002), 2.

70. Season 3, Episode 14, 'Bad Girls'.

71. A. Susan Owen, 'Vampires, Postmodernity and Postfeminism: *Buffy the Vampire Slayer*', *Journal of Popular Film and Television*, 27/2 (1999), 26.

72. Grosz, *Volatile Bodies*, p. 177.

73. Sarah Gilligan, 'Performing Postfeminist Identities: Gender, Costume, and Transformation in Teen Cinema', in Melanie Waters (ed.), *Women on Screen: Feminism and Femininity in Visual Culture* (Basingstoke: Palgrave, 2011), p. 167.

74. Gilligan, 'Performing Postfeminist Identities', p. 167.

75. Renold and Ringrose, 'Schizoid subjectivities?', 390.

76. Battis, 'Willow as Hybrid Hero', 2.
77. Season 3, Episode 2, 'Dead Man's Party'.
78. Season 4, Episode 4, 'Fear Itself'.
79. Season 4, Episode 14, 'Goodbye Iowa'.
80. Season 4, Episode 16, 'Who Are You?'.
81. Battis, 'Willow as Hybrid Hero', 19–20.
82. Rhonda Wilcox, *Why Buffy Matters: The Art of Buffy the Vampire Slayer* (London: I. B. Tauris, 2005), p. 220.
83. Season 4, Episode 22, 'Restless'.
84. Battis, 'Willow as Hybrid Hero', 20.
85. Season 6, Episode 20, 'Villains'.
86. Season 6, Episode 21, 'Two to Go'.
87. Season 6, Episode 22, 'Grave'.
88. Battis, 'Willow as Hybrid Hero', 3.
89. Battis, 'Willow as Hybrid Hero',17.
90. Battis, 'Willow as Hybrid Hero', 10.
91. Season 7, Episode 21, 'End of Days'.
92. Season 7, Episode 22, 'Chosen'.
93. Season 5, Episode 11, 'Triangle'.
94. Ana Carolina De Barros, '"Gay Now": Bisexual Erasure in Supernatural Media from 1983 to 2003', *Journal of Bisexuality*, 20/1 (2020), 108.
95. Em McAvan, '"I Think I'm Kinda Gay": Willow Rosenberg and the Absent/Present Bisexual in *Buffy the Vampire Slayer*', *Slayage: The Journal of Whedon Studies*, 6/4 (2007), 9.
96. Powell, *Deleuze and Horror Film*, p. 72.
97. Season 7, Episode 13, 'The Killer in Me'.
98. McAvan, 'I Think I'm Kinda Gay', 13.

Chapter 5

1. An earlier version of this chapter appears as 'The Monstrous Girl: Teen Witches, Power and Fourth-Wave Feminism', in Helen Gavin (ed.), *Women and the Abuse of Power* (Bingley: Emerald, 2022). Reprinted with permission and in accordance with Emerald Publishing's policies on open access and republishing.
2. Michel Foucault, *Abnormal: Lectures at the Collège de France, 1974–1975* (trans. Graham Burchell) (London: Verso, 2016), p. 211.
3. Karen Barad, 'Nature's Queer Performativity', *Qui Parle*, 19/2 (2011), 149.

4. Nicola Rivers, *Postfeminism(S) and the Arrival of the Fourth Wave: Turning Tides* (London: Palgrave, 2017), p. 8, p. 22.

5. Rivers, *Postfeminism(S) and the Arrival of the Fourth Wave*, p. 24.

6. Rivers, *Postfeminism(S) and the Arrival of the Fourth Wave*, p. 4.

7. Prudence Chamberlain, *The Feminist Fourth Wave: Affective Temporality* (Basingstoke: Palgrave, 2017), p. 3.

8. Chamberlain, *The Feminist Fourth Wave*, p. 3.

9. See Sue Jackson, 'Young feminists, feminism and digital media', *Feminism and Psychology*, 28/1 (2018), 32–49, for a detailed discussion of this issue.

10. Jackson, 'Young feminists, feminism and digital media', 36.

11. Jackson, 'Young feminists, feminism and digital media', 34.

12. Jessica Taft, *Rebel Girls: Youth Activism and Social Change Across the Americas* (New York: New York University Press, 2010), p. 8.

13. Taft, *Rebel Girls*, p. 8.

14. This is, of course, distinct from witch texts more broadly, which have engaged with feminist themes since at least the nineteenth century.

15. Rivers, *Postfeminism(S) and the Arrival of the Fourth Wave*, p. 19.

16. Michel Foucault, *The History of Sexuality, Volume 1: The Will to Knowledge* (trans. Robert Hurley) (New York: Pantheon, [1976] 1978), p. 93.

17. Foucault, *History of Sexuality*, p. 92.

18. Foucault, *History of Sexuality*, p. 94.

19. Karen Barad, 'Posthumanist Performativity: Toward an Understanding of How Matter Comes to Matter', in *Material Feminisms* (Bloomington IN: Indiana University Press, 2008), p. 135.

20. Barad, 'Posthumanist Performativity', p. 135.

21. Barbara Creed, *The Monstrous Feminine: Film, Feminism, Psychoanalysis* (Abingdon: Routledge, 1993), p. 105.

22. Creed, *The Monstrous Feminine*, p. 105.

23. Casey Ryan Kelly, 'Camp Horror and the Gendered Politics of Screen Violence: Subverting the Monstrous-Feminine in *Teeth* (2007)', *Women's Studies in Communication*, 38/1 (2016), 87.

24. Cherise Huntingford, 'Burn the Witch', in Richard Greene and Rachel Robison-Greene (eds), *American Horror Story and Philosophy: Life is but a Nightmare* (Chicago IL: Open Court, 2018), e-book, n.p.

25. See Stacy Alaimo, *Undomesticated Ground: Recasting Nature as Feminist Space* (Ithaca NY: Cornell University Press, 2000), for a more thorough exploration and deconstruction of these views.

26. Abigail Bray and Claire Colebrook, 'The Haunted Flesh: Corporeal Feminism and the Politics of (Dis)Embodiment', *Signs*, 24/1 (1998), 37.

27. Bray and Colebrook, 'The Haunted Flesh', 56.

28. Season 3, Episode 1, 'Bitchcraft'.

29. Barad, 'Posthuman Performativity', p. 136.

30. Karen Barad, *Meeting the Universe Halfway: Quantum Physics and the Entanglement of Matter and Meaning* (Durham NC: Duke University Press, 2007), p. 93.

31. Barad, 'Nature's Queer Performativity', 149.

32. Ann K. Brooks, 'Agential Realism in a Community-Based Organization in Mexico: An Ethico-Onto-Epistemology of Emancipatory Learning', *Adult Education Quarterly*, 69/1 (2019), 46.

33. Gilles Deleuze and Félix Guattari, *A Thousand Plateaus: Capitalism and Schizophrenia* (trans. Brian Massumi) (Minneapolis MN: University of Minnesota Press, 1987), p. 22–3.

34. J. Muñoz-Delgado, A. M. Santillán-Doherty, R. Mondragón-Ceballos and H. G. Erkert, 'Moon Cycle Effects on Humans: Myth or Reality?', *Salud Mental*, 23/6 (2000), 35.

35. Ingrid Johnston-Robledo and Joan C. Chrisler, 'The Menstrual Mark: Menstruation as Social Stigma', *Sex Roles*, 68 (2013), 12.

36. Jane M. Ussher, *Managing the Monstrous Feminine: Regulating the Reproductive Body* (London: Routledge, 2006), p. 50.

37. Ussher, *Managing the Monstrous Feminine*, p. 51.

38. Margaret A. McLaren, *Feminism, Foucault, and Embodied Subjectivity* (New York: SUNY Press, 2002), p. 4.

39. Foucault, *The History of Sexuality*, p. 92.

40. Part 1, Chapter 1: 'October Country'.

41. Barad, Meeting the Universe Halfway, p. 33.

42. Part 1, Chapter 1: 'October Country'.

43. Patricia Meyer Spacks, *The Adolescent Idea: Myths of Youth and Imagination* (London: Faber & Faber, 1981), p. 289.

44. Spacks, *The Adolescent Idea*, p. 4.

45. Part 4, Chapter 36: 'At the Mountains of Madness'.

46. Soili-Maria Olli, 'The Devil's Pact: A Male Strategy', in Owen Davies and Willem de Blécourt (eds), *Beyond the Witch Trials: Witchcraft and Magic in Enlightenment Europe* (Manchester: Manchester University Press, 2004), p. 100.

47. Foucault, *Abnormal*, pp. 209–10.

48. Foucault, *Abnormal*, p. 211.

49. Marilyn J. Westerkamp, 'Engendering Puritan Religious Culture in Old and New England', *Pennsylvania History: A Journal of Mid-Atlantic Studies*, 64 (1997), 107.

50. Carol F. Karlsen, *The Devil in the Shape of a Woman: Witchcraft in Colonial New England* (New York: WW Norton, 1998), p. 163.

51. Westerkamp, 'Engendering Puritan Religious Culture in Old and New England', 108.

52. Westerkamp, 'Engendering Puritan Religious Culture in Old and New England', 108.

53. Ussher, *Managing the Mostrous Feminine*, p. 1.

54. Stacy Alaimo, 'Trans-Corporeal Feminisms and the Ethical Space of Nature', in *Material Feminisms*, p. 238.

55. Alaimo, 'Trans-Corporeal Feminisms and the Ethical Space of Nature', p. 238.

56. Alaimo, 'Trans-Corporeal Feminisms and the Ethical Space of Nature', p. 239.

57. Adkins, *Deleuze and Guattari's* A Thousand Plateaus, p. 210.

58. Joshua Delpech-Ramey, 'Deleuze, Guattari, and the "Politics of Sorcery"', *SubStance*, 39/1 (2010), 14.

59. Ben Woodard, *Slime Dynamics* (Alresford: Zero Books, 2012), p. 14.

60. 'Female Freedom and Fury in The Witch', *Atlantic* (2016), *www.theatlantic.com/entertainment/archive/2016/02/robert-eggers-the-witch-female-empowerment/470844/* (last accessed 5 November 2019).

61. Laurel Zwissler, '"I Am That Very Witch": On the Witch, Feminism and Not Surviving Patriarchy', *Journal of Religion and Film*, 22/3 (2018), 1.

62. Zwissler, 'I Am That Very Witch', 7.

63. McLaren, *Feminism, Foucault, and Embodied Subjectivity*, p. 116.

64. Foucault, *Abnormal*, p. 207.

65. Delpech-Ramey, 'Deleuze, Guattari and the "Politics of Sorcery"', 15.

66. Season 1, Part One, 'The October Country'.

67. Patricia Hill Collins, *Black Feminist Thought: Consciousness and the Politics of Empowerment* (Abingdon: Routledge, [2000], 2009), p. 51.

68. Collins, *Black Feminist Thought*, p. 81.

69. Awad Ibrahim, 'Body Without Organs: Notes on Deleuze & Guattari, Critical Race Theory and the Socius of Anti-Racism', *Journal of Multilingual and Multicultural Development*, 36/1 (2015), 16.

70. Deleuze and Guattari, *A Thousand Plateaus*, p. 159.

71. Claudio Celis Bueno, 'The Face Revisited: Using Deleuze and Guattari to Explore the Politics of Algorithmic Face Recognition', *Theory, Culture & Society*, 37/1 (2020), 82.

72. Bueno, 'The Face Revisited', 83.

73. Amanda Kay LeBlanc, '"There's nothing I hate more than a racist:" (Re)centering whiteness in American Horror Story: Coven', *Critical Studies in Media Communication*, 35/3 (2018), 281.

74. Elizabeth Grosz, *Volatile Bodies: Toward a Corporeal Feminism* (Bloomington IN: Indiana University Press, 1994), p. 164.

75. Season 3, Episode 3, 'The Replacements'.

76. LeBlanc, 'There's nothing I hate more than a racist', 282.

77. Season 2, Episode 3, 'Boy Parts'.

78. Kinitra D. Brooks, *Searching for Sycorax: Black Women's Hauntings of Contemporary Horror* (New Brunswick NJ: Rutgers University Press, 2017), p. 6.

79. Brooks, *Searching for Sycorax*, p. 7.

80. In Yvonne P. Chireau, *Black Magic: Religion and the African American Conjuring Tradition* (Berkeley CA: University of California Press, 2003), p. 3.

81. Carolyn Morrow Long, *Spiritual Merchants: Religion, Magic, and Commerce* (Knoxville TN: University of Tennessee Press, 2001), p. xvi.

82. For example, the web series *Juju* (2019–present) focuses on three witches of colour who must navigate both young adulthood and their newly found magical powers.

83. Chireau, *Black Magic, p.* 12.

84. In McLaren, *Foucault, Feminism, and Embodied Subjectivity*, p. 37.

85. McLaren, *Foucault, Feminism, and Embodied Subjectivity*, p. 39.

86. McLaren, *Foucault, Feminism, and Embodied Subjectivity*, p. 39.

87. McLaren, *Foucault, Feminism, and Embodied Subjectivity*, p. 40.

88. Chireau, *Black Magic*, p. 13.

89. McLaren, *Foucault, Feminism, and Embodied Subjectivity*, p. 40.

90. Bray and Colebrook, 'The Haunted Flesh', p. 36.

91. Erica McWilliam, 'The Grotesque Body as Feminist Aesthetic?', *Counterpoints*, 168 (2003), 215–16.

92. Grosz, *Volatile Bodies*, p. 21.

Conclusion

1. Hayden White, *Tropics of Discourse: Essays in Cultural Criticism* (Baltimore MD: Johns Hopkins University Press, 1978), p. 72.

2. Gilles Deleuze and Félix Guattari, *A Thousand Plateaus: Capitalism and Schizophrenia* (trans. Brian Massumi) (Minneapolis MN: University of Minnesota Press, 1987), p. 239.

3. Patricia MacCormack, 'Unnatural Alliances', in Chrysanthi Nigianni and Merl Storr (eds), *Deleuze and Queer Theory* (Edinburgh: Edinburgh University Press, 2009), p. 136.

4. MacCormack, 'Unnatural Alliances', p. 136.

5. MacCormack, 'Unnatural Alliances', p. 139.

6. Deleuze and Guattari, in Elizabeth Grosz, *Volatile Bodies: Toward a Corporeal Feminism* (Bloomington IN: Indiana University Press, 1994), p. 225, n.3.

7. Lennard J. Davis and David B. Morris, 'Biocultures Manifesto', *New Literary History*, 33/3 (2007), 418.

8. Stacy Alaimo and Susan Hekman, 'Introduction: Emerging Models of Materiality in Feminist Theory', in Stacy Alaimo and Susan Hekman (eds), *Material Feminisms* (Bloomington IN: Indiana University Press, 2008), p. 9.

9. Kelly Hurley, *The Gothic Body: Sexuality, Materialism, and Degeneration at the* Fin de Siècle (Cambridge: Cambridge University Press, 1996), pp. 33–4.

10. Deleuze and Guattari, *A Thousand Plateaus*, p. 275.

11. See Carol J. Clover, Men, *Women and Chain Saws: Gender in the Modern Horror Film* (Princeton NJ: Princeton University Press, 1992) for more on this convention.

12. Emily Temple, 'There's a new *Buffy the Vampire Slayer* sequel coming, but will it be any good?', *Lithub* (2 August 2021), *https://lithub.com/theres-a-new-buffy-the-vampire-slayer-sequel-coming-but-will-it-be-any-good/* (last accessed 5 August 2021).

Select Bibliography

Adkins, Brent, *Deleuze and Guattari's* A Thousand Plateaus: *A Critical Introduction and Guide* (Edinburgh: Edinburgh University Press, 2015).

Alaimo, Stacy, and Susan Hekman, *Material Feminisms* (Bloomington IN: Indiana University Press, 2008).

Allison, David B., and Mark S. Roberts, 'On Constructing the Disorder of Hysteria', *The Journal of Medicine and Philosophy*, 19/3 (1994), 239–59.

Aloi, Peg, 'A Charming Spell: The Intentional and Unintentional Influence of Popular Media Upon Teenage Witchcraft in America', in Hannah E. Johnston and Peg Aloi, *The New Generation Witches: Teenage Witchcraft in Contemporary Culture* (Aldershot: Ashgate, 2007), pp. 113–27.

Barad, Karen, *Meeting the Universe Halfway: Quantum Physics and the Entanglement of Matter and Meaning* (Durham NC: Duke University Press, 2007).

—— 'Nature's Queer Performativity', *Qui Parle*, 19/2 (2011), 121–58.

—— 'Posthumanist Performativity: Toward an Understanding of How Matter Comes to Matter', in Stacy Alaimo and Susan Hekman (eds), *Material Feminisms* (Bloomington IN: Indiana University Press, 2008), pp. 120–54.

Bartky, Sandra Lee, 'Foucault, Femininity and the Modernization of Patriarchal Power', in Katie Conboy, Nadia Medina and Sarah Stanbury (eds), *Writing on the Body: Female Embodiment and Feminist Theory* (New York: Columbia University Press, 1997), pp. 129–54.

Battis, Jes, '"She's Not All Grown Yet": Willow as Hybrid/Hero in *Buffy the Vampire Slayer*', *Slayage: The Journal of Whedon Studies*, 2.1/5 (2002), 1–6.

Braidotti, Rosi, 'Mothers, Monsters and Machines', in Katie Conboy, Nadia Medina and Sarah Stanbury (eds), *Writing on the Body: Female Embodiment and Feminist Theory* (New York: Columbia University Press, 1997), pp. 59–79.

—— 'Teratologies', in Claire Colebrook and Ian Buchanan (eds), *Deleuze and Feminist Theory* (Edinburgh: Edinburgh University Press, 2000), pp. 156–72.

Brain, Robert, 'Materialising the Medium: Ectoplasm and the Quest for Supra-Normal Biology in *Fin-de-Siècle* Science and Art', in Anthony Enns and Shelley Trower (eds), *Vibratory Modernism* (Basingstoke: Palgrave: 2013), pp. 112–41.

Braude, Ann, *Radical Spirits: Spiritualism and Women's Rights in Nineteenth-Century America* (Indianapolis IN: Indiana University Press, 2001).

Bray, Abigail, and Claire Colebrook, 'The Haunted Flesh: Corporeal Feminism and the Politics of (Dis)Embodiment', *Signs*, 24/1 (1998), 35–67.

Brooks, Kinitra D., *Searching for Sycorax: Black Women's Hauntings of Contemporary Horror* (New Brunswick NJ: Rutgers University Press, 2018).

Brumberg, Joan Jacobs, *Fasting Girls: The History of Anorexia Nervosa* (London: Vintage, 2000).

Buckley, Chloé Germaine, *Twenty-First-Century Children's Gothic: From the Wanderer to Nomadic Subject* (Edinburgh: Edinburgh University Press, 2018).

Budgeon, Shelley, 'Identity as an Embodied Event', *Body & Society*, 9/1 (2003), 35–55.

Bullen, Elizabeth, 'Inside Story: Product Placement and Adolescent Consumer Identity in Young Adult Fiction', *Media, Culture & Society*, 31/3 (2009), 497–507.

Claudio, Celis Bueno, 'The Face Revisited: Using Deleuze and Guattari to Explore the Politics of Algorithmic Face Recognition', *Theory, Culture & Society*, 37/1 (2020), 73–91.

Chandler, Emily, '"Loving and Cruel, All at the Same Time": Girlhood Identity in The Craft', *Girlhood Studies*, 9/2 (2016), 109–25.

Chireau, Yvonne P., *Black Magic: Religion and the African American Conjuring Tradition* (Berkeley CA: University of California Press, 2003).

Cixous, Hélène and Catherine Clément, *The Newly Born Woman* (trans. Betsy Wing) (London: I. B. Tauris, 1996).

Clark, Stuart, *Thinking with Demons: The Idea of Witchcraft in Early Modern Europe* (Oxford: Oxford University Press, 1999), e-book.

Collins, Patricia Hill, *Black Feminist Thought: Consciousness and the Politics of Empowerment* (Abingdon: Routledge, [2000] 2009).

Corcoran, Miranda, and Steve Gronert Ellerhoff (eds), *Exploring the Horror of Supernatural Fiction: Ray Bradbury's Elliott Family* (London: Routledge, 2020).

Creed, Barbara, *The Monstrous Feminine: Film, Feminism, Psychoanalysis* (Abingdon: Routledge, 1993).

De Barros, Ana Carolina, '"Gay Now": Bisexual Erasure in Supernatural Media from 1983 to 2003', *Journal of Bisexuality*, 20/1 (2020), 104–17.

Deleuze, Gilles, and Félix Guattari, *Kafka: Toward a Minor Literature* (Minneapolis MN: University of Minnesota Press, 1986).

—— *A Thousand Plateaus: Capitalism and Schizophrenia* (trans. Brian Massumi) (Minneapolis MN: University of Minnesota Press, 1987).

Delpech-Ramey, Joshua, 'Deleuze, Guattari, and the "Politics of Sorcery"', *SubStance*, 39/1 (2010), 8–23.

Driscoll, Catherine, *Girls: Feminine Adolescence in Popular Culture and Cultural Theory* (New York: Columbia University Press, 2002).

Dudenhoeffer, Larrie, *Embodiment and Horror Cinema* (Basingstoke: Palgrave, 2014).

Dyrendal, Asbjorn, James R. Lewis and Jesper Aa. Petersen, *The Invention of Satanism* (Oxford: Oxford University Press, 2016).

Elliott-Smith, Darren, *Queer Horror Film and Television: Sexuality and Masculinity at the Margins* (London: I.B. Tauris, 2016), Kindle edition.

Falzon, Christopher, et al., *A Companion to Foucault* (Oxford: Blackwell, 2010).

Foucault, Michel, *Abnormal: Lectures at the Collège De France* (trans. Graham Burchell) (London: Verso, 2016).

—— 'About the Beginning of the Hermeneutics of the Self: Two Lectures at Dartmouth', *Political Theory*, 21/2 (1993), 198–227.

—— *The History of Sexuality, Volume 1: The Will to Knowledge* (trans. Robert Hurley) (New York: Pantheon, [1976] 1978).

—— 'Nietzsche, Genealogy, History', in Paul Rabinow (ed.), *The Foucault Reader* (New York: Random House, 1984), pp. 76–100.

—— *Psychiatric Power: Lectures at the Collège de France, 1973–1974* (trans. Graham Burchell) (Basingstoke: Palgrave, 2003).

Franklin, Ruth, *Shirley Jackson: A Rather Haunted Life* (New York: W. W. Norton, 2016).

Garland-Thomson, Rosemarie, *Extraordinary Bodies: Figuring Physical Disability in American Culture and Literature* (New York: Columbia University Press, 1997).

Gasser, Erika, *Vexed with Devils: Manhood and Witchcraft in Old and New England* (New York: New York University Press, 2017).

Genz, Stéphanie, and Benjamin A. Brabon, *Postfeminism: Cultural Texts and Theories* (Edinburgh: Edinburgh University Press, [2009] 2018).

Gibson, Marion, *Witchcraft Myths in American Culture* (Abingdon: Routledge, 2007).

Gill, Rosalind, 'Postfeminist Media Culture: Elements of a Sensibility', *European Journal of Cultural Studies*, 10/2 (2007), 147–66.

Gilligan, Sarah, 'Performing Postfeminist Identities: Gender, Costume, and Transformation in Teen Cinema', in Melanie Waters (ed.), *Women on Screen: Feminism and Femininity in Visual Culture* (Basingstoke: Palgrave, 2011), pp. 167–81.

Ginzburg, Carlo, *Ecstasies: Deciphering the Witches' Sabbath* (trans. Raymond Rosenthal) (New York: Pantheon, 1991).

Greene, Heather, *Bell, Book and Camera: A Critical History of Witches in American Film and Television* (Jefferson NC: McFarland, 2018).

Grodal, Torben, *Embodied Visions: Evolution, Emotion, Culture, and Film* (Oxford: Oxford University Press, 2009).

Grosz, Elizabeth, *Volatile Bodies: Toward a Corporeal Feminism* (Bloomington IN: Indiana University Press, 1994).

Halberstam, Jack, *Skin Shows: Gothic Horror and the Technology of Monsters* (Durham NC: Duke University Press, 1995).

Hawkins, Sunny, *Deleuze and the Gynesis of Horror: From Monstrous Births to the Birth of the Monster* (London: Bloomsbury, 2020).

Helgren, Jennifer, *American Girls and Global Responsibility: A New Relation to the World During the Early Cold War* (New Brunswick NJ: Rutgers University Press, 2017).

Heymans, Peter, 'Eating Girls: Deleuze and Guattari's Becoming-Animal and the Romantic Sublime in William Blake's Lyca Poems', *Humanimalia*, 3/1 (2011), 1–30.

Hinton, Perry R., 'The Cultural Construction of the Girl "Teen": A Cross-cultural Analysis of Feminine Adolescence Portrayed in Popular Culture', *Journal of Intercultural Communication Research*, 45/3 (2016), 233–47.

Hoppenstand, Gary, and Ray B. Browne, *The Gothic World of Stephen King: Landscape of Nightmares* (Bowling Green OH: Bowling Green State University Press, 1987).

Huntingford, Cherise, 'Burn the Witch', in Richard Greene and Rachel Robison-Greene (eds), *American Horror Story and Philosophy: Life is but a Nightmare* (Chicago IL: Open Court, 2018), e-book, n.p.

Hutton, Ronald, *The Witch: A History of Fear, from Ancient Times to the Present* (New Haven CT: Yale University Press, 2017).

Hruschka, Daniel J., *et al.*, 'Biocultural Dialogues: Biology and Culture in Psychological Anthropology', *ETHOS*, 33/1 (2005), 1–19.

Ibrahim, Awad, 'Body Without Organs: Notes on Deleuze & Guattari, Critical Race Theory and the Socius of Anti-Racism', *Journal of Multilingual and Multicultural Development*, 36/1 (2015), 13–26.

Jancovich, Mark, *American Horror in the 1950s* (Manchester: Manchester University Press, 1996).

Karlsen, Carol F., *The Devil in the Shape of a Woman: Witchcraft in Colonial New England* (New York: W. W. Norton, 1998).

Kearney, Mary Celeste, 'Birds on the Wire: Troping Teenage Girlhood Through Telephony in Mid-Twentieth-Century US Media Culture', *Cultural Studies*, 19/5 (2005), 568–601.

King, Stephen, *Danse Macabre* (London: Hodder & Stoughton, [1981] 2006).

Kokesh, Jessica, and Miglena Sternadori, 'The Good, the Bad, and the Ugly: A Qualitative Study of How Young Adult Fiction Affects Identity Construction', *Atlantic Journal of Communication*, 23/3 (2015), 139–58.

Larner, Christina, 'Was Witch-Hunting Woman-Hunting', in Darren Oldridge (ed.), *The Witchcraft Reader* (2nd ed.) (Abingdon: Routledge, 2008), pp. 171–9.

LeBlanc, Amanda Kay, '"There's nothing I hate more than a racist:" (Re)centering whiteness in *American Horror Story: Coven*', *Critical Studies in Media Communication*, 35/3 (2018), 273–85.

Levack, Brian P., *The Witch-Hunt in Early Modern Europe* (Abingdon: Routledge, [1987] 2016).

Lippert, Conny, 'Nightmares Made in America: Coven and the Real American Horror Story', in Rebecca Janicker (ed.), *Reading American Horror Story: Essays on the Television Franchise* (Jefferson NC: McFarland, 2017), p. 182–99.

Long, Carolyn Morrow, *Spiritual Merchants: Religion, Magic, and Commerce* (Knoxville TN: University of Tennessee Press, 2001).

McAvan, Em, '"I Think I'm Kinda Gay": Willow Rosenberg and the Absent/Present Bisexual in *Buffy the Vampire Slayer*', *Slayage: The Journal of Whedon Studies*, 6/4 (2006), 1–20.

McLaren, Margaret A., *Feminism, Foucault, and Embodied Subjectivity* (New York: SUNY Press, 2002).

Moseley, Rachel, 'Glamorous Witchcraft: Gender and Magic in Teen Film and Television', *Screen*, 43/4 (2002), 403–22.

Murphy, Bernice M., '"The People in the Village Have Always Hated Us": Shirley Jackson's New England Gothic', in Bernice M. Murphy (ed.), *Shirley Jackson: Essays on the Literary Legacy* (Jefferson NC: McFarland, 2005), pp. 104–26.

Nash, Ilana, *American Sweethearts: Teenage Girls in Twentieth-Century Popular Culture* (Bloomington IN: Indiana University Press, 2006).

Olli, Soili-Maria, 'The Devil's Pact: A Male Strategy', in Owen Davies and Willem de Blécourt (eds), *Beyond the Witch Trials: Witchcraft and Magic in Enlightenment Europe* (Manchester: Manchester University Press, 2004), pp. 100–16.

Ormrod, Joan, 'Endless Summer (1964): Consuming Waves and Surfing the Frontier', *Film & History: An Interdisciplinary Journal of Film and Television Studies*, 35/1 (2005), 39–51.

Owen, Alex, *The Darkened Room: Women, Power and Spiritualism in Late Victorian England* (London: Virago, 1989).

Palladino, Grace, *Teenagers: An American History* (New York: Basic Books, 1996).

Pinedo, Isabel Cristina, *Recreational Terror: Women and the Pleasures of Horror Film Viewing* (New York: State University of New York Press, 1997).

Piran, Niva, *Journeys of Embodiment at the Intersection of Body and Culture: The Developmental Theory of Embodiment* (Cambridge MA: Academic Press, 2017).

Powell, Anna, *Deleuze and Horror Film* (Edinburgh: Edinburgh University Press, 2005), e-book.

Priest, Hannah (ed.), *She-Wolf: A Cultural History of Female Werewolves* (Manchester: Manchester University Press, 2017).

Projansky, Sarah, and Leah R. Vande Berg, 'Sabrina, the Teenage . . .?: Girls, Witches, Mortals, and the Limitations of Prime-Time Feminism', in Elyce Rae Helford (ed.), *Fantasy Girls: Gender in the New Universe of Science Fiction and Fantasy Television* (Lanham MD: Rowman & Littlefield, 2000), pp. 13–40.

Purkiss, Diane, *The Witch in History: Early Modern and Twentieth-Century Representations* (Abingdon: Routledge, 1996), Kindle edition.

Reiches, Meredith W., 'Adolescence as a Biocultural Life History Transition', *Annual Review of Anthropology*, 48 (2019), 151–68.

Rivers, Nicola, *Postfeminism(S) and the Arrival of the Fourth Wave: Turning Tides* (London: Palgrave, 2017).

Rodgers, Beth, *Adolescent Girlhood and Literary Culture at the Fin de Siècle: Daughters of Today* (Basingstoke: Palgrave, 2016).

Russell, Jeffrey B., and Brooks Alexander, *A New History of Witchcraft: Sorcerers, Heretics & Pagans* (London: Thames & Hudson, 2007).

Savage, Jon, Teenage: *The Creation of Youth, 1875–1945* (London: Chatto & Windus, 2007).

Scahill, Andrew, *The Revolting Child in Horror Cinema: Youth, Rebellion and Queer Spectatorship* (Basingstoke: Palgrave, 2015).

Schiff, Stacy, *The Witches: Salem, 1692: A History* (London: Weidenfeld & Nicolson, 2015).

Schubart, Rikke, *Mastering Fear: Women, Emotions, and Contemporary Horror* (London: Bloomsbury, 2018).

Sedgwick, Eve Kosofsky, *Tendencies* (London: Routledge, 1994).

Shildrick, Margrit, *Embodying the Monster: Encounters with the Vulnerable Self* (London: Sage, 2002).

Silverman, Kaja, 'Fragments of a Fashionable Discourse', in Tania Modleski (ed.), *Studies in Entertainment: Critical Approaches to Mass Culture* (Bloomington IN: Indiana University Press, 1986), pp. 139–51.

Spacks, Patricia Meyer, *The Adolescent Idea: Myths of Youth and Imagination* (London, Faber & Faber, 1981).

Spooner, Catherine, *Fashioning Gothic Bodies* (Manchester: Manchester University Press, 2004).

Staiger, Janet, *Perverse Spectators: The Practices of Film Reception* (New York: New York University Press, 2000), e-book.

Stephens, Walter, *Demon Lovers: Witchcraft, Sex, and the Crisis of Belief* (Chicago IL: University of Chicago Press, 2002).

Strain, Christopher B., *The Long Sixties: America, 1955–1973* (London: Wiley-Blackwell, 2016).

Truzzi, Marcello, 'The Occult Revival as Popular Culture: Some Random Observations on the Old and the Nouveau Witch', *The Sociological Quarterly*, 13/1 (1972), 16–36.

Ussher, Jane M., *Managing the Monstrous Feminine: Regulating the Reproductive Body* (London: Routledge, 2006).

Warin, Megan, *Abject Relations: Everyday Worlds of Anorexia* (Baltimore MD: Johns Hopkins University Press, 1978).

Westerkamp, Marilyn J., 'Engendering Puritan Religious Culture in Old and New England', *Pennsylvania History: A Journal of Mid-Atlantic Studies*, 64 (1997), 105–22.

Wilcox, Rhonda, *Why Buffy Matters: The Art of Buffy the Vampire Slayer* (London: I. B. Tauris, 2005).

Wood, Robin, 'An Introduction to the American Horror Film', in Barry Keith Grant (ed.), *Robin Wood on the Horror Film: Collected Essays and Reviews* (Detroit MI: Wayne State University Press, 2018), pp. 73–110.

Yi Sencindiver, Susan, '"It's Alive!" New Materialism and Literary Horror', in Kevin Corstorphine and Laura R. Kremmel (eds), *The Palgrave Handbook to Horror Literature* (London: Palgrave, 2018), pp. 483–97.

Zika, Charles, *The Appearance of Witchcraft: Print and Visual Culture in Sixteenth-Century Europe* (Abingdon: Routledge, 2007).

Zwissler, Laurel, '"I Am That Very Witch": On the Witch, Feminism, and Not Surviving Patriarchy', *Journal of Religion and Film*, 22/3 (2018), 1–33.

Index

Aguirre-Sacasa, Roberto, 16, 172–3
Alaimo, Stacy, 13, 33–4, 179
Alexander, Brooks, 93
Aloi, Peg, 141
American Horror Story: Coven, 16, 17, 26, 163, 164, 165, 167, 168–71, 178, 185–6, 188, 189, 193, 200, 201
'April Witch, The', 4, 14, 56, 80–7, 101, 218n75, 219n79
Archie Comics, 100, 104, 136, 172
Atakora, Afia, 17, 163, 188–92, 193

Balan, Jane, 43
Barad, Karen, 13, 16, 27, 34, 86, 164, 167–8, 170–1
Bartky, Sandra Lee, 134
Battis, Jes, 151, 154, 155, 157
Beach Party, 102
Beatrice of Nazareth, 43
becoming-animal, 84–5, 110–12, 185–6, 199
Bell, Book and Candle, 11, 101, 208n50
Bewitched, 18

Blake, Kendare, 202
Blood on Satan's Claw, 12
bioculturalism, 12–13, 20, 24–7, 28, 29, 30, 97, 198, 199
bisexual erasure, 158
bisexuality, 158–9
bobby-soxers, 14, 57, 60–1, 67
body without organs, 45, 122–3
Borden, Lizzie, 107
Bradbury, Ray, 4, 14, 56, 78–87, 101, 218n71
Bradbury, Mary, 218n71
Braidotti, Rosi, 34, 38
Braude, Ann, 50
Brooks, Kinitra D., 186–7
Browne, Ray B., 116
Brumberg, Joan Jacobs, 42
Buckland, Raymond and Rosemary, 93
Buckley, Chloé Germaine, 95, 104
Budgeon, Shelley, 132, 134
Buffy the Vampire Slayer, 15, 128, 136, 150–60, 199, 202
Bullen, Elizabeth, 95, 102

Carrie, 6, 15, 92, 105, 106, 116–24, 131, 166, 173, 199, 223n
Carrie – A Period Piece, 117
Catherine of Siena (Saint), 42, 43
Cemetery Boys, 208n51
Chandler, Emily, 142, 143
Charmed, 18, 186
Chireau, Yvonne, 189, 190
Circe, 81
Cixous, Hélène, and Catherine Clément, 70, 72
Clark, Stuart, 8–10
Collins, Patricia Hill, 183
Columba of Rieti (Blessed), 42, 43
Conjure Women, 17, 163, 164, 165, 167, 188–92, 193, 201
Conversion (novel), 218n64
Craft, The, 15, 16, 26, 128, 136, 141–50, 151, 160, 199
Creed, Barbara, 12, 38–9, 118, 169
Crucible, The, 4, 14, 26, 56, 65–78, 79, 80, 87, 96, 169, 172, 199

Danse Macabre, 117
De Barros, Ana Carolina, 158
De Palma, Brian, 117, 118
DeCarlo, Dan, 100
Deleuze, Gilles, and Félix Guattari, 13, 29, 34–7, 39, 45, 48, 51, 83–5, 109, 110–14, 121–3, 149, 152, 159, 164, 171, 180, 182, 184–5, 201
Delpech-Ramey, Joshua, 51
Demonic pact, 8, 16, 163, 164, 175–82
Devil, 2, 8, 10, 32, 43, 46, 47, 51, 76, 174–6, 177, 181, 182
Devil in Massachusetts, The, 4, 14, 26, 56, 57–78, 79, 80, 87, 88, 131, 166, 169, 199, 216n

Disney, 11, 64, 102
Driscoll, Catherine, 17, 22, 37, 52
Dudenhoeffer, Larrie, 40
Dyrendal, Asbjorn, 93

Eggers, Robert, 177
Eller, Jonathan R., 218n71
Elliott-Smith, Darren, 6, 117

Fancher, Mollie, 43–4
Fasting girls, 43–5
Fausto-Sterling, Ann, 63
Faxneld, Per, 48, 216n40, 217n48
Fear Street, 201
Foucault, Michel, 13, 16, 22–3, 29–33, 44, 47–8, 50, 70, 73, 103, 122, 133, 138, 164, 167, 176, 181–2, 190
Ford, Michael Thomas, 17, 196
Fox Sisters, 50
Freud, Sigmund, 7, 40, 67, 68–9, 72, 149, 216n40

Gage, Matilda Joslyn, 11, 97
Gardner, Gerald, 93
Garland-Thomson, Rosemarie, 145
Gasser, Erika, 46, 73
Gladir, George, 100
Gibson, Marion, 57
Gidget, 102
Gill, Rosalind, 129
Gilligan, Sarah, 152
Gilman, Charlotte Perkins, 11
Girl on the Broomstick, The, 12
Ginger Snaps, 12
Ginzburg, Carlo, 2
Goth, 137–8, 141–3, 145–9
Grodal, Torben, 24, 26, 30

Grosz, Elizabeth, 27–9, 31, 81, 109, 121, 192, 193

Hack, Robert, 172, 173
Halberstam, Jack, 11
Hawkins, Sunny, 131
Helgren, Jennifer, 102
Hekman, Susan, 13, 33–4
Heymans, Peter, 84
Hinton, Perry R., 23
Hobbs, Abigail, 59, 60
Hoffman, Alice, 18, 19, 208n50
Hoppenstand, Gary, 116
How to Hang a Witch, 218n64
Howe, Katherine, 218n64
Hurley, Kelly, 41, 65, 78, 80, 118
Hutton, Ronald, 9
hysteria, 14, 56, 65–78, 173, 216n40

I Married a Witch, 11
I Was a Teenage Werewolf, 112
Ibrahim, Awad, 184
In Every Generation, 202
Initiation of Sarah, The, 220n16

Jackson, Shirley, 15, 92, 105, 107–16
Jacob, Sarah, 43
Jancovich, Mark, 101
Jennifer's Body, 12
Juju (TV series), 232n82
Junior Miss, 62

Karlsen, Carol F., 178
Kearney, Mary Celeste, 4, 7
King, Stephen, 15, 92, 105, 116–24
Kiss and Tell, 62
Knapp, Elizabeth, 46–7, 181
Kokesh, Jessica, 95
Kristeva, Julia, 38

LaVey, Anton Szandor, 94
Lemke, Thomas, 32–3
lesbian, 140, 159
Lewis, James R., 93
Lewis, Mercy, 59
Life Begins for Andy Hardy, 100
long 1960s, the, 15, 91, 92, 93
Love and Other Curses, 17, 196–8
Love Finds Andy Hardy, 100
lycanthropy, 111–13

makeover, 128–30
maleficium, 8, 60, 108, 109, 111
Malleus Maleficarum, 10
Mather, Adriana, 218n64
McAvan, Em, 159
McLaren, Margaret A., 44, 181
medium, 13, 42, 49–53
menarche, 12, 17, 24, 63, 64, 98, 118, 119, 122, 131, 173, 179
Michelet, Jules, 97
Miller, Arthur, 4, 14, 56, 65–78, 79, 80, 82, 96, 107, 173, 199, 218n64
Morgan, Jack, 39–40, 41, 118
Moseley, Rachael, 129–30, 137
Murphy, Bernice M., 107

Nash, Ilana, 7, 57, 58, 62
neopagan, 93
new materialist, 13, 14, 34, 40, 41, 86, 164
Night of the Demons, 12

occulture, 93
Owen, Alex, 49

Palladino, Grace, 57, 58, 59, 60, 93
Parris, Betty, 59, 72

perverse readership, 15, 92, 105, 106, 115, 117
perverse reception, 106–7
Petersen, Jesper Aa., 93
Petry, Ann, 190
Pinedo, Isabel Christina, 115, 123
Piran, Niva, 98–9
postfeminism, 127, 129
Powell, Anna, 37, 39, 40
Practical Magic, 18, 19
Priest, Hannah, 113
premenstrual syndrome (PMS), 69, 173
Projansky, Sarah, 137, 140
puberty, 12, 14, 24–6, 62, 63, 65–78, 81, 98–9, 113, 119–20, 131, 137, 172–3
Puritan, 9, 19, 59, 61, 62, 71, 72, 76, 96, 99, 107, 177–8, 181
Purkiss, Diane, 76, 110, 128
Putnam, Jr., Ann, 59, 64, 66–7
Putnam, Sr., Ann, 67

queer, 17, 105, 117, 118, 123, 155, 158, 195, 197, 207–8n50

race, 11, 59, 109, 113, 129, 142, 144–5, 182–92, 197
Rachel Dyer (1828), 11
Reiches, Meredith W., 26
Rivers, Nicola, 165
Rodgers, Beth, 52
Russell, Jeffrey B., 93

Sabrina the Teenage Witch (comics), 15, 92, 100–5, 136
Sabrina the Teenage Witch (TV series), 15, 19, 26, 128, 136–41, 160
Saducismus Triumphatus, 107

Salem witch trials, 10–11, 14, 56, 57, 59, 61, 65, 78, 107, 168, 218n71
Salem Witchcraft (1867), 11
Satan's Cheerleaders, 220n16
Satan's School for Girls, 220n16
Satanism, 93–4
Scahill, Andrew, 105
Scarrie – The Musical, 117
Schiff, Stacy, 75
Schubart, Rikke, 5, 25
Scream, 12
Sedgwick, Eve Kosofsky, 15, 106
sexuality, 4, 5, 9, 10, 11, 15, 16, 22, 59, 61, 62, 77, 78, 82, 92, 138, 141, 143, 146, 155, 158–60, 169, 184, 186, 197
Shildrick, Margrit, 38
Silverman, Kaja, 138, 139
Spacks, Patricia Meyer, 175
Speare, Elizabeth George, 4–5, 6, 15, 91, 96–100
Spiritualism, 49–50
Spooner, Catherine, 143, 149
Staiger, Janet, 15, 106
Starkey, Marion L., 4, 14, 56–78, 79, 80, 82, 88, 199, 216n40, 217n41, 218n64
Stephens, Walter, 9
Sternadori, Miglena, 95
Strain, Christopher B., 15, 91, 92, 93
subdebutante, 1–2

Taylor, Martha, 43
Teen Witch (film), 15, 128, 130–6, 137, 139, 141, 148, 153, 160, 200
teenager, invention of, 2, 3, 7, 12, 57–9

Teeth (film), 169
Thomas, Aiden, 208n51
Tituba, 76
Tituba's Children, 65
Tituba of Salem Village, 190
transgender, 18, 140, 158, 183, 196,
    208n51
'Traveler, The', 56, 79, 80, 81, 83
trope, 6, 7, 55–6, 196
Truzzi, Marcello, 94

uncanny, 22, 40, 76
Upham, Charles Wentworth, 11
Ussher, Jane, 69, 98, 122, 173

vagina dentata, 168–70
Valerie and Her Week of Wonders, 12
Vande Berg, Leah R., 137, 140
veneficium, 108, 109
Vodou, 188
Voodoo, 185, 188–9

Warin, Megan, 44, 45

Warren, Mary, 59, 71–2, 74
We Have Always Lived in the Castle,
    15, 92, 105–16, 124, 196, 199
West, Kristina, 19
'West of October', 14, 56, 79, 80, 87
Westerkamp, Marilyn J., 177–8
White, Hayden, 6–7, 55
Wicca, 5, 93, 119, 141
Williams, Abigail, 59, 67, 74–7, 173
Witch, The (2015), 16, 163, 164, 165,
    167, 177–82, 193, 201
Witch of Blackbird Pond, The, 5, 6, 15,
    26, 91, 96–100, 105, 124, 166,
    200
Witch of New England, The (1824), 11
Wizard of Oz, The, 11
Wood, Robin, 18
Woolf, Virginia, 11

Yi Sencindiver, Susan, 41

Zika, Charles, 9
Zwissler, Laurel, 180–81